A PROPOSITION TO

Theory of History and Social Evolution

ROBERT KENOUN

Note for Librarians: A cataloguing record for this book is available from Library and Archives Canada at www.collectionscanada.ca/amicus/index-e.html

ISBN: 978-1-4196-6473-1

FOREWORD

The ideological position of the author in this book is merely scientific and does not belong to any political party. However, he validates these political ideologies against what he believes is a scientific theory for the evolution of the social organism in the integration process of history. His criticism of current and past policies of U.S. and other superpowers is meant only to produce better and more sensible policies toward other societies and in general toward humanity. The author believes the science behind social evolution, which points to a deterministic finality that we all share together, if taught to all of humanity, will change the process of history and create a less violent and self-regulated process.

This book is dedicated to my parents:

Gabriel and Shooshan

to my two sons:

Ramiel and Ramman

and to my fiancé:

Nenita

who has been so patient with me in this process

ACKNOWLEDGEMENTS

Ever since I was a young man, I always wondered how to make sense of the process of history. My logic was simple; if society is composed of humans and humans are built with basic material components and there are laws that govern the behavior of these components, then these laws must have some influence in the behavior of complex living systems. The "theory of history" proposed in this book has been developed in isolation from the work accomplished by other experts to maintain its originality. I spent years thinking and organizing my thoughts to write this book and if I have not used proper and popular terminologies in some cases, I apologize to my readers. My readers may also realize that English is not my first language and that I received some help from a few individuals to bring this book to a level presentable to the public.

I will start by thanking my younger son Ramman, a student of journalism at Northern Illinois University, who was the first to edit this book. Ramman was instrumental in encouraging me to finish this book. Working full time for a demanding corporation and coming home to spend the remaining hours of the day writing had been an exhausting process and there were times that I was ready to give up, but Ramman's encouragement kept my enthusiasm up.

Next on the list is Jamshid Mohammadi Ph.D. and Dean of the Department of Civil Engineering in Illinois Institute of Technology (IIT). I know Jamshid from high school, which makes him a close friend of mine and I respect him immensely for his intelligence and knowledge. Jamshid's opinion in validating the concepts presented in this book was reassuring and very important to me and gave me a higher degree of confidence for publishing my thoughts. Jamshid also made many positive comments of how to make this book better, but I was too tired and impatient to implement all of his suggestions.

The next person on the list is Barbara Ardinger Ph.D. in literature and English language. Barbara is a very well-read person and she has a vast knowledge in almost any subject pertaining to liberal arts and history. Barbara took the challenge of proof reading this book and she made quite a difference. Because the subject of this book was new to her, occasionally, we had our disagreements and I had to be stubborn and deviate from her advice to preserve the content of the material over the form. Therefore, I assume the responsibility of editorial mistakes and apologize to my readers if the text does not meet their standards. Many thanks to all of these contributors.

Robert Kenoun

TABLE OF CONTENTS

Chapter 1

Theoretical foundation of the process of history

Chapter 2

Structural similarities of human and the social organism

Chapter 3

The effect of environment on the course of history and social evolution

Chapter 4

Human nature and its influence
on the course of history and social evolution

Chapter 5

The Social organism and its behavioral characteristics
in the integration process of history

Chapter 6

The social organism and its behavioral characteristics in the disintegration process of history

Chapter 7

Misrepresentation and misconceptions of our social evolution in recent history and issues of concern as we go forward

PREFACE

When Bohr proposed the atomic model for subject matter in 1913, it was an extraordinary breakthrough for the scientific community. At that time, it was assumed that the atomic model was the basic structure of every living thing and inanimate objects in the universe. When accelerators became available some years later, physicists were able to break the core of the atom and find newer and smaller particles. This work gave birth to elementary particle physics, which explores the micro-world of the subject matter. Research in elementary particle physics is intended to identify the smallest and simplest system in the hierarchy of matter that, in theory, can no longer be broken into smaller parts. Today, many sub-atomic particles have been identified, but have we found the smallest and simplest particle of all? No one can claim this with certainty.

Opposite the micro-world, we have the universe, which its immense size and complexity has been the subject of research for thousands of years by almost every civilization on earth. Today, scientists and astrophysicists continue to search for ways to look even deeper into the space in the hope that they may find better clues to explain this immense system. Their focus is to understand the origins of the universe, its limitations, and its behavior as the largest system known to us.

The two areas of research at these two ends of the spectrum complement one another, and any discovery in either one would bring about much greater understanding and clarity of the behavior of all other systems that fall somewhere within this spectrum. After all, the universe and all other systems are made up of these simple elementary particles and the laws governing these particles must somehow influence the behavior of all systems, regardless of their complexity.

Today, physicists also work very hard to generalize the theories of physics that pertain to the forces of nature that currently are explained by independent theories. General theories are theories with expanded domains that are capable of both explaining and predicting the behavior of systems, large or small, under a variety of conditions.

Bear in mind that without expansion of our sensory limitations through innovations such as the microscope, the telescope and many others, none of today's scientific achievements in the various branches of science would have been possible. Further expansion of our sensory limitations would result in newer discoveries that would lead to greater generalization of our theories about the behavior of systems across the spectrum. However, regardless of how much we expand our sensory limitations, we would still be limited by our human comprehension, which is bounded by a three-dimensional world. Consequently, understanding the behavior of our universe from a forth, fifth, or other dimensions, would remain limited to our abstract and mathematical approaches and nothing more. Furthermore, all of the efforts that we put into explaining our three-dimensional world, whether can be explained in a simpler way in other dimensions, is also something that we may never find out.

Our theories help us to predict the behaviors of systems that surround us. Predicting behavior gives us the ability to control and manipulate our environment to our advantage. Through these theories, we have built various sciences, a knowledge system and our civilization.

But sciences move very slowly, and at some point, it is not satisfying to an inquisitive mind that is searching for the truth and unanswered questions. A search for unanswered questions by science opens up the doors to the fields of philosophy and religion. Throughout history, many philosophical beliefs have been reformed or proven wrong by the advancement of science. Does this mean that some time in the future there will be no philosophical beliefs because most of them will have been supported or rejected by science? It is unlikely that this will happen, at least not in foreseeable future. As science advances to new frontiers, it brings along many more unanswered questions to be discussed in philosophical debates. However, science continues to remain the only tool we have to uncover the truth, one step at a time. It is possible that in the future, scientific discoveries in different scientific fields may find more common ground for a more general theory that explains the behavior of any system, regardless of its size, shape, form, and degree of complexity. As we generalize our theories, we may have much better understanding of the world that we live in. This would include ourselves, our social system and its evolutionary process that we call history.

Our focus in this book is to construct a theory that explains the process of history and the behavior of social systems, utilizing theories that are generally applied to the behavior of non-living and less complex systems. After all, a living system's basic components are those of non-living systems. Therefore, any scientific approach to explain their behavior must include all the laws that apply to their subsystems as well.

It is a fact, that experts in various fields of science, such as physics and microbiology, can reach agreement over issues related to these sciences with much greater consensus than can specialists in the field of social sciences. This is generally because social sciences lack the scientific foundation of the true sciences.

Most of the disagreements arising from debates on the behaviors of social systems are the result of individual perspectives and belief systems.

It is possible that by providing a scientific basis for the behaviors of a social system, we would be able to minimize the personal bias, reduce conflicting opinions, and pave the way for much better understanding of historical processes. Through this understanding, we would be able to set responsible behavioral standards not only for ourselves, but also for the policies of our states, to assist our social evolution to attain its predetermined goals.

Constructing a theory to explain social evolution and the process of history is truly an enormous task that must be handled by teams of scientists from every scientific discipline, as it is beyond the ability of any individual to tackle this problem single handedly. History and social evolution can be studied using two methodologies. The first and most popular methodology in use today is the *microanalysis* of history that focuses on gaining an insight into future historical processes by analyzing the details of past and present events. Since this methodology lacks any scientific basis, it is incapable of deriving concrete conclusions of future historical processes. Through this methodology, historians (with the exception of Karl Marx who have come close to explaining social evolution) have not been able to construct a single theory that describes our social system and its evolutionary process, and most of the time, they form personal views of historical processes that are not generally supported by majority of their colleagues. Clearly, this indicates that microanalysis methodology may not be a sufficient and appropriate approach in achieving this objective, due to the vast number of variables that are involved in the behaviors of social systems and historical processes. This makes it very difficult, if not impossible, to construct a theory that explains the entire process. This difficulty leads us to believe that we need to change our approach and construct a new methodology to analyze social evolution.

The proposed breakthrough approach to studying social evolution is founded on this fact that a social system is a living entity in itself, one that pursues its own evolutionary aspirations and goal seeking processes, which may be in conflict with the goals of its subsystems. It appears, however, that in the long run the aspirations of the larger system would always subdue those of its subsystems by bringing them under its control, which suggests that these subsystems (human beings) are not in total control of their history as they think they are. In this proposition, we would argue that the ultimate driving force behind a social system's evolutionary process, with all of its complexities, is the pursuit of a simple goal. This goal is the same goal that most simplistic systems in nature also pursue in their evolutionary process—seeking maximum stability by attaining the lowest state of internal energy, in connection with a given environmental condition.

This will lead us to a second, and new, way of thinking about the process of history. We will call it the *macroanalysis of history*. Macroanalysis is a methodology based on the laws of nature and systems as well as on a few other principles related to the evolutionary patterns of living systems and similarities in their structural organization.

This methodology, bring about a new level of clarity in understanding historical trends and processes. When we use macroanalysis methodology, we recognize that the finality of history (in terms of a social system's organizational structure) and the nature of relational bonds that will eventually develop among its subsystems (humans) are all deterministic goals, and are tied to the notion of the lowest state of internal energy, which is not subject to permanent change by the subsystems. However, the process by which these goals are achieved would remain unpredictable, chaotic and subject to intervention by subsystems from time to time.

We would also argue that the process of history is a reversible process and that the only force that is capable of defining the direction of this process on a permanent basis is the environment of the social system. The environment can set one or another course of evolution for a social system both being goal-seeking processes, deterministic in their finality, yet chaotic in their processes. We will refer to these processes as "*integration and disintegration process of history*".

The macroanalysis of history is capable of predicting the outcome and the main trends of social evolution pertaining to integration and disintegration processes. This methodology, can teach us that social evolution in integration process of history is a goal-seeking process and regardless of how hard we try to avoid its goals, they will be achieved through other processes or we would adopt and implement them out of necessity. This is due to the fact that evolutionary goals of a social system, the social system being the supreme living system, would take precedence over its subsystems' conflicting goals. This is an important derivation from the macroanalysis of history that can lead us to a better understanding of social evolution.

I have made an attempt in this book to apply some of the well-known theories from other sciences and disciplines to propose a theory for history and its intricate process, and through logical arguments, I have tried to make some sense out of this enormously complex and chaotic process. Hopefully, the arguments presented in this book will appeal to my readers and would trigger further debates on this subject. Such debates might result in greater understanding of history, social evolution and sociobiology as scientific processes. Finally, I hope that this new approach in understanding the social evolution and history will give birth to a new social consciousness that will assist humanity in accelerating their journey to the finality of their history with minimum casualties.

Robert Kenoun

CHAPTER I

Theoretical foundation of the process of history

In this chapter, we will discuss some of the fundamental laws of physics and their implications in the behavior of systems. These definitions will then be used throughout the book as they apply to the subjects under discussion. At the end of this chapter, we will have a summary of what we have discussed.

System: A *system* is a structure composed of substructures with a particular bond or relationship among them that exhibits a distinct characteristic or behavior that is distinguishable from its surrounding structures. Systems can be categorized in many different ways. Systems can be *ordered* or *non-ordered* structures; and within the category of ordered structures, we can have *living* and *non-living* systems. We may also have non-material systems that we call *symbolic systems*. Some of the simplest systems known to us are atoms and molecules, and among more complex systems, we can name biological systems such as animals, humans, and their society. Other types of systems are those that have been created by humans themselves; these are systems we deal with on a daily basis. All of these systems, without exception, are ordered systems. Some fall under the category of material systems, such as computers, cars, etc., and others, under symbolic systems, such as language, music, mathematics and law.

Subsystem: A *subsystem* is a substructure that is part of a larger structure. A subsystem also has its own distinct characteristics. A subsystem may contain other smaller structures within itself, each distinguishable from its surrounding structures by its own unique characteristics. Therefore, each system may contain an array of systems and subsystems within one another. For example, let us take our society as a system. In our society, there are living (human) and non-living structures (machines and buildings). Within living structures, there is a multitude of organs, such as brain, heart, etc. and molecules of water, as one of their main structural components. Within the molecule of water, we will find atoms of hydrogen and oxygen, and the breakdown of the systems can go on and on. Each one of these structures and sub-structures has its own distinct behavioral characteristic.

Parallel and serial systems: Parallel systems are similar or non-similar systems that interact with each other, but they are not part of the same hierarchy in their level. For example, humans may be considered *similar parallel systems* because they are not part of each other, but they could be part of another complex system, such as their society. As an example of *non-similar parallel systems,* we may consider a man with all of his belongings, such as his car, his computer and his house, all interacting parallel systems yet not part of the same hierarchy. Another example is the multitude of organs within the human body that are similar and non-similar, yet they are all parallel systems that interact with each other and are part of a larger system. Parallel systems do not necessarily carry the characteristics of each other. In *serially connected systems,* however, the physical characteristics of all lower level systems always transcend to the high level system and affect its behavior as well as its evolutionary process. Human intelligence transcends to higher system level (society) and makes it an intelligent organism.

An alternate definition for parallel and serially connected systems can be defined based on the notion of system boundaries, which we will discuss shortly. In this definition, we propose that the external boundaries of parallel systems are, in the physical sense, completely separated. If one of the systems is removed, the remaining parallel systems would not lose mass, though they may experience alteration of their state of energy and functionality. In contrast, in serially connected systems, where the external boundary of one system is entirely within the boundary of another, if the system within is removed, the encompassing system experiences loss of mass and a change in the state of energy and functionality. Let us assume that a system is composed of family members: a father, mother, two adult children and a newborn baby. When the father, who used to be the breadwinner of the family, passes away, the mother, who had been a housewife until now, is forced to work to support her family. The older children assume greater responsibility to help their mother; and the baby spends more time in the daycare than ever before. Evidently, the loss of the father in this family disturbed its functionality and resulted in a loss of mass in the system. To revive the functionality of the system (the family), all earlier relational bonds established among family members and their supporting external systems, such as daycare and employer, have had to be redefined. In addition, each family member now assumes a greater level of responsibility toward other members of the family that would increase their internal stress, which is associated with their internal energy.

Complexity of a system: The complexity of a system is the degree to which it can be broken down into smaller and simpler systems. Since the simplest (indivisible) system in the nature is unknown to us, the degree of complexity of a system remains a relative number. For example, human society may be several degrees higher in complexity than individual human beings, for being part of its organization. As systems become increasingly more complex, their behavior becomes increasingly difficult to predict, due to the evolvement of relational bonds of their subsystems in all levels. Moreover, assuming that each one of these subsystems has its own evolutionary process, one can imagine how cumbersome it would be to analyze the net result of this dynamic process in all system levels upon the top-level system.

Hierarchy of subject matter: It seems that there is a natural tendency in the subject matter to form structures and combine them to form even more complicated structures. These levels of structures or systems are called the hierarchy. The following example shows the hierarchy of a complex system, which contains every subsystem to its left.

....Atoms, Molecules, Cells, Heart, Human Being, Human Society.......

An atom is one of the simpler systems in the hierarchical chain that leads to human society. Both ends of this hierarchical chain have been left open purposely to indicate that the simplicity and complexity of these systems in the hierarchical chain can still continue to further extremes. Figures 1-1 and 1-2 show the graphical representation of two complex systems, one having only one level of parallel subsystems, the other having two.

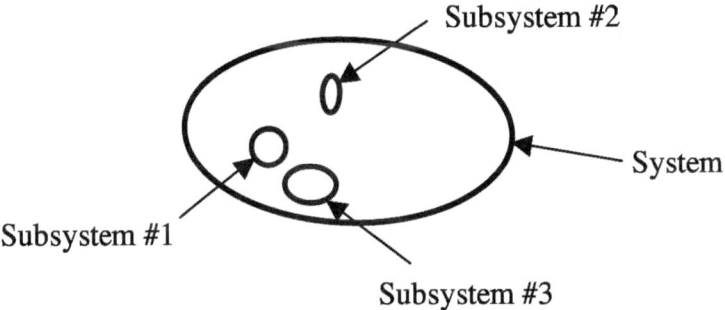

Figure 1-1 A two level system

In Figure 1-1, three subsystems are shown within the larger system.

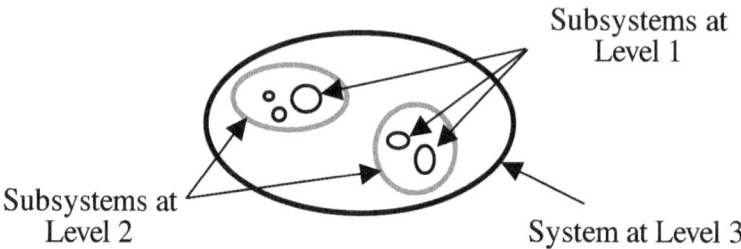

Figure 1-2 A three level system

In Figure 1-2, all systems whose boundaries fall entirely within another system are serially connected and subsystems of the same level have parallel connections.

Metasystems or multilevel systems: Based on the definitions given above, each system contains less complicated systems. The complexity and behavioral characteristics of these subsystems are functions of their level in the chain of hierarchy in reference to the system itself. The higher in the hierarchy, the more intricate their behavior. Since any system can be broken down into simpler systems, we can assert that every system is indeed a *multilevel system*. For example, an atom is a multilevel system because it is composed of electrons, neutrons, and protons, all of which can further be broken down into simpler systems of subatomic particles.

Human society as a system is composed of human beings, material objects, symbolic systems, etc. Each of these categories can be further broken down into lower multilevel systems and subsystems. Furthermore, a multilevel system is composed of both parallel and serially connected systems, which means that there are a multitude of similar and non-similar systems at every system level in the hierarchy of the system. Every one of these systems form relational bonds with parallel and serially connected systems and interacts with them in their evolutionary process.

Isolated systems: An *isolated system* is a system that has no relationship, bond, or any open communication channel with any other system around it or in its environment. Such a system does not exchange mass, energy, or information with its surrounding systems and no external forces affect its physical or mental state. Therefore, this system remains in its physical or mental state (whatever it may be) for eternity. From the viewpoint of physics and thermodynamics, such a system and its environment are only hypothetical and do not exist in consensual reality. Note also that in the classification of thermodynamic systems, a distinction has been made in the field of physics, between isolated and closed systems, in terms of the nature of their relational bonds and the type of exchange they establish with other systems. A closed system, then, would be open to the exchange of energy, but not mass. Thus far, no such distinction has been made for social systems as thermodynamic systems. Therefore, we may use both terms (isolated and closed, also equivalent political terminologies) interchangeably in our future discussions of social systems, i.e., social systems that lack any relationship with other similar systems, with the exception of their environment.

Non-isolated or open system: Unlike isolated systems, *open systems* exchange mass, energy and information with their surrounding systems. As a result, they affect one another's steady state conditions. In other words, open systems can influence each other's evolutionary courses. If two or more systems of similar or dissimilar nature are not isolated from each other, they are bound to interact with one another. The type of interaction depends on the level of complexity of the two systems. For example, if we immerse a glass of cold water in a bathtub filled with warm water, the cold and warm water will exchange thermal energy until both reach the same temperature. This interaction between cold and hot mediums is a physical interaction. For biological systems such as human beings, the interaction may be emotional or rational and for more complex systems such as societies, the interaction may be cultural and economical.

Relational bonds: Theoretically, every subsystem within a multilevel system interacts with parallel and serially connected systems in its surroundings. Let us define this interaction/connection by a new term: *relational bond*. It is these relational bonds in every subsystem level that define and influence the characteristics of every succeeding system in the hierarchy. Figure1-3 shows a system hierarchy with three subsystems in its lower level, having parallel relational bonds. Going down two levels, we find elements of subsystem #1 having their own parallel relational bonds. Finally, as shown in Figure 1-3, there are two levels of serial relational bonds, one between the top-level system and subsystem #1, and second between subsystem #1 and one of its own elements.

As subsystems can be identified by their level in the hierarchy of a system, relational bonds can also be assessed in the same manner. For example, a Nth level system in a hierarchy will have ($N^{th} - 1$) levels of serial relational bonds with its subsystems. To show how these low level relational bonds can play an enormously important role in defining the behavioral patterns of the ascending systems, we can use the example of a simple isomer constructed of carbon and hydrogen. Without changing its basic elements, we can make a whole range of different compounds, from methane (CH_4), to ethane (C_2H_6), to propane

(C3H8), and many others, merely by changing their relational bonds, which are of parallel nature. In methane, one carbon has relational bonds with four hydrogen atoms. In ethane, two atoms of carbon have a relational bond with each other, as well as additional relational bonds with three hydrogen atoms independently. Due to these alterations, the resulting compounds have different physical and chemical characteristics. In general, any time the relational bonds of subsystems undergo an alteration; the result is a change in the behavioral characteristics of all ascending or encompassing systems.

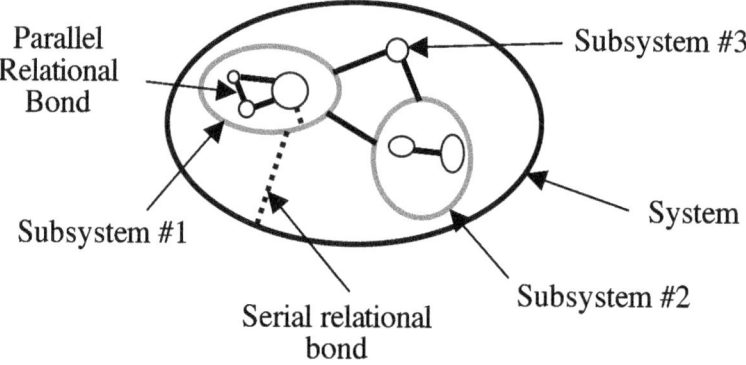

Figure 1-3 Relational bonds within system hierarchy

Cross-relational bonds: We can also define a set of relational bonds and interactions between the elements of one system with systems of higher order or their subsystems. These are *cross-relational bonds*, which may be weaker in some cases and stronger in others. For example, a philosopher from one society may publish a book describing a revolutionary system of thought, influencing the thinking process of a large population of his readers in other societies, which would then alter their relational bonds and the attitude of their societies. Another example is the direct relational bond that individual human beings have with nature at the same time that they are a subsystem of their society that itself has a relational bond with nature. This argument shows that sometimes subsystems of a system can establish relational bonds with systems of a higher order, whether they are part of that system hierarchy or not, by skipping the intermediate system. Figure 1-4 shows a cross-relational bond between the elements of one system and other systems that are not necessarily part of the first system's hierarchy.

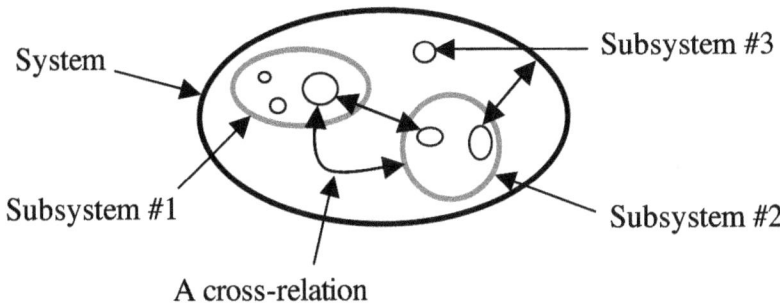

System

Subsystem #3

Subsystem #1

Subsystem #2

A cross-relation

Figure 1-4 Cross-relational bonds

Relational bonds and their evolutionary process: The properties of relational bonds among non-living systems are invariant in time and space and are defined by the natural laws of thermodynamics and physics. This is not true for living systems. Living systems are dynamic in terms of transforming their physical and relational bond properties with the passing of time or changes in their environment. This means that these properties have evolutionary processes that are tied to the evolutionary processes of all systems that are connected to them. An example in this regard may be seen in international relations. For those of us who are old enough to remember the intensity of the Cold War between the Soviet Union and the West, it is hard to believe that those formerly hostile relations have been replaced with friendly relations. If we consider these two blocs of nations as living entities, we see that they have gone through major changes internally to be able to develop today's relational bonds they hold with each other. Hence, if a system undergoes an internal change through an evolutionary process, it is bound to change all of its relational bonds with all other surrounding systems. This is also true that when a relational bond undergoes an evolutionary process and imposes itself upon a system, it forces that system to evolve in such a way to adapt to the new imposed condition.

Boundary conditions: While all systems are separated from one another by their boundaries, it is still through these boundaries that systems interact with each other. Moreover, it is through these boundaries that systems establish communication channels with each other and impose new conditions upon one another that can affect their evolutionary processes. The interaction of systems through their boundaries may produce such outcomes as physical transformation, energy exchange, and even behavioral modification. The *boundary of a system* may not always be a notable physical separation between that system and the others. In contrast, it may be an expanded boundary in both space and time, in comparison to their actual physical limitations. Boundaries of this type can be the gravitational fields of planets and the electromagnetic fields produced around charged particles and objects. Therefore, when two objects of this nature approach each other, they start affecting each other before they even come into a physical contact. These extended boundaries for systems are not limited to objects alone, as living beings also have extended boundaries, which we will discuss later. In a single system, shown in Figure 1-5a, there is only one boundary that separates the system from its environment. In multilevel systems, however, there are at least two boundaries embracing every system level. Figure 1-5b shows a second order system with two boundaries surrounding it. The first boundary separates the system from the lower level system, the second from the higher level system.

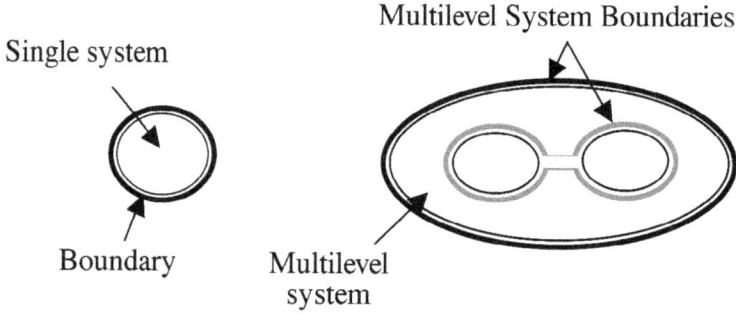

Figure 1-5a   *Figure 1-5b*
Figure 1-5 Boundaries of a system

Figure 1-5b also shows in a symbolic way how two parallel systems of the same type can be in communication with each other via mass, energy, information, or other means. This communication channel between two parallel systems may eventually lead to their unification, as one system, and produce uniform boundary conditions surrounding them.

To conclude this section, we argue that there are no isolated systems in nature and that all systems are multilevel systems, with the exception of the first that is unknown to us. Each system has at least two boundaries with lower and higher level systems. Figure 1-6 shows the hierarchy of these boundaries as systems become more complex.

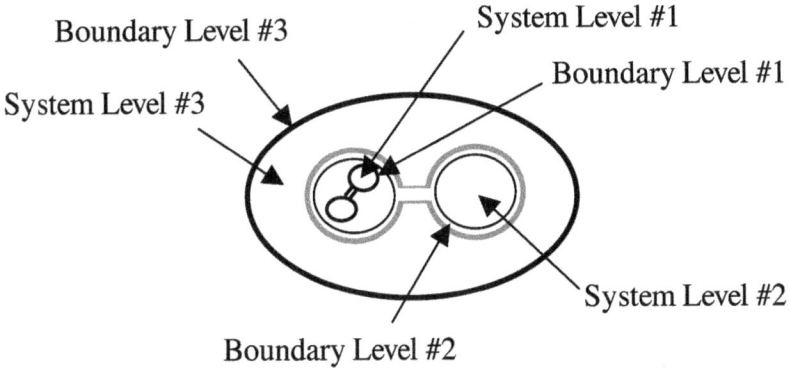

Figure 1-6 Boundaries of multi-level systems

As shown in the figure, system level #2 is surrounded by boundary level #1 and #2, and system level #3 is surrounded by boundary level #2 and #3. Because the boundary conditions of a system dictate its physical state and evolutionary course, any changes in these conditions can produce a physical transformation in that system or a diversion from the system's original evolutionary course. Since all systems are part of a system hierarchy, any physical transformation at one system level sets a new boundary condition for the next level system, followed by a transformation in that system level. This may set off a chain reaction that can propagate throughout the system hierarchy, as every system tries to adjust to its changing boundary conditions.

Boundaries of humans and animals as systems interacting with their environment: Following our earlier discussions regarding the impact of the boundary conditions on the physical and behavioral characteristics of a system, at this time we need to define the nature of these boundaries and their domain for living systems. The brain, as the sole modifier of behavioral characteristics in these systems, responds to two sets of stimulating signals, those generated internally by communication with other organs and signals received by the senses from the external world. Interpretation of these signals by the brain results in generation of proper responses and transformations in the biological structure and composition of the living organism. Like some of the systems we discussed earlier, the boundaries of a living system are not limited to a physical line that separates the system from its environment. For these systems, the entire domain that the system is capable of sensing and comprehending a change in environment is defined as their boundaries. For example, in the frequency domain, human beings are capable of hearing sounds between 20 Hz and 20,000 Hz, down to zero decibels. In the visual domain, we sense all light frequencies between infrared and ultraviolet. Adding to these domains, other domains generated by the sense of smell, taste, or touch, we will end up with a relatively large sensory domain whose boundaries extend far beyond our physical boundaries.

Note that humans and animals may not have the same boundary limits because of variations among the strengths of their senses. Therefore, to define the outer boundary of a living system, we propose that it starts at the surface of the skin and stretches to as far as the strength of the senses allows reception of information from space, time, or frequency domain.

According to our definition of system response, a transformation or behavioral change in a system would take place only when boundary conditions change or are hit by a stimulus. For example, when living systems perceive a dangerous situation from a distance, they produce chemicals such as adrenaline (a physical transformation), which flows into their blood stream to prepare them for the fight-or-flight response. Social systems also have boundaries that separate them from each other according to the uniqueness of their cultural, socioeconomic, and political systems, and as they are exposed to each other, the outcome may be transformation, and eventual unification of their societies. Due to advancements in the fields of science and technology, the boundary limits of human beings and social systems continue to expand in all the aforementioned domains.

Physical laws behind the integration and unification of systems: The boundary of a system is the interface between the system and its environment. Any environmental change would affect the boundaries of the system before it produces a transformation or qualitative change in the composition of the system itself. When the boundaries of two systems that are qualitatively different intersect, a duality of conditions is imposed upon regions or segments of the boundary shared by the systems. Such duality when it is on a permanent basis is unacceptable in the physical world. What we mean by "duality" is the physical characteristics of entities that are situated in the shared boundary in order to satisfy the conditions imposed upon them by both systems as well as the environment surrounding them. For example, one system may demand that a molecule in the shared region or boundary holds a temperature of 100 degrees Centigrade, whereas the other system dictates that it be 50 degrees Centigrade. We know that this is not a possible scenario in nature. To eliminate unrealistic conditions imposed upon these entities, the two systems need to exchange energy and mass in order to homogenize and integrate. When homogenization, or transformation, is complete, a new system will emerge with a single boundary that imposes a unity of conditions upon all entities within the system and those in its surrounding environment. In other words, the conflicting physical characteristics imposed upon those entities in the shared boundaries will converge into a unique set of requirements and new physical characteristics dictated by the new homogenized system. As we can see, the homogenization of interacting systems becomes a deterministic outcome whose purpose is to eliminate conflicting conditions imposed upon entities on the shared boundaries. Natural systems are open systems that make them susceptible to interacting with other systems by exchanging mass, energy, and information. It should be noted that interaction that takes place between two or more systems would immediately propagate throughout the hierarchy of systems to redefine all relational bonds pertaining to all subsystems with respect to their surrounding systems, whether they are parallel or serially connected with each other. When interactions between systems are complete, the newly emerged system will reach a steady state condition with respect to its environment, and the state of the internal energy of the system would reach the lowest state (homeostasis), again under given environmental conditions. We will expand on this notion in further detail in upcoming discussions. In conclusion, the final state of the merger of systems can be defined by homogenization, equalization or assimilation of one system into another. For example, the economic integration of two states would result in eventual assimilation of the two nations, with the production of one set of economic, political, and ideological values in dealing with the rest of the nations. This phenomenon was observed during the Cold War in both East and West camps.

The steady state condition of a system and its transformation mechanism:
As we have seen, all open systems will interact with other systems, either by imposing new boundary conditions on surrounding systems or exerting forces on each other. These forces, or imposed conditions, are latent in the relational bonds that have evolved among them. Depending on the type and complexity of the interacting systems, the nature of these forces may vary from electromagnetic to emotional/psychological, economical, or political. However, the outcomes of all system interactions are determined by the system that encompasses the interacting subsystems. To resolve conflicting boundary conditions as a result of interactions, the encompassing system would set up an evolutionary process not only for itself but also for all of its subsystems.

After the resolution of any boundary conflicts, the system would reach a *steady state condition*, with *stability* and a *minimum state of internal energy* under given environmental conditions. When a system is in the steady state condition, it will remain steady as long as the boundary conditions surrounding the system remain unchanged. If a change occurs at any point in time in one of the boundary conditions, the system will become unstable, at which time it has no other alternative but to transform itself and adapt to newly imposed conditions. This process would then continue to propagate throughout the hierarchy of the system, as every subsystem seeks its own steady state condition and makes its own necessary transformations. This suggests that, at least in theory, any change in one of the boundary conditions of a multilevel system at any level will force the entire hierarchy of the system to undergo changes. In Figure 1-6, we can see that system level #1 is affected by only one boundary condition, which is boundary condition #1. Systems level #2 and #3 are affected by two boundary conditions (#1 and #2) and (#2 and #3), respectively. Therefore, if the external environment of system level #3 imposes a new condition on that system, it will transform and adapt and, as a result, will enforce new conditions on its lower boundary, which is shared by system level #2. System level #2 will then transform and adapt to these changes and exert its own condition on its shared boundary with system level #1. This will go on until transformation and adaptation hit the lowest subsystem level in the hierarchy. This chain reaction does not have to start at the top-level system and propagate downward; it can also start from the bottom and propagate upward. Theoretically, if a change occurs in the middle of the system hierarchy, it can also propagate in both directions until every connecting system completes its transformation and adapts to its new environment. The extent of transformation in any subsystem level is defined and limited by the system's least amount of stored internal energy as a function of newly imposed boundary conditions. The steady state condition may not be the desired state by any system or subsystem level in the hierarchy, but it is a compromise state imposed on them by the highest order of boundary or system level.

Systems respond differently to changing environmental conditions, some with slower responses, some with faster. We call this the response time of the system. Other systems may exhibit resistance toward transformation and continue to store energy within their structure until they have no choice but to transform.

Moreover, any system transformation requires time, and the larger and the more complex the system, the larger the duration of its transformation. As an example, if we place an alloy rod in a very hot environment, the core temperature of the rod will not immediately be elevated to the temperature of the environment. This is due to the slow conduction rate of the heat from the surface of the rod to its core. If sufficient time is provided, the core temperature will rise to the temperature of the environment and the process will halt. Obviously, when a process comes to a halt, it means that all transformations in all system levels have been completed and the system has adapted to its new environment by reaching a new steady state condition. We realize that this requires some time to be accomplished. In this process, transformations at all system levels are as follows. The elevation of temperature in metal rod would results in phase transformation of the alloying elements, followed by increased levels of atomic vibration at lower system level (atomic elements), and jumping of electrons into higher orbits of the atoms, at sub-atomic level. Human beings and their societies are no exception to these laws and they behave in a very similar manner with respect to their environmental changes, and interaction among themselves. We will discuss this in greater detail in later chapters.

A system's reaction to changing boundary conditions or external forces: Any transformation within a system is the result of the application of external forces upon the boundaries of that system. External forces may change over time and force the system into continuous adjustments. The nature of transformation process within a system is a function of the magnitude difference of the applied forces over their time interval ($\frac{\Delta F}{\Delta t}$). For example, if this ratio is large, a system's transition to the next steady state condition is likely to be violent or chaotic before it reaches that state, whereas when this ratio is small, the transition to the next state is likely to be smooth and nonviolent. When a process becomes violent, it means that a system has to absorb or release a large amount of energy in a short time, in order to achieve a steady state condition. If we take the heated rod of the previous example and immerse it into a tank of cold water, we will notice a splash of water due to evaporation at the surface of the rod. This is because the elevated heat on the surface of the rod cannot instantly be absorbed into the water, due to slow rate of heat transfer in the water medium. However, if all the heat in the metal rod were introduced at a slower rate into the water, the heat would have been easily absorbed by the water, without a splash or evaporation of water. Hopefully, with this example we have clarified system's response to the rate of changing external forces.

In the case of living systems, rapid environmental changes (which are external forces) can result in the extinction of a species because the living system (the species) would not be able to adjust quickly enough to its new environment. However, when environmental changes occur at a more moderate pace, the living systems may have enough time to make proper adjustments to their genes (this is called mutation) and survive in their new environment. Therefore, mutation in living systems is a transformation (called also adaptation) initiated by environmental forces, in which the living system reaches a new steady state condition in its new environment. Every system, regardless of the degree of its complexity, responds to changing environmental forces in its own way, but all systems, living or nonliving, share the same fundamentals of adapting to change.

Behavior of a system: A system's response to environmental conditions and external forces can be called *system behavior*. Different terminologies used in various scientific fields have come to provide the same meaning when we analyze system behavior. Behavior is the response of a system to a stimulus, external force, changing environmental conditions, or imposition of new boundary conditions. It is this process by which a system changes or transitions from one state to another in response to a stimulus. Nonliving and non-ordered systems respond only to forces that are associated with their mass and energy, whereas living and ordered systems respond not only to environmental forces but also to information stimuli. In the case of a nonliving but ordered structure, like a computer, this system responds to information stimuli. In living systems, like human beings, the exchange of the ideas and thoughts can become a powerful stimulus in altering behavior.

Internal energy of a system: When a system rests at the steady state condition, it retains a level of *internal energy* that remains constant as long as its boundary conditions do not change. When boundary conditions change and the system has to transition from one state to another, the state of its internal energy also changes and the system either releases or absorbs energy from its surrounding systems. Let us consider the structure of an atom. When an atom is heated, the electrons of its lower orbit tend to jump to its higher orbit as part of the absorption of the energy. When the atom is cooled down, the electrons jump back to the lower orbit by releasing their energy in the form of radiation. The level of energy retained in the system (the atom) can be correlated directly with the boundary conditions imposed upon it. The important derivation of this discussion is that the notion of internal energy of a system can be substituted for the notion of the system's boundary conditions. In the upcoming arguments, we will be using this notion more frequently than the notion of boundary conditions. We also need to emphasize that systems inherently oppose absorbing additional energy into their structures, unless they are forced to do so by their surrounding systems. In other words, systems strive to keep their state of internal energy at the minimum level at all times.

Stability of a system: Before we define the stability of a system, let us review the concept of the steady state condition. Every system can be put into a steady state condition with any level of internal energy by the exertion of forces or the imposition of certain conditions upon its boundary. In the steady state, the system remains stable as long as the external forces remain unchanged. The partial stabilities associated with every steady state condition may not be the optimum stability the system can have. To examine whether a steady state condition with partial stability is indeed the most desired stability for a system with a minimum level of internal energy, we can remove the external forces exerted upon the system and see what happens. If in its steady state condition, the system happens to have an undesired level of internal energy, it will release the excessive energy and find a path to a new steady state with the least amount of stored internal energy and optimum stability. In states associated with optimum stability, the magnitude of the external forces exerted upon the system are either zero or lower than the forces exerted upon the system in other steady state conditions. In an abstract way, in Figure 1-7, we see an evolutionary process for a system that is driven by external forces that have produced a condition with the minimum internal energy at point A of the process. At this position, the system rests in optimum stability, as compared to all other positions in this process (which makes the notion of stability only a relative measurement).

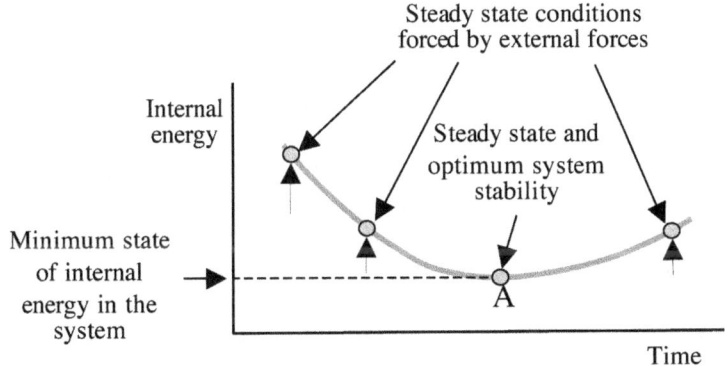

Figure 1-7 Stability and internal energy of a system

When the internal energy of a system rises, most of the absorbed energy is passed on to its subsystems, which pass part of that energy to their own subsystems, and so on throughout the hierarchy of the system. While subsystems also show resistance to absorbing unwanted energy, they have no choice but to abide by the rules of the system, which are based on the principles set by the laws of nature. The high level system always enforces the rules upon its subsystems so that all parallel subsystems hold equal levels of internal energy. This produces a more desirable outcome from stability point of view for the system itself. In upcoming sections, we will discuss these principles in greater detail. In summary, in any partially or optimally stable condition, as shown in Figure 1-7, we have a system that has a different level of internal energy, and the energy this system passes on to its subsystems is equally distributed among its members at every subsystem level. When the internal energy of a system changes, it also affects all of the relational bonds set at all levels among its subsystems.

To show this, let us take water as a system with H_2O molecules as its subsystems and molecular forces as their relational bonds. When water is heated, it absorbs the energy and passes it on to its subsystems. At the beginning of this process, despite an increased level of molecular agitation and molecular distances (due to increased level of stored energy), the nature of the relational bonds among the molecules is not impacted in any significant way and water remains as a stable system. When the absorbed energy increases beyond a certain threshold level, the water molecules start breaking up, due to excessive stored energy within molecular structure, followed by a drastic change in the characteristics and nature of the molecules' relational bonds. This is the stage when liquid water is no longer stable and changes phase to a gaseous state (water vapor). As is evident, the absorbed energy by the system has affected the stability of the system and the relational bonds of its subsystems.

We mentioned the term "threshold level". When we recognize a threshold, we realize that the nature of the relational bonds developed among the subsystems in a particular steady state condition do not immediately alter following a small change in the system's internal energy caused by changes in environmental conditions. They could be affected, but not enough to make a phase transformation a necessity yet. We may assert, therefore, that the stability of a system is tied to the relational bonds of the subsystems, and as long as external forces are not large enough to alter the nature of these relations in a significant way, the system may remain relatively stable, despite absorbing or releasing some of its energy. This implies a tolerance level that is unique to every system before any transformation takes place in its organization.

In upcoming sections, we will introduce a new notion in regard to the state of internal energy of a system and the distribution of this energy among its subsystems. We will then show that when subsystems refuse to equalize the state of their internal energy, they produce stresses among themselves that keep the system's internal energy at an undesirably higher level. Any additional energy that remains within the system now undermines the stability of that system.

Let us apply these notions to a much more complex system, such as a society with unjust socioeconomic relations. "Unjust" means "unequal," and inequality equates to stressful relational bonds among human beings as the subsystems of the society and the outcome of these relational bonds translates to instability at the society level. But what stops an unstable society from transforming itself to become optimally stable? The law enforcement agencies take on this task to keep the society from falling into the chaos of transformation and force the society to maintain a steady state condition with partial stability. Obviously, partial stability is a less desirable state from the state of optimal stability, which is attainable through socioeconomic equality at the human level. However, when stress levels among peoples continue to rise, followed by increased levels of stored energy as a result of anger, frustration and difficulty to survive in the society, even a massive police force cannot stop the transformation process. It is in these circumstances that society reaches its threshold level and erupts into civil unrest, revolution, or war to modify the existing socioeconomic relations among its subsystems, and thus transit to a more stable society. In the next section, we will show why equality in subsystem level equates to lowest state of internal energy for the system itself.

The first and the second law of thermodynamics as they apply to systems:
The *first law of thermodynamics* states that the total energy of the universe is constant, and that when systems interact with each other and exchange energy, the energy may flow from one system to the other or change from one form to another. However, the total level of energy within the universe always remains the same. The *second law of thermodynamics*, or the law of entropy, states that the entropy of an isolated system will continue to increase until that system reaches an equilibrium state. From nature's point of view, however, equilibrium is equivalent to chaos and disorder. This is different from the perception of equilibrium from the viewpoint of ordered structures, which include living systems. Taking the entire universe as an isolated system, according to this law, at some point in time the universe will reach a state of equilibrium and the resulting homogeneity will lead to the termination of every interaction and energy exchange within its structure. This is called the heat death of the universe. The second law of thermodynamics suggests that the entropy of the universe continually increases on the positive scale as it nears that state. But in the mean time, as systems within the universe continue to interact and exchange energy with each other, they form structures that are generally in negation of the second law of thermodynamics. Ordered structures and living organisms are systems that maintain negative entropy. In the case of living organisms, particularly human beings, as we continue to build structures and form larger organizations, the entropy of these entities continues to become even more negative.

But with a little careful analysis, we can purge such a theoretical contradiction. Part of our explanation is that a portion of the exchanged energy between two systems becomes unavailable as it dissipates in the form of heat or friction. The remaining part of the energy that flows from one system to the other can then be used to lower one system's entropy at the expense of the other system's elevation of entropy. This means that we can construct orderly structures by extracting energy from other systems and create disorder in those systems of much larger magnitude. Now this would satisfy the second law of thermodynamics so that in this process the overall entropy of the universe has continually increased due to the dissipation factor. Yet, within its structure, the systems have adopted orderly and disorderly structures with much greater disparity in their entropy levels. Ordered structures and living systems, if left unsupported by their surrounding systems or their environments, will be exterminated over time, as nature and the second law of thermodynamics do not support them.

The phenomenon, known as "pollution," is exactly what human beings and their societies do to their environment to maintain negative entropy and to survive. Pollution cannot be stopped, as it is a consequence of maintaining every ordered structure built by us. However, it can be managed and controlled in a much more efficient way.

Implications of the laws of thermodynamics in system behavior: Based on the notion of conservation of energy (the first law of thermodynamics), if one system releases energy, another has to absorb it. Isolated systems do not exchange energy. However, when they become open to each other, the larger system that encompasses them starts to impose its will upon those subsystems and force them to exchange energy. It is through this process that the larger system's internal energy drops to a minimum level and the system achieves maximum stability, when its subsystems hold equal states of internal energy. As we discussed in the previous section, the second law of thermodynamics (entropy) tells us that in any energy exchange between two systems, some of the energy leaves the systems and becomes unavailable. It is solely for this reason that the larger system loses some of its internal energy to gain greater stability. The lost energy may appear in the form of friction, heat, or even loss of human life, depending on the type of the system.

Let us make an attempt to prove this notion. Suppose that the dual level system A, as shown in Figure 1-8, contains three parallel subsystems, each having a different level of internal energy before they open up to each other. Simplistically, the internal energy of system A, labeled E_{AI} (prior to the energy exchange process between its subsystem), can be shown by the following equation, in which K is a constant energy not related to the stored energy in the subsystem level.

$$E_{AI} = E_1 + E_2 + E_3 + K$$

The value of K goes up in multilevel systems that have a higher degree of order and complexity. This value represents the entire stored energy in the system below the top subsystem level.

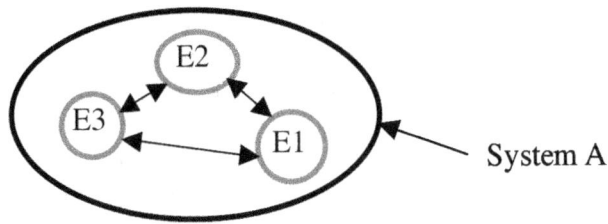

Figure 1-8 Parallel systems engaged in energy exchange

If we designate E_{12}, E_{13}, and E_{23} as dissipated energies related to the process of energy exchange between every two systems, then these dissipated energies will reach their maximum levels at the end of the process when all three subsystems attain equal levels of internal energy. This is the time when system A reaches its minimum level of internal energy because the dissipated energies have reached their maximum levels. At the end of the process, each subsystem will theoretically have the same level of internal energy, as calculated below:

$$E_{eq} = \frac{\left(E_1 + E_2 + E_3 - \left(E_{12M} + E_{13M} + E_{23M}\right)\right)}{3}$$

where E_{12M}, E_{13M}, and E_{23M} are the maximum dissipated energies between each two systems. We can then calculate the final internal energy of the system as follows:

$$E_{AF} = E_1 + E_2 + E_3 - \left(E_{12M} + E_{13M} + E_{23M}\right) + K = 3E_{eq} + K$$

$$E_{AF} < E_{AI}$$

It is clear that the internal energy of system A at the end of the process is less than its internal energy at the beginning of the process. An important conclusion that can be derived from these simplistic calculations is that, a state of equality between subsystems, results in the maximum elevation of entropy in the surrounding environment of the system, which conforms to the second law of thermodynamics. Furthermore, it also supports the notion that the high level system's objectives in reaching a state of internal energy that is at the minimum level and provides optimum stability will supersede the intention of all subsystems that are in contradiction with system objectives. Moreover, we can also conclude that the outcome of this process is deterministic and dictated by the laws of nature. To achieve these goals, the high level system imposes its own conditions upon all parallel systems that are one level below its own level. This notion holds true throughout the hierarchy of the system, as every subsystem will do the same to its own lower-level parallel subsystems. Let us not forget that subsystems also struggle not to accept an elevation to their internal energy, but they find themselves unable to challenge the will of the high level system or to change the boundary conditions it imposes upon them. This notion also supports the earlier notion of uniformity of boundary conditions surrounding the interacting systems as they unite and equalize to eliminate contradictory requirements imposed upon their boundaries. If for some reason the energy exchange between subsystems were to be restricted, tension would build up between the subsystems. This would also leave the larger system at a lower degree of stability.

The degree of stability of a system is directly proportional to the difference in the state of internal energy between its subsystems. This can be observed in complex systems such as human beings and their societies. In living organisms such as animals, the lowest state of internal energy can be interpreted as the perceived survival needs of the living organism, which would include the energy resources and life support systems. Animals and human beings demonstrate these needs by being territorial. By marking a territory, an animal or a group of animals protect and control the available resources for their own exclusive use. Protecting these resources for future needs relieves an animal from potential stresses arising from its search for energy.

This has not changed, even for the modern humans or the so-called the "civilized man." Modern humans are still territorial beings, but instead of marking their territory with their body fluids (as animals do), they mark them on a piece of paper called a "map." By doing this, nations try to protect their resources, technologies and economies to serve themselves only. If they happen to have a surplus of any life support system that others may need, they do not give it up unless they get something in return. Therefore, the lowest state of internal energy for a living organism (animal, human, or society) is related to security and survival of the living organisms and connected with the constant flow of energy and life support systems that they need. This would require development of means to safeguard and control the supply of energy to their organisms, and overcome the threat presented by the environment or other humans or societies that might wish to take over their protected resources. In the modern world, these controlling means are manifested in money, power, and (on a larger scale) political affiliations, a strong economy, and a strong military. The sense of insecurity in man is the result of his starvation days during his evolutionary process, which has dominated his behavior from prehistoric times until present. As properties of subsystems transcend to higher system levels, such as societies, they, too, exhibit these security concerns in their behavioral patterns.

From these arguments, we can thus conclude that the global social organism, with the support of the laws of nature, would eventually manage to optimize its stability by enforcing equality among all of its subsystem, which are societies and their subsystems, human beings. However, in this process, the global social organism faces resistance from societies and individuals that have a lower state of internal energy (or wealth of resources) and are not willing to support the global social organism's intended goals to attain maximum stability and security. Such resistance from a minority of subsystems would produce a great deal of stress among them that would raise the internal energy of the system itself and drive it into instability. However, this would not concern the global social organism, as it would resolve the differences among its subsystems through violent processes.

Entropy, the force behind the existence of all systems and their evolutionary processes: If we could eradicate the second law of thermodynamics (entropy) and leave only the first (conservation of energy), we would have a very different world in which every process that ever occurred would be one hundred percent efficient because there would be no dissipation or loss of energy. One system in this new world would release energy and the other would absorb all of it. But is this a possible scenario? Let us go back to the example in Figure 1-8. In that example, we noticed that when the three systems opened up to one another, a larger system encompassing them instantly forced the three subsystems to exchange enough energy until they reached a state of equality. At the end of that process, the system itself reached the minimum state of internal energy.

If the second law of thermodynamics was not in existence and there were no dissipation of energy, then even if the interaction between the three subsystems had taken place and reached the state of equality, the state of internal energy of the encompassing system would have not changed at all. This is because all of the exchanged energy would have remained within the encompassing system; only redistributed among the three subsystems. With this logic, the system itself will remain indifferent to enforcing the energy exchange process among its subsystems because it will gain nothing from the process. If a system plays no role or has no relational bonds with its subsystems, its existence becomes irrelevant. Now, taking the system out of the picture, it becomes the choice of the subsystems whether or not to initiate the energy exchange process among themselves. If they do, then they form a larger system, which we have already demonstrated to be irrelevant. Therefore, the only logical outcome for their relationship would be to have no relationship, which means they would remain as isolated systems, content with their state of internal energy, whatever it may be. At this point, we can treat any one of these subsystems as an independent system with its own subsystems, and through the same logical deduction, prove that these systems are also irrelevant in relation to their own subsystems. This process continues throughout the hierarchy of systems until no system remains that is relevant. This would disassociate every complex system in our universe from its basic building blocks, which are unknown to us. To clarify this concept, let us think of the second law of thermodynamics (entropy) as a field that exerts a force on every mass and energy exchange between systems, just as a gravitational field exerts its force upon any mass within its field, or an electrical field applies a force to any charged particle in its field. For readers with a lesser degree of scientific background, we can provide another example to grasp the workings of the second law of thermodynamics; this law is analogous to the tax law. Assume three merchants having several products that they would like to trade among themselves for money. They start with a limited amount of money, say $1,000. When the first trade takes place between two of them, part of the exchanged money goes to the government in the form of sales tax. Then comes the next trade with the remaining money. Again, some of the money goes to the government as sales tax. If sufficient amount of trade takes place between these merchants, most of the money will eventually end up in the hands of government and the merchants will end up with nothing. In this example, the sales tax that ends up in government's hand is analogous to the dissipated energy, and the trade of merchandise between these merchants is the energy exchange between systems. Finally, the tax law resembles the second law, which demands a part of every exchange between systems. To conclude this discussion, it seems that the laws of thermodynamics in association with the notion of the lowest state of internal energy (a state demanded by every system), are behind all evolutionary processes that take place in our universe. These laws are also responsible for the formation of all relational bonds among systems and their interactions. It is through the development of these relational bonds that systems with greater complexity and with newer characteristics are born and continue to evolve into more complicated systems.

Definition of a process: All of the matter in the universe is ruled by one single process, which started at the beginning of time (the so-called initial conditions) and will terminate at a distant future. Everything in between is just an intermediate stage of this infinitely long evolutionary process. It is only intelligent beings, such as humans, who wonder what this really means. To satisfy their curiosity and understand their environment, they study the behavior of matter in limited ways and in short time periods, form opinions and epistemological views of the evolving world. To study a process, we define a beginning and an end to that process, within which a major event such as a transformation, mutation or a physical or chemical reaction takes place. Based on these observations, we develop theories to explain the behavior of matter under those limited circumstances. The sum of these theories empowers us to understand and form opinions regarding the behavior of matter not only in a limited way, but also in a broader way that applies to the most complex systems.

Processes such as history, which is the evolution of social systems, can never be replicated in the laboratory or observed in their entirety and need to be studied based on limited observation, logical deductions, and application of theories that are regarded as natural laws. Since our emphasis in this book is on the process of history, we need to define a starting and ending point for history. For the starting point, we can imagine the formation of the smallest groups of humans and for the end of history, we can visualize the integration of the whole world into one social system that has reached optimum stability and has terminated the struggle among its subsystems. We would like to call this the end point in the evolutionary process of social system or the *finality of history*. Obviously, this would not mean that process of history would halt at this point, as the struggle between social organism and its environment (nature) will continue forever. But let us not forget that such a finality for a social system, despite being deterministic, is conditional and depends upon the support of its environment in order to materialize. If this environmental support is not available, it will severely affect the relational bonds of humans and throw the evolution of social organism in a totally different direction, yet seeking deterministic goals. We will discuss this subject in greater detail in later chapters.

Complex systems and complex evolutionary processes: It is obvious that structures with a greater level of complexity in their organization, such as multilevel systems or living organisms, have much more complicated evolutionary processes than those with simpler structures. A *complex system* has multiple layers of subsystems, each having a particular relational bond with parallel and serially connected systems and subsystems. When the environment or the boundary condition of a complex system changes, a qualitative change has to take place within the system to adjust to the new environment. This will require that subsystems redefine their relational bonds with each other at every system level.

Because each subsystem level has to use a specific process to achieve the goal of redefining relational bonds, we can therefore assign this process to the subsystem level and call it a sub-process. The sum of all sub-processes in all subsystem levels in the hierarchy of the system forms a complex process. From this argument, we may conclude that a complex system will definitely have a complex evolutionary process that would be much more difficult to understand and predict its behavior, when compared to simpler systems. However, despite complexity of these systems both structurally and behaviorally, with a closer look, most of them are seen to exhibit general trends that make them predictable.

One such complex system is our social system, with its enormously complex evolutionary process. What seems to be less predictable, however, is the sequence of events pertaining to the completion of evolutionary processes related to each subsystem level that lead the social evolution to its finality. For example, a grade school math teacher might give a perfect grade to any student who comes up with the correct answer when adding numbers 2, 3 and 4, regardless of what order they were added in. This is exactly what we mean by variations in the sequence of events, through which the finality of social evolution materializes with any permutation of sub-processes involved in driving it. Obviously, when a complex evolutionary process with numerous variations leads to the same finality, there can be only one explanation for it: the finality is influenced and guided by the fundamental laws of nature.

Deterministic evolutionary processes and equifinality: When the characteristics of a system undergoing an evolutionary process is predictable in every point in space and time, that system has a *deterministic process*. A projectile would be a good example in this case, where its positions both in space and in time can be easily predicted along its trajectory before it hits the target. In some other evolutionary processes such as an equifinial process, a system may take different evolutionary paths that all cease at a predetermined finality, where all of the characteristics of the system at that finality are known in their entirety. A system with equifinal process is a system that will eventually reach its lowest state of internal energy (optimum stability point), irrespective of its initial condition and its evolutionary path. To demonstrate this concept, let us assume that a small ball is thrown into a spherical bowl, as shown in Figure 1-9. As we can predict, the final destination of this ball after it whirls around the bowl many times will be at the bottom of the bowl, where the ball comes to rest and attains its lowest state of internal energy. The sum of forces exerted upon the ball from every direction at this point is zero. At this point, the ball has lost all of its kinetic and potential energy and it rests at its condition of optimal stability.

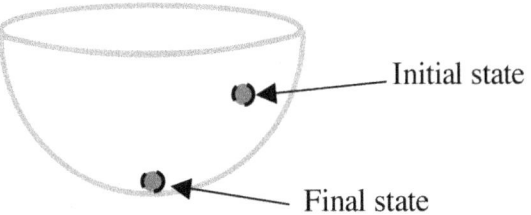

Figure 1-9 An equifinal evolutionary process

Note that every time that this ball is thrown into the bowl under different initial conditions, it will eventually reach the same destination through different routes. In this example, as easy it is to predict the final state of the ball it is equally difficult to predict the path this ball travels before it stops at its final destination. What makes this ball rest at the bottom of the bowl, time after time, is the imposition of constraints on its freedom and the forces that pull it toward that finality, regardless of where it may be in its evolutionary process around the inside of the bowl. In this case, the constraints are the inner surface of the bowl and the gravitational force. The question is: can anyone change the finality of this process? The answer is no, not if we deal with natural laws and the forces of nature, such as the gravitational force in this instance. For example, if we throw the ball with a higher initial speed and in different directions, would that make any difference in its final resting position? Absolutely not. The only thing that we have done is to increase the duration of its process.

In earlier sections, we stated that the laws of nature apply to all systems indiscriminately and that they influence the behavior of those systems regardless of how complex they may be. We have talked about the electromagnetic fields, gravitational fields, and the laws of thermodynamics, particularly the second law and its influence on every system at every level. We have discussed how this law is responsible for the development of all relational bonds between the elements of systems in all levels of system hierarchy. All of this means that no system in our universe can have an evolutionary process that is without constraints and exists in total freedom. Constraints that are imposed and enforced upon systems by the laws of nature in most cases result in deterministic outcomes in their evolutionary processes.

Now we have come to a point to declare that living systems, including our social system, are no exception to these laws and as a result, their evolutionary process is not free from restrictions and constraints. In fact, their evolutionary process looks very much like our example, where the finality of their evolutionary process is set by the natural laws and forces of nature. For example, it is the second law of thermodynamics (entropy) that drives the evolutionary process of a social system to its optimum stability (a state desired by all systems) and minimum state of internal energy when its subsystems are forced to achieve equilibrium or equality among themselves. Therefore, we can claim that social evolution is indeed an equifinal and a deterministic process in its finality, even though it could be circumstantial within the process itself. Circumstantial situations may arise not only from within the social system, but also from the environment that supports it. A war initiated by an aggressive nation may delay achieving the state of finality of social evolution on a global scale, but it will not deter it from attaining that state in the long run. If the environment of a social system stopped supporting it due to diminishing life support systems, then the social evolution would take a self-destructive path, yet again a deterministic process in its finality, but it will remain circumstantial within its process.

To further clarify the definition of determinism in finality and not in the process itself, let us assume that we can restart our history repeatedly to compare the historical processes. To our surprise, we will find that not a single historical process matches another, regardless of how many times we restart our history. However, at the end of each process, we may (surprisingly) find that all processes have guided the social organism to reach a state of stability in which its attributes in terms of structural organization, development of specific relational bonds among its subsystems, and its relationship with its environment, resemble each other. The difference between these historical processes is only in their chronological events, the sequential development and maturation of their organization, and the total length of the process, all of which are caused by circumstantial situations before stability is reached. The socioeconomic evolution and integration of human societies on a global scale is, in fact, a deterministic and equifinal process.

Despite the unpredictability of historical processes, it is not hard to envision the finality of human society on earth in terms of development of relational bonds between humans and their environment. In the view of many, irrespective of how many times we destroy our own civilization, annihilate our societies or obliterate human races, what is left at the end must be treated equally or the struggle will continue. Struggle will go on until we realize that the key to stability of human society lies in establishing harmony and just treatment of all of its members, in all subsystem levels.

Realization of this fact and recognition of the social organism as a living entity in search of stability can lead us to better understanding of the causal relationship between the historical events of the past and present. Furthermore, it would enhance our ability to understand and manage future historical processes so we can accelerate the advancement of the society toward a state of stability and put an end to the struggle of man against man. The good news is that human beings and the social organism are, to some extent, self-aware and self-regulating systems that can influence their own evolutionary course by obtaining knowledge. But the bad news is that human beings are not an exception to system laws and behave like all other systems that work to keep their own state of internal energy at the minimum level. This thrusts people into confrontations, whether at the individual or social level. Up to this point in our history, any relative equality that has been achieved at human and societal level has been through violence and confrontational processes.

Whether this will continue to be the same in the future will depend on our understanding of history and on our positive response to its deterministic finality. The experience of two world wars in Europe and the loss of more than 55 million lives in the Second World War led to the unification of these societies and formation of EU subsequent to war. How many lives have to be lost through violent behavior on a global scale to unite the world? Billions? The violence in our historical processes seems to be inevitable, and it can only get worse with the world population growing and energy resources depleting. If energy resources start to run out, this will trigger a new round of competition, even among the closest allies, to capture and manipulate energy resources, regardless of where they may be.

In the final analysis, if we are able to understand the principles, causes, and rationales behind the events that created our history, then we should be able to assist its process to achieve certain outcomes, in line with its intended goals, in order to avoid human catastrophes and minimize the destruction of order. Alternatively, we can leave it to the natural processes or the social organism itself to lead us to the state that it seeks, which would be extremely lengthy and very costly to all of us. From this point on, when we use the terms "determinism" or "deterministic process" as they apply to the social system, we refer only to the finality of the process and not the entire process itself.

Evolutionary processes of isolated and open systems: In an isolated system, where no external forces interfere with the state of the system, no evolutionary process takes place within the system. Any initial state the system had adopted before it entered into isolation would remain as its final state. This assumes that the system is immune to the implications of natural laws. However, when we isolate the system from other systems but not from the implications of natural laws, that system will adopt an evolutionary process that focuses on its internal conditions and the development of certain relational bonds among its subsystems that will lead the system to achieve its lowest state of internal energy. This evolutionary process is deterministic in finality, and when the system acquires that state, it remains in that state for eternity.

In open systems, the evolutionary process becomes far more complex as environmental forces continue to evolve dynamically and affect the evolutionary process of the system in such a way that its finality starts to become a moving target. But having a finality that becomes a moving target by no means implies that the evolutionary process is no longer deterministic. On the contrary, determinism applies to the state of internal energy of the system and not to external circumstances. The external forces only set a different finality for the system to pursue, but for any of these finalities, there is only one deterministic outcome that would evolve internal to the system and put the system in its best position with respect to its internal energy level and stability. Therefore, evolutionary processes related to the open systems also remain deterministic in their finality. We must bear in mind, however, that when external circumstances or forces that apply to the open system change rapidly, they may not give sufficient amount of time for a system to achieve one finality before it is forced to pursue another.

Chaotic and random processes: One attribute of a complex system is its complex evolutionary process. Obviously, this complexity is due to the large number of variables, subsystems, and sub-processes that are all involved in the main process. Systems are always trying to redefine their relational bonds with all surrounding systems and subsystems. In this chaotic period of the evolutionary process, predicting the behavior of the system with a single set of rules becomes a cumbersome task. However, let us not forget that regardless of how complex a system may be, it is still built from matter and its process must be guided by natural laws. Therefore, despite the chaotic behavior of some evolutionary processes associated with complex systems, the general trend, direction, or outcome of the process influenced by the natural laws may be predictable.

Chaos theory suggests that systems with a greater sensitivity to initial conditions may produce different outcomes in their evolutionary process. This may be true for abstract and mathematical systems that do not obey the laws of nature, but real systems that obey these laws behave differently. For example, they always seek the lowest state of internal energy that is their state of optimum stability, which means that real systems are goal-oriented. The misconception about random behavior of real systems comes from our inability to formulate their behavior, particularly when systems are complex and have lengthy evolutionary processes like our social evolution. Nonetheless, there may be real systems that are sensitive to their initial conditions and produce a multitude of outcomes as an indication of their randomness. But this is only possible if all outcomes can provide the same degree of stability and state of internal energy to the system. It is only then that the restrictions imposed upon the system by natural laws would be lifted. This is because every outcome would equally satisfy the natural laws, and would not mean that those outcomes have been excluded from implications of natural laws. As a result, such a process becomes a truly random process. If a process is not proven random according to our definition, it is expected to be deterministic at the end of its evolutionary process. Therefore, any conclusions we draw regarding the randomness of its process by observing its transitional states may be misleading and inaccurate. Examples of random processes are the landing of a die on any one of its faces, or the landing position of a ball thrown from a height over a horizontal plane, as shown in Figure 1-10a. In the latter case, the ball may adopt numerous positions (finalities) on the horizontal plane when it becomes stationary, resulting in the storage of the same level of internal energy within its structure. That is, it can land anywhere. The laws of nature remain indifferent to these finalities, as all become equally acceptable states.

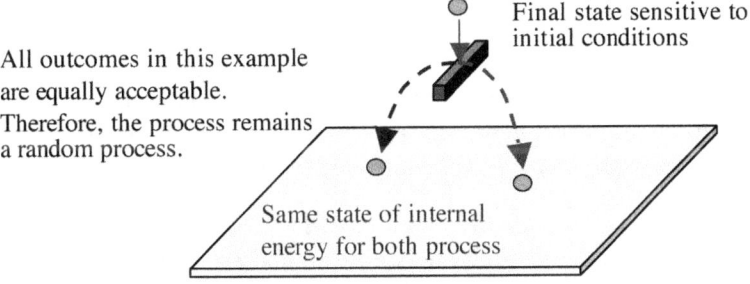

Figure 1-10a An example of random process

Figure 1-10b shows a two-stage process. The first part illustrates a sub-process that is sensitive to its initial condition, combined with a second sub-process that is insensitive to its initial conditions, yet sensitive to its final state. Therefore, the combination of the two-stage process in Fig.1-10b would become a deterministic process even though it may seem to be a chaotic or random process anywhere in between. Our conclusion from the above argument is that, although some processes may seem to be chaotic, they may be goal-seeking processes. It is only our limited assessment of their entire process that leads us to the wrong conclusions. We may also conclude that a chaotic behavior is primarily observed between the initial and final conditions of a process where the system has not yet reached its stability. Chaotic behavior can also be observed in systems that are in the process of transforming from one phase or state to another and where the behavior of the system cannot be formulated by only one set of rules, but by many rules associated with those phases.

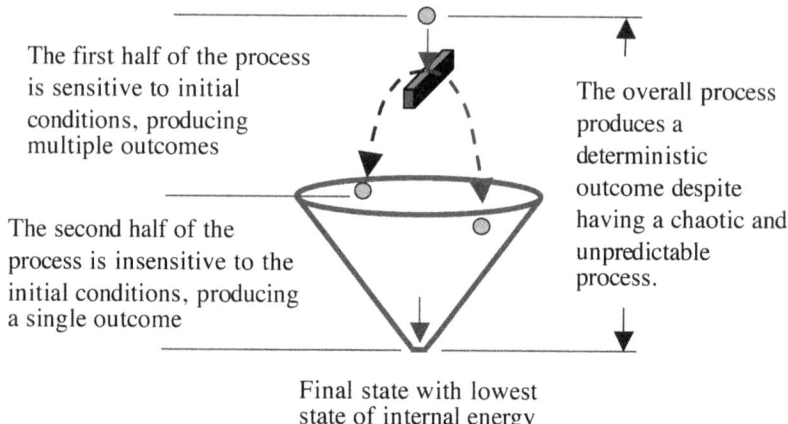

The first half of the process is sensitive to initial conditions, producing multiple outcomes

The overall process produces a deterministic outcome despite having a chaotic and unpredictable process.

The second half of the process is insensitive to the initial conditions, producing a single outcome

Final state with lowest state of internal energy

Figure 1-10b An example of a deterministic process

In any transformative process, one of the major events that takes place is among subsystems trying to redefine their relational bonds at all hierarchical levels. After transformation process is completed and new relational bonds have emerged, the system may become more predictable once again.

Taking water as an example, we may say that when water is in the gaseous state, its molecules are free and can bounce around at any direction and speed. Therefore, there is more chaotic behavior in water vapor than it is in liquid water. But this is not what we are defining as chaotic behavior. Even though the molecules of water in the gaseous state exhibit a greater chaotic behavior in terms of their motion, gases do follow rules that make them predictable. This means that there is a set of well-defined relational bonds among the subsystems that makes the behavior of the system predictable. This is not true in the transformation stage, where the relational bonds of the liquid and gas may both apply simultaneously, making the system more unpredictable. A chaotic process is one that lacks rules and regulations that define its behavior and evolutionary process.

Chaotic behavior in social evolution can be attributed to the instability of the society as a system striving to become stable by enforcing equality among its subsystems. The root cause of instability in social systems is socioeconomic inequality among their subsystems that manifests itself in the form of social unrest, which takes many forms, ranging from criminal behavior to revolution and acts of war, each with a different magnitude of chaos in its process. In some chaotic behaviors of social systems, where the magnitude of the difference in subsystem's energy levels are huge, in a short period of time a large amount of energy is exchanged between the subsystems, in order to move the system to its stability as quickly as possible. In reality, the chaotic behavior of a society is the consequence of accumulated stresses among its subsystems resulting from un-equal levels of energy stored within them. The only way that the social system can release that tension and achieve an optimum state of stability is to force its subsystems to exchange energy, which results in the modification of their relational bonds.

Transformation of a system and alteration of relational bonds at the sub-system level: When the absorbed or released energy within a system exceeds a threshold level, the transformation of the system from one state to another be-comes a necessity. This leads to the alteration of its subsystem's relational bonds. Let us take the example of water again. When its temperature exceeds 100 degrees Centigrade, water changes its state from liquid to vapor. This change of state eliminates the stresses accumulated among water molecules due to excessive absorption of energy and brings about a new stability to the system itself. The transformation of a system affects the relational bonds of its subsystems at all levels. Transformation is not limited to non-living systems, but also applies to living systems.

When corrupt government officials and wealthy individuals and corporations affiliated with them continue to set policies to make themselves richer and richer and leave the rest of the population of their society in despair, the stress level among these socioeconomic classes will rise until it reaches a point where transformation becomes unavoidable. In this case, people rebel against the government and overthrow it by force, if peaceful political processes fail to produce desired results. After the new revolutionary government assumes political power, it revises the failed socioeconomic policies of the past government and mends the broken political ties of the previous government with other societies if necessary. Most of the relational bonds among the members of the society also undergo changes brought about by healthcare practices, labor laws, education policies, etc.

Ordered systems: As the second law of thermodynamics reminds us, nature has the tendency to increase its entropy, which means it raises its level of disorder with every interaction that takes place between systems. If this is true, then the emergence of living systems with *ordered structures* in nature poses a difficult question. The question is: *How does an ordered structure evolve in na-*

ture? To answer this question, let us remind ourselves that any ordered system in nature has a level of stored energy in its structure that is less than the total energy that has been consumed to create it. Naturally, the consumed energy, which contributes to the elevation of entropy in the universe or nature, exceeds the decline of entropy caused by the formation of that ordered structure. As a result, the net amount of entropy remains positive in the universe and in accordance with the second law of thermodynamics.

Now that we have established that ordered structures can exist in accordance with all the laws of nature, how we can define an ordered structure? It is very difficult to come up with a single definition for ordered structures that covers all living and non-living systems. One property that seems to be common to all of these systems is the stored energy in their structure. This is partly due to having diverse relational bonds among their subsystems, particularly at the highest subsystem level. Systems with a diversity of relational bonds among their subsystems can produce non-isotropic characteristics, either in their behavior, their form factors or both. If these systems are capable of performing work, which we know it would require energy, then they need to replenish their lost energy by taking it from their environment. Examples of such systems are living beings and machines, and the difference between them is in their self-consciousness. If an ordered system does not provide a function or perform work, then it may preserve its stored energy for a much longer time before it eventually collapses.

Let us now explore some of these concepts through examples. A crystal is an ordered structure because all of the atoms in its structure follow a certain rule in organizing themselves in its lattice. The entropy in this structure is less positive than a structure that its atoms are randomly organized. Crystals exhibit non-isotropic behavior due to the formation of a variety of electromagnetic forces between their atoms (diverse relational bonds). A non-isotropic behavior refers to the formation of a variety of physical characteristics in every plane or direction. Let us take numerous small but perfect crystals and randomly organize them into a new structure, called an amorphous structure. Such a system would lack the definition of an ordered structure because the randomness in orientation of crystals would produce isotropic characteristics in all directions and planes despite having perfectly ordered systems in its sub-subsystem level. Therefore, it is critical that such diversity in relational bonds exist, at least, in the top subsystem level of an ordered system to be considered an ordered structure. A crystal does not perform any work on its own, and therefore it does not need to consume energy but only preserve what is stored in its structure. In contrast, other ordered structures such as human beings and the machines built by them, have the tendency to consume energy to maintain their structure and perform work.

Note also that complex ordered systems are those that are constructed upon layers and layers of ordered system that make up their hierarchy. This is particularly true in regard to human beings, as they tend to grow and integrate into larger systems, or organisms, such as their society. People also tend to reorganize their natural environment and build non-living ordered structures and integrate them into their society either for their convenience or to better control their environment. A human society in an urban environment with factories, transportation systems, etc., is an example of such an integrated system. The energy requirement to maintain this huge structure, including its residence, is much greater than the energy its population needs to survive. Obviously, as long as this huge ordered system can extract enough energy from its environment to continue its growth to an even larger ordered structure, it will continue to do so. The moment the energy resources fall short of what is needed to maintain that large structure, the system will start disintegrating to minimize its dependence on the energy, or it will vanish all together due to a lack of energy. As we understand the basic reason behind the existence of the ordered systems in connection with energy resources and life support systems of their environment, we will better comprehend and appreciate their behavior in manipulating these resources.

Ordered systems with optimized structures: The second law of thermodynamics prevents any process, or the work performed by a system, from achieving efficiency levels of 100 percent because a portion of the energy the system uses to perform a task gets dissipated through the generation of heat or friction. The operational efficiency of living system, as well as every ordered structure that they create, can approach the limit of 100 percent efficiency, but it can never achieve it. Systems that can approach such limits of efficiency must have been optimized rigorously; among them are living beings. The question is: what was the necessity behind the evolutionary process of almost every living being that led that being to evolve with such degree of operational efficiency? The answer is easy: the scarcity of natural resources in the life forms environment. These animals had to be extremely efficient to minimize their dependence on the resources in order to survive. Birds, for example, have porous and hollow bones to make flying an easier task. Animals living in Polar Regions preserve their body heat with layers of fat and fur. The aerodynamic shape of sea animals facilitates the efficiency of their movement in the water.

This argument brings us to some other logical deductions that may or may not be acceptable to some readers. If energy resources in the environment were influential factors driving the evolutionary processes (such as evolvement into efficient structures) of all living beings, then it is also possible that shortage of resources had a major influence in the development of the sensory organs of the living beings and on the development of their brain and cognitive ability. Let us assume that a living organism with no ability to move or perceive its environment is confined to one location. Obviously, if the energy resources this organism needs cannot be found or do not flow through this location on a continuous basis, this organism would not be able to survive. If resources were available, however, then there would be no need for the organism to mutate into anything else and it could remain in its primitive form. However, when resources start becoming scarce, the organism may evolve into a mobile organism to allow it to search for resources elsewhere. Again, if the organism is capable of finding vital resources within the range of its mobility, then there would be no necessity for it to evolve into a more complex life form, and it would remain a mobile organism only. If mobility was not enough, then the organism would need other means to help it perceive its environment better and search for hidden energy resources it needs. It is at this point that the organism would evolve with sensory organs, a brain, and cognitive ability.

It is logical, then, to believe that the sequence of the evolution of all life forms, starting with the simple organism, has been to evolve with mobility first and then add sensory, brain and cognitive abilities. It is also reasonable to conclude that a living organism will do anything to survive, from evolving with mobility and a brain for better understanding of its environment, to building reproductive and defensive systems and collaborating and integrating with similar systems...all to improve its chances of survival.

The scarcity of resources in the environment has affected the biological and psychological developments of living organisms. For example, human beings are capable of storing energy in their bodies in the form of fat to be used in later times because during their evolutionary process they starved from time to time. This biological development would have not been necessary if resources were always available. The psychological impact of starvation has resulted in insecurity in humans, and animals in general. This insecurity is the main reason why animals continuously search, collect, and store energy (food). Even modern day human beings can hardly depart from the behavioral pattern associated with their insecurity, despite the fact that there may be an abundance of energy resources available to them for consumption.

In conclusion, the structures of living organisms have evolved with a high degree of efficiency in order to function and survive in an environment that lacks sufficient resources for everyone. Society, which is at the early stages of its evolutionary process as a higher-level living organism, is following in the footsteps of human evolution in optimizing its own structure and operational efficiency. All ordered structures (such as cars and other products) that are built by human beings tend to have evolutionary processes of their own, which continue to become more and more efficient, simply because humans try to replicate what nature has given them in their own evolutionary process.

Transcendence of all subsystem properties to the system level: In the hierarchy of matter, as we move from the simplest subsystem in the hierarchy toward higher system levels, we find new characteristics and properties in each higher level system that are not present in the lower level systems. We also find that all of the properties of the lower level systems in the hierarchy are retained in the high level systems. Figure 1-11 shows what we have just discussed. In this figure, P1, P2, and P3 are the collections of all properties pertaining to the corresponding systems. Subsystem level 2 has all the properties of subsystem level 1, including its own additional set of properties, P2, which are not present in subsystem level 1. System level 3 possesses all of the properties of subsystems at level 2 with an additional set of new properties, P3, again not found in any of the lower level systems.

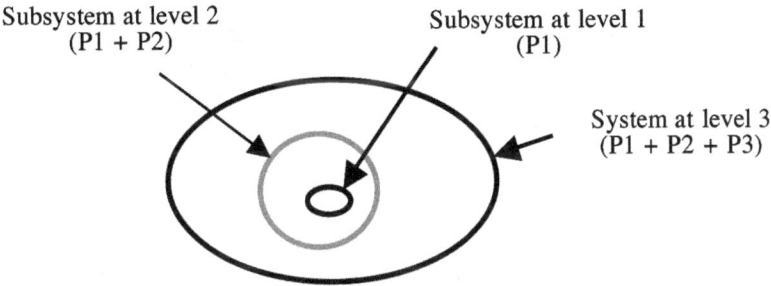

Figure 1-11 transcendence of system properties

As an example, one of the components of the human body is water. This component boils and evaporates at 100 degrees Centigrade, whether as an independent system or as part of a larger system. Therefore, humans could not possibly survive in temperatures above 100 degrees Centigrade. As the top-level system, the human body has other characteristics that none of its components and subsystems possess, characteristics such as intelligence, cognitive ability, and emotion are among few of them. Newer system properties always arise by formation of relational bonds among parallel subsystems one level down. For example, looking at a higher order system, such as a society, and comparing it to its subsystems (individual human beings), we find that society is a living organism with intelligence, cognitive ability, and emotions because the lower level subsystems have all of those properties. However, newly generated characteristics in the society, such as technology, culture, and economy, are not applicable to its subsystems, i.e., individual human beings. These new characteristics are the product of their relational bonds in the society.

The technological advancements of today's world would have not been possible if it were not for the formation of society. The division of work in our society has created expertise to improve productivity, which has eliminated the need for every individual to seek for the daily energy he or she needs to survive. As a result, the burden of energy supply to all members of the society is placed upon a smaller percentage of the population, which lets others use their time for other social needs. This division of work has led to the creation of military, educational, and cultural institutions, to name just a few, and it has also helped the advancement of science. As systems emerge from integration of subsystems, their behavior becomes much more complicated and difficult to predict due to the accrual of properties from all subsystem levels. That is why it is easier to predict the behavior of a human being than to forecast the behavior of a society and its evolutionary process.

Determinism and chance: A deterministic process is a process that generates predictable states, if the initial conditions and forces that apply to the system throughout its evolutionary process are well known. Systems cannot be predicted if their initial conditions or the nature of the forces that affects them are unknown. Moreover, predictability becomes increasingly more difficult with every level of added complexity in the system's organization, which means the larger the number of subsystems and subsystem levels in the hierarchy of the system the more unpredictable its behavior. In these cases, the behavior of the systems and finality of their processes may be estimated using non-exact sciences and probability theory. In other cases, despite having a non-exact knowledge of details of subsystem behavior, the final state of the system's evolutionary process may be accurately predicted. For example, let us take a volume of gas that is trapped in a cylinder with a moveable piston. We know if we reduce the volume of the chamber to half while keeping all other physical parameters the same, such as temperature, the pressure will double. This is a predictable and deterministic outcome using simple calculations. This outcome can be studied using a more detailed methodology, which is to calculate the total force applied by the impact of gas molecules that hit the walls of the cylinder and generate the pressure. The number of molecules trapped in the chamber may be billions, and even with the fastest computers, it would be impossible to come remotely close to such calculations. But simply because we are unable to calculate and predict the position of every single molecule at each particular time, it does not make the overall behavior of the trapped gas unpredictable. Therefore, the best answer that we can provide to this problem at this time would be that the number of molecules impacting the piston doubles when we reduce the volume to half. The fact is that all of the processes in nature are more or less deterministic, if not throughout the process, then in their finality. It is only our lack of knowledge and inability to deal with large number of variables and systems that makes them nondeterministic to us. Terms such as chance, statistics and probability describe ways of estimating the outcome of a process or an event, using mathematical tools such as the statistics and probability theory.

To show how the level of knowledge can affect the outcome of a research study, let us consider a scientist who is studying the motion of a projectile but is unaware of the presence of the air in his test environment and how the movement of the air can affect the outcome of his experiment. When air is stationary and there is no wind, all of the projectiles that he releases under the same initial conditions will repeatedly hit the same spot. However, when air is moving, the projectiles will hit different spots within a circle (target) depending on the speed of the wind and its direction. For this scientist who is unaware of the effects of the wind on his projectile, a completely deterministic outcome and process will turn into a stochastic process. The results of his study will indicate that there is a greater probability that the projectile will hit the center of a circle (target) and an increasingly lower probability as one moves away from that center. If this researcher had known about the movement of air and its effect on the motion of the projectile, and had incorporated this information in his calculations, his study would have shown deterministic outcomes for the motion of the projectile. This is exactly what happens in any scientific discipline that deals with a large number of variables and undiscovered phenomena that affect the behavior of the systems under study. Consequently, based on the two examples discussed here, a process can be called deterministic when an exact knowledge exists to predict the behavior of the system under any circumstances or when we know the response of the system for any stimulus. When this knowledge is not exact, the outcome of a system's behavior becomes uncertain, or stochastic. Going one step further, when no knowledge can remotely describe the behavior of a system, the outcomes seem to be equally probable, or simply random. Therefore, the seemingly random or stochastic outcome in regard to the behavior of a system by no means eradicates the existence of an exact knowledge that is capable of predicting its behavior.

Open-loop and closed-loop systems: We should not confuse the definition of the open and closed systems with *open-loop and closed-loop systems*; they are entirely different. Please refer to the earlier definition to remind yourself of the definition of open and closed systems. Open-loop systems do not participate in their own course of evolution and are merely driven by external forces. In other words, no part of the system's current output (in the form of a force) is fed back or reapplied to the system as new input, to drive the system forward in its evolutionary path. In contrary, a closed-loop system takes part in its own evolutionary process by exerting its own forces upon itself either discretely or on a continuous basis. The result is; an evolutionary process that is partly driven by the forces of the system itself, which means that the current state of a closed-loop system is impacted by its own previous states.

In systems theory, *feedback* is a term that is often used to indicate that there is an open path between the output and the input of a system. This path is a communication channel through which information or physical properties are exchanged.

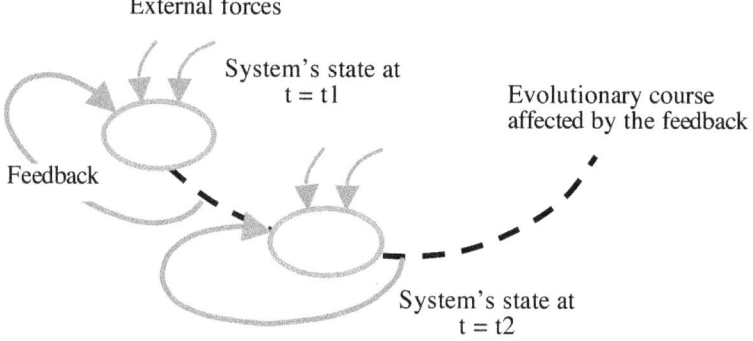

Figure 1-12a A closed-loop system

Figure 1-12a shows a closed-loop system that applies its own forces at each stage of its evolutionary process to set the conditions for the impending states of the system.

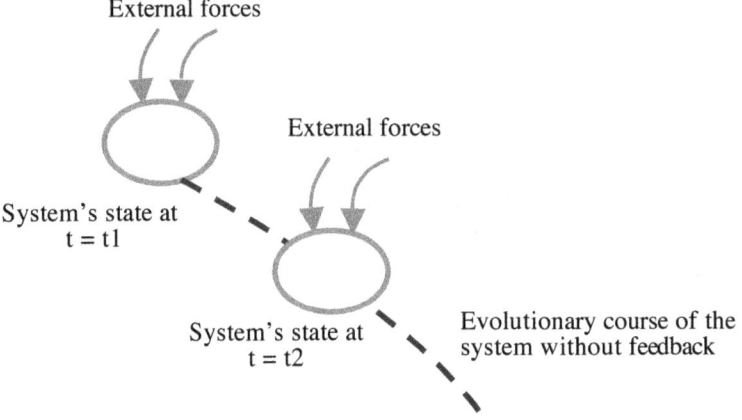

Figure 1-12b An open-loop system

In contrast, the system in Figure 1-12b is operating as an open-loop system, and its evolutionary path is merely driven by external forces. Although the two systems have started at the same initial conditions, note how their evolutionary paths have diverged due to the self-involvement of the system shown in Figure 1-12a in its own evolutionary process. Thermostat/furnace is a good example of a closed-loop system. In this closed-loop system, the furnace continues to provide warm air to the house until it receives a signal from the thermostat indicating that the room temperature has risen to the level of temperature setting. The furnace then stops operating until it receives a new signal that the temperature has fallen. Social systems and human beings are other examples of closed-loop systems because their planned activities designed for today are expected to have certain outcomes in their future.

Cybernetic and self-regulating systems: Closed-loop systems that are goal-oriented are called *self-regulating systems*. For a system to be goal-oriented, it needs a *feedback mechanism* to keep track of its current status so that it can make proper adjustments to its behavior in order to achieve its goal. There are two types of feedback, positive and negative. When feedback is positive, it supports the direction of the evolutionary process and produces either acceleration and expansion or deceleration and contraction. Examples of positive feedback are population growth and the multiplication of cancerous cells. When feedback is negative, it opposes the direction of the process by either halting it or reaching a steady state condition. Examples of such processes include controlling the room temperature or water level in a tank.

Imagine a predator adjusting his path to follow every maneuver his prey makes. This process would have not been possible without sensory organs and perceptive ability in both predator and prey. In general, most life forms are equipped with sensory organs and perceptive abilities and to a lesser or greater degree, can be considered self-regulating systems. This self-regulating characteristic of living organisms helps them modify their behavior, adapt to changing environments, search for food, and defend themselves against others. Human beings, unlike many other living organisms, are capable of coordinating their activities to react to feedbacks connected with future events (which may be perceived to be dangerous) and plan accordingly to avoid those future events.

This difference between human beings and other living beings comes from human's cognitive capacity and knowledge of their environment. This characteristic of human beings also transcends to the higher level systems, which is their society. Human society is thus another example of a goal-seeking system whose evolutionary process is not only influenced by natural laws, but also by self-regulation. For example, self-regulation at the level of the social organism might be an international effort to control and protect the natural environment from pollution or an effort to stop population explosion. Both of these responses need long-term planning and are based on feedback that is not imminently life threatening, but may present serious threats in the distant future. Human beings and social organisms continue to struggle to protect themselves from life-threatening situations and maintain a stable and secure environment for their survival. To achieve this stability, they continue to expand their knowledge of their environment to make a better assessment and interpretation of today's feedbacks connected with tomorrow's events. This knowledge gives them enough lead time to prepare for corrective measures to avoid or minimize threats. All of these actions are to protect the social organism from slipping into an uncontrollable situation that may be life-threatening not only to itself, but also to its own subsystems (human beings). In general, human beings and social organisms are capable of interfering in their own evolutionary processes and setting their own environmental conditions, rather than allowing circumstances and miscellaneous factors set the conditions up for them.

To show the impact of the human involvement in his own evolutionary process, let us consider Charles Darwin's theory of evolution and the notion of survival of the fittest based on natural selection. In the past, human beings had a shorter life span than they have today. This was partly due to their vulnerability to incurable diseases that allowed natural selection to be the dominant factor in deciding who would live and who would not. Recent advances in the field of medicine, urbanization and sanitation, however, have weakened the influence of nature in the selection process and added the human factor, which has set up a new course for the evolution of human beings and their societies. As human knowledge continues to advance to higher and higher grounds, so would his ability to predict and control more distant futures based on today's feedbacks, which will diminish the influence of nature to control his destiny. Obviously, this would also hold true for the evolutionary process of social organism. Let us not forget that our environment is not limited to the nature that supports us but also includes all other individuals and societies that surround us. Therefore, we must respond responsively to all the feedbacks that we receive from our surrounding systems.

Social evolution on earth is a goal-seeking process that aims at integrating all of the societies of the world and all human beings into one single community or organism, in which all members at all system levels would have equal rights with predefined relational bonds with each other. There is sufficient evidence in our historical process to support this notion. The question is, can individuals and social organisms use this knowledge to interfere in this process and regulate it? Suppose that the world leaders, particularly those of the advanced nations, understood the process of history, realized the inevitability of its finality in terms of evolvement into a single organism (a global society), and decided to interfere with the process in a positive way. To start, they might help underdeveloped nations with their economies and education as well as terminating their influence in the manipulation of hostility among them and begin assisting those nations to improve their standard of life, so that they can join the global community as significant members. This course of action in self-regulating our historical process would definitely change the course of our social evolution and avoid historical events that may have been different and undeniably more violent. If these leaders choose not to participate in this self-regulating process, the natural course of social evolution would attain its intended goals anyway, but it would be through trial and error, possibly through violence, and a much more complicated and lengthy process. What deters humans from fully adopting the first approach can be found in their dominant instinctive behavior over their rational behavior, which has been formed over millions of years of struggle for survival in their environment and further fortified by the laws of systems.

The question is: is there any optimism for human beings and their societies, to deviate from their instinctive behaviors and insecurities and adopt more rational solutions to their problems and self-regulate their social evolution? The answer is probably *yes*. In smaller scales, self-regulation is already taking place and will continue to strengthen as social evolution proceeds to its next stages where global society, as a single entity, would be highly self-regulated system.

To maintain its stability and security, which will be of benefit to all human beings, society will foresee upcoming changes and will act upon them in a logical and rational manner.

Perceptions of survival by living and non-living systems: When the environment surrounding a non-living system changes, that system either transforms itself into a different physical state or changes its form to adapt to its new environment without resistance. This is due to the fact that non-living systems have no preference for maintaining specific relational bonds between any parallel or serially connected systems in their own structure or their surrounding environment. As a result, they can adapt to all conditions as their environment dictates. Unimaginable hot and cold conditions produce no preference to non-living systems, only changing their physical state. The collisions of planetary systems and galaxies are by no means the end of their existence, but only a new beginning. Living systems, by contrast, can tolerate only minute environmental changes before they collapse due to alteration or loss of critical relational bonds among their subsystems. The existence of a living system is so critically dependent upon all the relational bonds of its subsystems that any damage to a few of these relational bonds would threaten its survival. That is why living systems always resist drastic environmental changes that may lead to alteration of the relational bonds of their subsystems and threaten their survival. For example, consider the human body, which can survive only within a certain ambient temperature range. If ambient temperatures fall outside these desirable limits, the body will perish. Therefore, any environmental change that does not fall into the narrow window of a living system's survivability may be perceived as life threatening. That is why living systems strive to control their environment or develop capabilities to adapt to changing environments. It is also logical to assume that control of the environment would become a more critical issue for living systems of a greater complexity, such as social systems. This is due to an added level of subsystems and the development of an additional level of relational bonds, which makes the system both more sensitive and more susceptible to environmental changes and, in general, less adaptable.

Self-involvement of living systems in their evolutionary process: Every system in our universe is surrounded by other systems and every system evolves at the same time that others do, which means that their evolutionary process are interdependent. In other words, a system's evolutionary process is tied to the evolutionary processes of all of its surrounding systems. These system interactions continuously set new boundary conditions or exert new forces upon one another that force them either to transform themselves or change their evolutionary paths. This continuous conformity of a system to its environment is called *adaptation*. When a system adapts through transformation, then a change in relational bonds of its subsystems becomes a necessity. We must also note that adaptation, which is the product of system interaction, is always accompanied by energy, mass and information exchange, and, depending on the rate of exchange, some of adaptation processes may be violent and some others non-violent as systems move from current to future states. Most of the systems, in particular living systems, have a built in delayed response to changing environmental conditions, to ascertain that incoming changes are permanent and not transitory. This will avoid unnecessary change to the relational bonds of their subsystems, until it reaches a point that they can no longer ignore environmental changes. If environmental changes take place in a much faster pace, then a swift response by the living systems might be necessary to avoid a major threat to their survival.

One of the most important topics in the theory of evolution is the evolution of life forms on our planet, especially the evolution of human beings. All physical and psychological states of human beings are products of continuous adaptation to the changing environment. The development of intellect, for example, has given human beings an opportunity to have greater influence in the alteration of their environment and, consequently, their own evolutionary process. With the rapid advancement of science in the field of the human genome and other frontiers, it is possible that, one day, human beings be able to set their own evolutionary course independent of their environment and also design living beings that are able to survive in environments other than human environment. It is hard to predict where this evolutionary process might take us and to what extent we might be able to control the environment that once controlled us.

As a living organism, society has its own evolutionary process, which we call *history*. Is history merely a sequence of unrelated events that repeat from time to time, or is it a meaningful and goal-seeking evolutionary process? History is the utmost complicated process for two reasons. First, because society is the most complex system in the hierarchy of the multilevel systems; and second, because its evolutionary process is so long that one can hardly make any sense out of it by analyzing it in short durations of time. However, based on the arguments that we have presented so far, it seems that the process of history (our social evolution), like other natural processes, is dominated by natural laws leading to deterministic finalities. Like all other systems, social systems evolve and adapt as they interact with other social systems and their environment. A social system is an intelligent entity, and if humans can interfere in their own evolutionary process, so can the social system. Therefore, it is not unrealistic to believe that social systems could plan their own evolutionary process and pursue their own finality.

Adaptation through the generation of directed gene mutations: Due to planetary and cosmic forces, the environment that supports life continuously changes. Sometimes these changes are so drastic that life forms (organisms) do not have a chance to adjust to new environmental conditions and are forced into the path of extinction. Other times, changes are relatively modest and life forms are capable of adjusting to their new environment and surviving. The accumulation of these gradual changes in the organism's biological make-up over time allows the organism to survive in its environment; this is referred to as the *evolutionary process*. In reality, not every single member of a particular life form is always capable, as other members, of surviving in the same environment. Those that survive carry genes that are best suited in the new environment. This selection process, as proposed by Charles Darwin in the 19th century, is called *survival of the fittest*. This theory suggests that when an environmental change occurs, only a part of the population of a particular life form, that possesses genes that best fit the emerging environment are able to survive, and the rest (with unsuitable genes) perish. Of course, the members of the surviving group are not all genetically identical, and there is always a distribution of mutated genes ready to be picked up in the next step of the evolution process as the environment changes again. The real question is, "is the mutation of genes merely a random process or is it random and at the same time a directed process?" Logically, if we believe that a life form is an open system and in constant communication with its environment, the mutation of genes that prepares the life form for its next stage of evolution cannot possibly be a random process. As our brain is capable of analyzing received data, it can become aware of coming environmental changes and prepare a number of genetic mutations that are suitable for the new environmental conditions. If gene mutation was merely a random process with no directivity, we would have seen a broader range of variations in the human species, to a point where some newborn humans might have resembled the newborns of our ancestors who lived millions of years ago. We do not observe these cases. Therefore, we propose that the mutation of genes in any life form is not a flat distribution, but rather a Gaussian distribution that its mean follows the environmental change indicator, which suggests directivity in gene mutation. If we accept this argument, then we have to also accept that this directivity in gene mutation is a result of a closed-loop communication between life forms and their environment.

Technological achievements of the last century and the release of polluting industrial by-products into the environment have affected the earth's environment to an extent that it will play a major role in the evolutionary process of every living system on earth. Environmental changes that were once natural are now combined with those generated by industrial by-products. The pollutants that we create and release in the environment have already affected our air, our water (the oceans) and the forests of the planet, and they have also hastened the extinction process of many life forms that have low tolerance to changes in the environment. Pollution may, however, provide a suitable environment for the growth of new life forms in the form of microorganisms that might affect us and other life forms in the long run. Figure 1-13 shows how some species may adapt and survive in emerging environments and how others may slowly perish. In these plots, we have picked an environmental indicator (which defines the environment) and placed it in the center, or mean, of the distribution curve. The distribution curve is a representation of gene variation among the population of a particular species. We have also assumed that most of the population of this species carries the most suitable gene for the current environment, represented by the indicator. The genes on the left side of the environmental indicator are those that are ready to be picked up by the environment as the environmental indicator start to move toward the left, which is a sign of change in the environment. The genes on the left side that represent the next generation of this species (those fit to survive) are not there merely by chance. They are there because the species was in a closed-loop relationship with its environment and anticipated the forthcoming changes and prepared for change by mutating genes in that direction. Figure 1-13a shows the inherent ability of a species to adapt to the rate of change represented by our environmental indicator as it moves to the left. As we can see, most of the population of this species possesses genes suitable for survival in the new environment. It is very likely that this species would continue to survive when the next environmental change arrives, as long as the rate of change does not exceed beyond its ability to cope. In contrast, Figure 1-13b shows a different species that is inherently incapable of mutating enough new genes in its population to sustain its survival, assuming that the rate of change in the environment of this species has remained similar to that of the first. Therefore, chances are that when the next environmental change arrives, this species will be in further trouble, as its surviving population will continue to shrink until it becomes extinct. When the rate of change in the environment is lower than that of the life form's inherent ability to adapt (managing the gene mutation in a proper direction at least equal to the rate of environmental change), the life form will survive and evolution will continue.

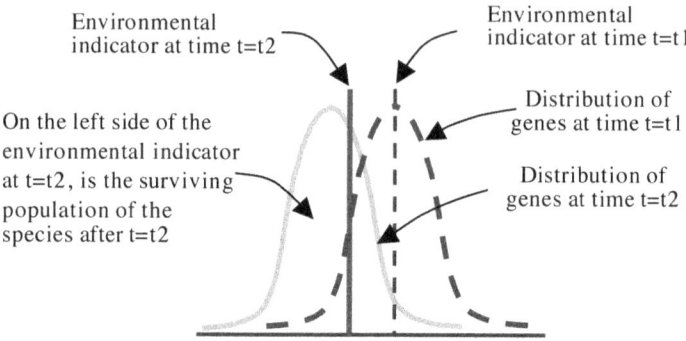

Figure 1-13a Successful adaptation of the species

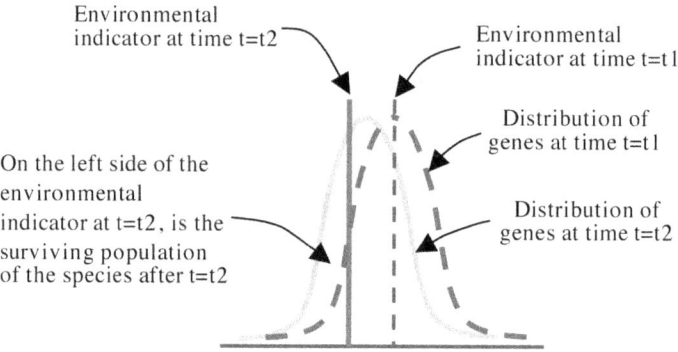

Figure 1-13b Failed adaptation of the species

The moment the rate of environmental change exceeds the ability of the life form to cope, the life form will be in the path of extinction.

Interference of humans in their evolutionary process: Is the robot an extension of human evolution? Will genetically enhanced human beings eventually replace present-day human beings and keep enhancing themselves in the course of their evolution? Is it possible that we are capable of creating more intelligent beings than ourselves? These questions trigger the following philosophical debates. If the theory of evolution is correct, and intelligent beings or systems have risen from unintelligent systems with no external interference, then it is possible that greater intelligence can rise from lesser intelligence, which leads to this conclusion that one day, humans may create beings more intelligent than themselves. But if we believe that intelligent beings can only be created by a

greater intelligence or a creator (God), then we would not be able to create anything better than ourselves; otherwise, the whole notion of God as a supreme
being will collapse immediately, because God Himself would be able to create
a God superior to Himself. In addition, if human beings cannot become more
intelligent over time, then we have not changed since the day we were created.
The latter notion seems static and incompatible with what nature really is, which
is dynamic. Moreover, it is also incompatible with the documented evidence of
the evolutionary process of human beings and their achievements throughout
the course of history. It is certainly possible that in the future, humans interfere
in their evolutionary process at the genetic level and produce human-like species with different qualities. They may even produce intelligent species that are
suited for different environments, so that the journey of scientific exploration
of nature on the frontiers, that present-day humans could never reach, can
continue. However, human involvement in his evolutionary process has to be
done with extreme care. Despite producing some positive results, they may also
create catastrophic consequences, not only from the point of view of survival,
but also by having a negative impact on the social evolution.

For example, let us assume that through scientific breakthroughs in genetic
engineering, we have been able to prolong the life of human beings from sev-
enty-five to two hundred years. The positive aspect of this change may be the
production of greater minds due to the continued accumulation of knowledge
by individuals, which may lead to greater discoveries. However, the question
of overpopulation would remain an issue and it would also produce a very
conservative society that would not want to adapt to a changing environment
as necessity dictates. This long-lived society may be stagnant because the older
population would be around and would not understand the necessities for social reforms and adoption of new ethical standards. To clarify this example,
suppose that such genetic engineering breakthrough for extending human life
had taken place one hundred and fifty years ago. Let us also assume that a
major part of that population has been surviving up to present time. Can we
imagine how the mentality of this portion of population that believed in the
slavery of blacks would have affected the social consciousness and social evolution of U.S. at present time? Certainly there would have been a lesser degree of
accomplishments in liberating the blacks with this population being around,
than what has been achieved today by younger generation and in the absence
of this population.

Genetic diversity (regardless how small) in humans and animals has provided
a chance for survival of the species in case of an environmental change or an
outbreak of an epidemic disease. The development of genetically superior be-

ings with identical genes, regardless of how carefully they may be designed or crafted, could pose a danger to their survival, in the event of an unforeseen environmental change. Therefore, diversity is the key to survival of any species when a hostile environment can change with very little advance notice.

Creationism: Many of the world's religions are based on the existence of a supernatural creative force known as God. Prophets who brought God into the life of lawless societies devised behavioral guidelines based on divine laws. What some religions offered human beings in exchange for their good behavior was an eternal life in God's kingdom. At the same time, these religions threatened punishment for those who disobeyed these divine laws. Because each prophet had a different understanding of God and His rules, this produced a disparity in religions, followed by separations of societies based on their religious convictions. As time passed, other interpretations of religious beliefs and divine laws were introduced to the members of the society and disparities within each religion began to grow and gain acceptance. Religious disparities have played key roles in shaping some of our major historical events, in the past and present, when societies became hostile to each other and eventually clashed. The root causes of these social conflicts may have not always been religion, but rather, economic and deterministic tendencies of integration of social systems that used religion as their catalyst. Since religion has been an inseparable element of our historical process and our social evolution, it is worthwhile to explore the fundamentals of religion. Our discussion is based on creationism, which certainly fits into the subject of this book.

Creationists believe that God created the entire universe. Of all the planets in the universe, He chose the planet earth to be the residence of His living beings, including humans, which He created in His own image, according to the story of creation in the Old Testament. It is believed by creationists that neither human beings nor other living organisms have undergone any changes in their organic structures from the day that they were created. In other words, creationism does not believe in the mutation of genes and rejects the theory of evolution because it contradicts the notion that God created human beings and other living beings. Believers of creationism further state that God created human beings and all other living beings on earth around ten thousand years ago, and since then no changes have occurred in their genetic composition. The theory of evolution, on the other hand, teaches that all living beings originated from a single cell and evolved into a diversity of life forms as each life form adapted to its changing environment. Contrary to religious beliefs that gives mankind a special status among all other living beings, theory of evolution does not grant any special status to mankind. Today, scientists can show the continuity of new life forms at the bacterial level. This suggests that either God has been continually involved in creating new life forms, or these life forms evolve from an evolutionary process. If we reject the involvement of God in creating new life forms on daily basis, then we have to accept the idea that life forms are a product of evolution and mutation of genes. If we accept that proposition, what would then stop us from believing that humans are also a product of evolution? This argument leads to the conclusion that either all living beings are the products of evolution or God has never stopped creating new life forms. Furthermore, if we believe that the date of creation does not go back beyond ten thousand years, then we may ask who created the extinct species that lived millions of years ago. Discoveries of the remains of ancient species show that the disappearance of these species was due to an unsupportive environment. Even if we believe that God created all of those life forms long before ten thousand years ago, then why would He let the environment take charge of their faith and destroy them? Perhaps they were just the products of evolution that thrived when their environment was supportive, and when it changed beyond their capacity to adapt, they perished.

It can be shown that, like creation, the extinction of species is also a continuous process that may go back as far as the beginning of life in the universe. Creationism based on existing evidence coming from the remains of the animals and laboratory experimentation is full of contradictions. Creationists will have additional problems to deal with if some day life forms are discovered on other planets. It seems that creationists are not capable of resolving the contradictions that are deeply rooted in their arguments. Further, they are not capable of refuting or countering the scientific evidence that is mounting against their theory on a daily basis.

If religion takes a stubborn stand against science, one day it will lose its legitimacy completely. For example, can a religion proclaim that the earth is the center of universe, that it is flat, and that the sun is circling around the earth? This was a widely popular belief from the time of Ptolemy (first century, CE) to the seventeenth century, when Galileo rejected it. Today, religion cannot convince even a single person of that notion. If the words of the Old Testament are incompatible with discoveries of science in regard to the creation of the universe and life, then in what way may God have been involved in the creation of the universe and life itself that would be more compatible with current knowledge? Is it possible that when God created our universe, He knew how it would evolve on its own that would include a diversity of life forms? Is it possible that the theory defining the relationship between the evolution of the species and their environment is part of God's wisdom, and maybe that

Darwin only discovered part of it? With this theory, human beings will lose their special place in God's kingdom. This will destroy the entire foundation of religion and life after death, but it would restore God's glory as the creator of everything that there is in our universe, including life, and would leave us with an abundance of mysteries pertaining to God's wisdom. Whether God exists or not, we may never find out, but the last thing that we humans want is to be further divided by religious beliefs and principles that are full of contradictions and unsupported by the evidence.

Artificial intelligence, genetic research, and their impact on the evolutionary process of human beings and their society: There is no doubt that some time in the future an enhanced version of the human being will be developed in the laboratory using technological breakthroughs in genetic engineering. The opposition to this area of research today comes from religious and political groups who consider it immoral. Others believe that man's interference in the natural course of evolution may result in grave and unintended consequences for the human race. It is natural for people to feel uncomfortable with the products that genetic engineering may deliver to society. Part of that fear is simple uncertainty about positive and negative aspects of such technology; people fear that one day, someone, particularly those in power, may misuse this technology. This fear regarding new technology is not unfounded. As we know, nuclear energy has been used for both constructive and destructive purposes. Communication systems that were designed to connect us with each other are being used to invade our privacy. Despite the misuse of these technologies, however, the positive effects of these technologies on the life of people tend to overwhelm the negative effects. Therefore, if we accept the fact that misuse of this technology is likely to happen sometime in the future, we should not abandon research and development in this field and ignore all positive aspects of this new technology that may change our lives for better. The only issue that would remain open for discussion would be a new technology's application in connection with the moral and ethical standards of the time.

Religious leaders seem to resist the idea of humans creating their own intelligent living beings. Perhaps to religious leaders, this would weaken the position of God as the sole creator, and for this reason they have raised the question of morality involved in this research. Obviously, religious leaders have their own insecurities regarding their belief system and their opposition to genetic research is just to prolong the life of religion. Aren't we delighted that Galileo and Darwin despite their religious convictions still believed in science and published their controversial discoveries.

Human cloning will become a reality one day, if not for the purposes of pure research, then out of necessity. What if one day, the resources of our planet start to vanish and we have no alternative but to look elsewhere in our solar system or galaxy for additional resources with which to preserve the human race? Such expeditions would require space travelers who would live longer than human beings do today, and they would have to be able to sustain their physical strength in the absence of gravitational force and be able to work and survive in environments that we could never survive in. When the survival of humanity starts to depend on these special (perhaps manufactured) beings for space exploration, the moral values pertaining to this issue will start to vanish and human cloning will become a reality.

The same goes for the artificial intelligence (AI). In the future, there will be machines that will think faster and better than we do and even present themselves as emotional beings. How are we going to deal with such sophisticated pieces of equipment? Are we going to respect their feelings, greet them and give them a break to rest when they say they are tired? Or will we treat them like slaves? The reality is that AI, robotics, and genetic engineering will emerge as a necessity and will become part of our lives and our historical evolution. We need to be cautious when implementing advanced technologies and at the same time train ourselves to deal with them appropriately. After all, who is to say that life can only be in the form that we currently accept and feel comfortable with? How confident are we about the notion that humans are the ultimate creation of nature and not an intermediate stage for the development of something bigger and better? Is it possible that through our scientific endeavors, we are paving the process of evolution to create the next generation of humans and machines that are superior to us? Is this evolution a deterministic process that is bound to happen? Since the course of social evolution depends upon the nature of its subsystems and their course of evolution, how will the course of social evolution be affected in a society that is composed of beings with different natures and characteristics? Will new kinds of beings be granted rights equal to those of human beings, or will they have to fight for their rights, as many of us have to overcome racist and selfish attitudes?

Are ordered structures and living systems packets of energy? Like all other systems, living systems engage in energy exchange with each other that can lead to their merger and unification. Based on our earlier discussions, this exchange of energy is enforced by the top-level living system and supported by the second law of thermodynamics (entropy) and the lowest state of internal energy that systems like to adopt. In this process, part of the exchanged energy dissipates and becomes unrecoverable. But what is the form of dissipated energy in the interaction of living systems, humans and their societies? As we know, energy exchange between societies and human beings take place through violence, most of the time, caused by their difference in socioeconomic or prosperity levels and occasionally for other reasons. Based on the reality of conflict, the dissipated energy then, must be connected with the destructive processes, which includes the destruction of society's infrastructure and human life. Upon destruction, the victims of the conflict release all of the stored energy within their structures as dissipated energy. This may lead us to the conclusion that, from the viewpoint of thermodynamics, human beings, their societies and the infrastructures of their societies are all packets of energy. In reality, this is not an unreasonable assumption, when we add up the total amount of energy required to raise and to train a newborn baby to become an adult with a certain mind set and belief system. When a human being is destroyed in a conflict, all of the energy that has been put into the nurturing and training of that human being goes to waste in the form of dissipated energy. The infrastructure of a society, also has stored energy in its structure that upon its destruction this energy is released and dissipated.

When the prosperity gap and cultural/ideological differences in conflicting social systems (social organisms) become wider, it will require a much larger dissipated energy before the two systems merge and integrate. Therefore, yes, human beings and social organisms are packets of energy because they are ordered structures and any ordered structure has stored energy in its organization.

What is the lowest state of internal energy for human beings and the social organism? Let us imagine that we are given an unlimited amount of money to spend and that we do not have to worry about having a job. With all this money, we can purchase anything we desire at any time, and we can also travel to any place in the world. Suppose that the world around us is secure and we feel no threat from anyone. Wouldn't it be nice to have a life like this, with no stress and no concerns about anything? Now let us imagine that we have a job that we do not like and that the pay is so low that we can hardly manage the rent and other expenses. In addition, imagine that we have not taken a vacation for a long time. Imagine living in a bad neighborhood where we cannot walk on the street without worrying about being robbed or killed. Obviously, the first living condition is a happier one, whereas people living under the conditions given in the second endure a great deal of stress in their lives and are not generally happy people. As we know, living under stress for long periods of time results in physical ailments like high blood pressure, heart disease, or other problems, depending on an individual's genetic vulnerability. This clearly tells us that, like other systems, human body does not like internal stresses.

We need to mention, however, that there are many types of stress that are not harmful to human body. For example, the physical stress exerted upon human body during exercise or intense mental activity in problem solving could have a positive effect on the physical and mental health, contrary to the stress associated with survival matters that can be harmful. Stressful circumstances that millions of human beings face on a daily basis include lack of resources to survive, not having control over their own lives, insecurity, life-threatening conditions and the stresses associated with mental exhaustion and overwork. These conditions are real and they exist almost in every society on our planet. This is why, from time to time, we observe sudden death among young men and women overstressed by their work, or witness how an individual is driven to commit suicide or murder another human being, simply because that individual has lost hope and control of own life. We can now conclude that the lowest state of internal energy for a human being is equivalent to the lowest level of internal stress in conjunction with survival matters. Internal stress would drop when human beings are provided with shelter and abundance of resources for their survival. It would drop even further, when their security and freedom is improved and they gain better control of their lives. The social organism is no different from a human being, and as a system, it strives to retain a minimum level of internal energy as the most desired state, which is to maintain sufficient resources to feed its subsystems (human beings) and other energy resources to develop and maintain its infrastructure for self-preservation. The social organism needs security, stability, a greater degree of freedom and control over the resources of its environment as human beings do. Political games that a social organism plays with similar systems as well as engagement in conflicting situations with these systems are all to achieve a better position for self-preservation. Human beings do the same in dealings with their own kind.

Theoretical history: Contrary to the popular belief that history may be a set of random events, we would argue that history, or social evolution, leads to predictable and deterministic outcomes. Based on our earlier discussions in this regard, such outcomes have been set and determined by the environment and by the principles of thermodynamics, unified boundary conditions, and a minimum state of internal energy. Theoretical history maintains that the finality of social evolution is achievable, regardless of circumstances that may evolve during its process. In other words, the finality of social evolution, the so-called predetermined state, is independent and insensitive to the evolutionary process itself. The finality of history can be imagined as a state that offers optimum stability and a minimal state of internal energy to the social system. Because every system has the tendency to acquire such a state, this state becomes an *attractor*, or a *gravitating point,* for any process the social evolution adopts. This means that the social system continues to look in that direction, regardless of how circumstances affect its process. For the social system to reach such a state, it needs to enforce its subsystems to exchange energy and achieve a state of equilibrium or equality among themselves at all levels of the hierarchy. This suggests that the system that is ultimately responsible for almost every energy exchange among its subsystems and at all levels is the top-level system, which is the global social organism. It is the energy exchange among subsystems that produce our historical events and results in the modification of our relational bonds, which consequently drives the global social organism toward its intended goal or its finality. Based on these arguments, we can further argue that while the theory of history cannot predict minor historical events, such as the death of a citizen in a driving accident, it can predict major trends leading to the outcome of social evolution and the integration of societies on a global scale. Along with this deterministic outcome, which is set by natural laws, there seems to be a second factor that influences social evolution. This factor pertains to the structural and organizational development of the social organism following the general rule of evolutionary patterns of living systems that seem to be acting deterministically. There is also a third deterministic factor that has an indisputable influence on historical processes; this is the environment of the social organism. This third factor can, in fact, alter the finality of social evolution and turn the process of history backward, from integration to disintegration. We will explore all of these in further details in the upcoming discussions.

A brief summary of this chapter: Let us now review and connect some of the concepts that have had significant influence in driving our social evolution. In general, social evolution, or the process of history, is nothing but an exchange of energy/mass/information between complex living systems and their environment, an exchange that also affects the entire chain of subsystems in the hierarchy of every participating system. Therefore, historical events are the products of these exchanges, as each system and subsystem in the hierarchy of systems struggles to attain the lowest state of internal energy and acquire optimum stability. For the living systems, this translates to survival and security. We argued that in the absence of the second law of thermodynamics (entropy) and the minimum state of internal energy, systems would have not existed and it is these laws that are responsible for the existence of every system and their interaction with each other. Moreover, it is these laws that grant priority to the top-level system to attain its lowest state of internal energy over its subsystems that seek the same objective. If this was not the case, systems would have collapsed one after another in every system hierarchy. As a result, all natural processes, including our history, become goal-seeking and directive processes, serving the top-level system, despite their seemingly chaotic behavior.

The principal conclusion that we are going to derive here may be shocking to some readers. We tend to believe that we are the driving force of our social evolution, which means that subsystems are in control of the system. Since laws of nature do not support this notion, it leaves us with no other alternative but to accept that the social organism is in control of its subsystems (human beings). This raises some questions, such as the following: *Is it possible that the social organism may be in full control of its own evolutionary process, which includes all of us in its plan, and is it possible that we humans may be serving its purpose unknowingly, thinking that we are in charge?* If we hesitate to believe this, we can look at our own bodies. How did these trillions of cells with different specialties evolved from a single cell and formed a new entity and what made them to do so, and why are they integrated and not free to go or fall apart? Does the social organism follow the same footsteps of human evolution? At the end of the process, will it capture every human in its sophisticated structural organization? This proposition seems to grant an authoritarian role to the social organism over its subsystem, human beings; we may not like this notion, but it is a reality. It is important that we demonstrate once more, why equality is a non-negotiable and deterministic outcome of social evolution at the finality of its process, enforced by the laws of nature. Figure 1-14a shows an unstable system at time zero. Note that none of the subsystems are at the same levels of internal energy at this time. System A contains two subsystems (B1 and B2) that are not in equal states of energy, which results in system A not being in its lowest state of internal energy. As a result, system A will impose its will upon subsystems B1 and B2 to exchange energy so that a part of their exchanged energy dissipates and leaves the system. At the same time, subsystems B1 and B2, which are not at their lowest state of internal energy, will exercise their authority over their subsystems to do exactly the same. This process will continue until each set of parallel subsystems, at every system level, achieves equality in the hierarchy of system A. When this happens, as shown in Figure 1-14b, the level of dissipated energy reaches its maximum level and the internal energy of system A its minimum level. At this stage, assuming no influx of energy is taking place between system A and its environment, system A reaches a steady state condition with optimum stability. This process is goal seeking and deterministic and is independent of the initial conditions and sequences of the processes. What we mean by *sequence of the process* is the irrelevancy of the primacy of the sub-processes in the final outcome.

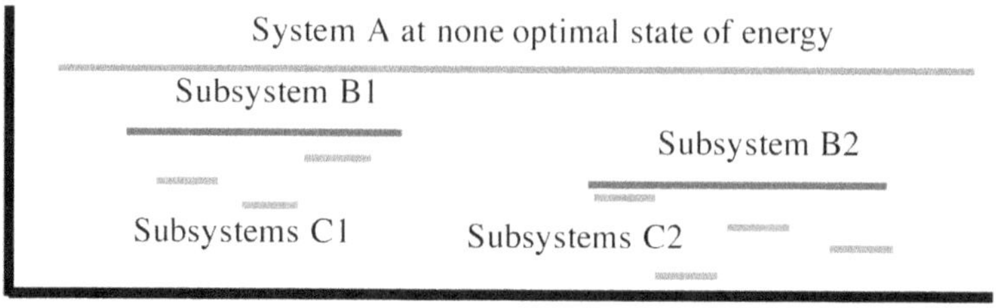

System A at none optimal state of energy

Subsystem B1

Subsystem B2

Subsystems C1   Subsystems C2

Figure 1-14a An unstable system
All parallel subsystems at none equal states of internal energy

Whether subsystems B1 and B2 reach their lowest state of internal energy first and then exchange energy among themselves to satisfy the state of internal energy for system A, or these exchanges take place in all system levels simultaneously, is unimportant, because they all lead to the same finality.

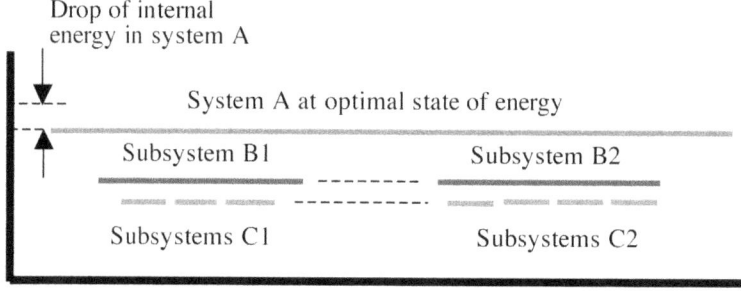

Drop of internal
energy in system A

System A at optimal state of energy

Subsystem B1   Subsystem B2

Subsystems C1   Subsystems C2

Figure 1-14b An optimally stable system
All parallel subsystems at equal states of internal energy

The other factor that is also important to discuss is the rate of energy exchange among subsystems that may point to the nature of events and historical processes. The X-axis (horizontal scale) of Figure 1-14c shows the difference between the internal energy levels of two systems. The further we go to the right of this axis, the larger this difference. The Y-axis (vertical scale) demonstrates the rate of energy exchange (amount of energy exchanged per unit time) between these two systems. The further we go up on this axis, the higher the rate.

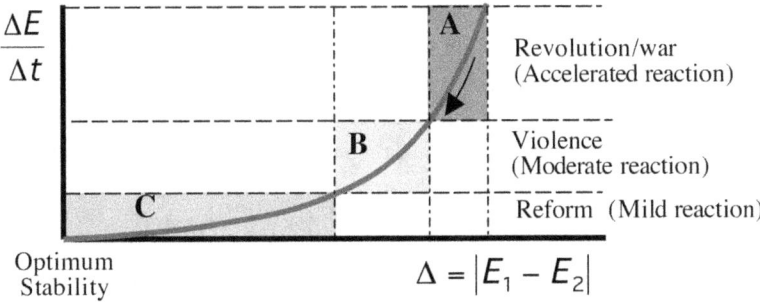

Figure 1-14c Internal energy gaps of living systems in connection with the type of interaction between them

As it is clear at the point of origin in this figure, the difference between the internal energies of the two interacting systems is zero, which means that the rate of energy exchange between them is also zero. At this point, the system that encompasses both systems is at its lowest state of internal energy and, consequently, at optimum stability. As we move further to the right on the X-axis, the absolute difference in the state of the internal energy of the two systems continues to increase, which results in a higher rate of energy exchange between them.

Earlier, we briefly touched on what constitutes the internal energy of the living systems like human beings and human societies. We will continue to expand on that notion in upcoming chapters, but for now, let us conclude our argument with what we have presented thus far. Since most historical processes (in the path of integration) are interaction of systems with different levels of energy exchange, the starting point of their interaction would be either at region A or B, in Figure 1-14c, proceeding to the last stage, C, in time. When this energy gap is large, the energy exchange may take place through violent processes, such as revolution or war, and usually, such a process does not take a long time from a historical point of view (region A) before it concludes. When the energy gap drops, so would the level of violence between them. In this case, the interaction between the two systems may be of moderate kind such as sporadic violence and criminal behavior (region B). This process is usually longer than the previous process, before the two systems approach the final stage of their interaction, in region C. In region C, the energy exchange takes place at a much slower pace and in a more peaceful manner, such as reform processes. This process is the longest before the encompassing system reaches its most desirable state of internal energy and achieves optimal stability. These processes will reverse when disintegration becomes the main path of historical process, caused by diminishing life support systems in the environment of living systems. In this scenario, the top-level system slowly disintegrates, loosening its grip on its subsystems and leaving them to survive on their own, which put these subsystems in competition with each other to manipulate the remaining resources of their environment. Assuming the initial condition of the state of energy of the system is optimal, this will take the system in a reverse path on the plot shown in Figure 1-14c, starting from region C all the way to region A.

Let us now consider important issues pertaining to the natural laws that we believe play a deterministic role in social evolution. One of these laws pertains to the manifestation and transcendence of all subsystem characteristics into high level systems, following the laws associated with the formation of multi-level systems. These characteristics then become the properties of the high-level system and play an influential role in its behavior and evolutionary process. For example, if human beings are intelligent constituents of the social organism, then the social organism can never be an unintelligent organism. If human beings cognitive ability and knowledge allow them to interfere in their evolutionary process, so would the social organism. If the structural organization of human body has proven to be effective in dealing with shortages of energy supplies in the environment, the social organism would also organize itself in the same manner and strive to optimize its operational efficiency and minimize its dependence on scarce natural resources. Finally, if the survival of human beings depends on the energy resources of their environment, so would the social organism. Let us keep in mind that social evolution both in integration and disintegration process, despite being chaotic, are directed processes and pursue deterministic outcomes and finalities.

In the next chapter, we will explore in more detail the connection between the social organism and its environment. We will also explore the connection between violent trends in our historical processes and human nature, which are the outcomes of human's evolutionary process in a hostile environment. We will discuss and compare the similarities of structural organization and operation of social organism to those of individual human beings and their ability to adapt to changing environments.

CHAPTER 2

Structural similarities of human and the social organism

In the previous chapter, we explored how natural laws have a grip on our social evolution, conducting it to a finality that will produce equality among all human beings and form a social organism that is optimally stable. But achievement of equality among members of a society does not make an operational social organism. To be operational, the social organism must evolve with a structural organization that can assign different tasks to select groups of individuals, from which other members of the society as a whole can benefit. Therefore, evolution of the social organism into an organized structure with a division of tasks among its members becomes a deterministic process. But what kind of structural organization would best fit the operation of the social organism? Before we answer this question, let us examine some of the similarities between human physiology and the elementary structural organization of the social organism. Obviously, in terms of its evolutionary process, the social organism is still in its infancy stage and not close to the maturity of a human being's structural organization, but even at this stage, we will find numerous and astonishing similarities between them. Later, we will discuss the influential factors that determine the pace of this process and whether or not the sequence of the evolutionary steps toward the creation of the social organism's structural organization maps those of the humans.

Human structural organization: Without getting into the details of human physiology, let us point to some of the major operational principles of human physical structure. Human physical structure operates through a single central control system, the brain. The brain is in full control of all organs and their activities on a continuous basis. The central nervous system is the communication channel between organs and the brain for the flow of information, so that the brain can regulate the activities of the organs in real time. All organs are made of cells, which are in need of nutrients to survive and function. These nutrients are carried and distributed by blood cells to every cell in the body through transportation channels called arteries and veins. The body is equipped with a mechanism called the immune system to defend itself against the invasion of undesired organisms and dangerous chemicals. The unused and undesired parts of digested food are expelled from the body by the kidneys, the colon, the lungs and the skin. Our sensory organs have helped us perceive our environment so we can search for energy resources; without cognitive abilities and physical mobility, this search would have been impossible to carry out. All of the organs in the body work together in harmony. The human body is made of a variety of cells that have a limited life span and have to be replaced with new ones to revitalize the functionality of the organs, and consequently, the entire body. Replacement cells are programmed to perform the same tasks. These are a few out of the many basic operational features of the living organism at the animal or human level. In the following section, we will show how the social organism, as a living being, also strives to duplicate the structural organization of a human being, adopted over millions of years of evolutionary process.

The social organism and its structural organization: Society is the next level of living organism that, in its evolutionary course, has evolved with government acting as the brain of the social organism and regulating its activities. Societies have evolved with distribution lines such as roads, airways, and railroad tracks (similar to arteries and veins) to support the delivery of energy resources (food being one of them) to the members of the society and its infrastructure. Like human body that discards the remains of the digested material, social organism also dumps the unwanted material into the sewer system or removes them by other means from its structure. The social organism has evolved with defensive mechanisms, using police and military forces, to protect itself from both internal and external enemies; similar to human body defending itself against invaders, using white cell. Communication systems have been evolving, particularly in the last few decades, to connect individuals with each other, forming a neural network on the scale of human being. In the future, communication systems might evolve into a central nervous system, connecting every living and non-living ordered system within the social organism to the central control system. The social organism has evolved with sensory devices to perceive its environment and take proactive measures to protect itself from other similar systems and its own hostile environment. Some of these sensory devices are weather satellites, spying agencies, and surveillance equipment. At this stage of evolution, the social organism has evolved with limited mobility by inventing transportation means such as airplanes and ships so that it can look for its survival needs elsewhere if necessary. The building blocks of the social organism, which are the individual human beings, have a limited life span and they are being replaced just as the body builds new cells to replace itself. The functionality of a newborn human cannot be determined at the time of his birth. However, the society's educational system assumes that role and takes the responsibility to train and educate individuals with a variety of skills to replace the older generations who are ready to retire. These are only a few examples of structural and functional similarities between human beings and their societies. These similarities may suggest that the evolution of the social organism's structural organization may be replicating human's structural organization.

The global social organism and its structural organization: The global social organism comprises many smaller social organisms (nations), all of which have adopted a similar structural organization for their operation, with one difference, that some of these nations are lagging behind others due to a disparity in their economic and technological expertise. It seems that these societies constitute the building blocks of a larger organism, the global social organism, and are analogous to individual human beings as members of their society and to cells as constituents of the human body. If social organism models human's structural organization as a preferred and efficient organization for its operation, the global social organism most likely will do the same and adopt the human model for its own structural organization. There are many indications that suggest that the structural evolution of the global social organism is also heading in that direction. Among these indicators is the establishment of the United Nations as the main body in which to discuss issues that concern nations. In the years to come, we will witness the transformation of this institution from a body that has been used to listen to the grievances of the nations, to an institution that can set top-level policies in world affairs and act as a central control system. In the years to come, we will also witness much greater cooperation among nations to a point that their economies, political systems, and defensive capabilities will merge to create a more harmonious global social organism. The European Union and its continued expansion is a sign of such a trend, which will be followed by similar trends in third world countries. The nervous system of the global social organism (communication systems) has been expanding to cover and connect its constituents throughout the world. Expansion of trade throughout the world, facilitated by improved transportation, has been serving as a supply line to deliver to every society the materials and goods that it lacks from the nations that have an abundance of them. A deterministic outcome of a true merger and integrative process of societies into a single organism is the consolidation of their operational methodologies and structural organizations. For example, merged nations will have a single constitution, a single government and defensive force, and a single judiciary and legal system. However, such mergers do not materialize with ease in the life of the global social organism. Let us not forget that major changes have to take place within the global social organism before such mergers become a possibility. The global social organism gets no preferential treatment from the laws of nature and even at this system level, these laws continue to exert their authority. For the global social organism to achieve its optimum stability and lowest state of internal energy, it must force its subsystems to reach equality, which in this case would be their level of prosperity. But before this equality materializes, a great deal of energy has to be exchanged between these societies, from which a part will be dissipative energy in the form of destructive processes. However, when the prosperity gap starts to close, the global social organism will be ready to emerge as a single organism, homogenizing the diversity of cultures and races around the globe and adopting the same structural organization for its operation as that of the human. The formation of global social organism can also be discussed from the viewpoint of systems and their natural tendencies to merge and grow, when energy resources are abundant to support their integration.

The galactic organism and its structural organization: This discussion may be a deviation from reality into fantasy, but it is meant to invigorate the mind of the reader. By logical deduction, from the evolutionary processes of the living systems, their integration, and their ever-growing system hierarchy, starting at the cellular level to an individual human being, followed by social organism and global social organism; could there be a higher level organism in the universe that encompasses multitude of civilizations around our galaxy (similar to ours) as its subsystems? Although there is no evidence of such an organism and its connection with our civilization, the possibility of its existence cannot be denied. When Indians were living in isolation on the American continent, they were allegedly unaware of the existence of other communities on the other sides of the oceans. Communities that already had found each other and had lived together for thousands of years. These communities did not know about Indians on American continent, not until the technological barriers of transportation were broken. On a larger scale, the same could be true about our isolation from outer space. We cannot refute the possibility that other civilizations in the universe may have already found each other and have established relational bonds to form a galactic organism with galactic intelligence and a central control system to conduct its operation. It is also possible that we may not be in isolation and already connected to such a galactic organism with a set of relational bonds that are beyond our understanding for the time being. Logically, we may also conclude that the galactic organism's evolutionary process, in terms of its structural organization and patterns of evolution, may resemble that of the evolution of its subsystems (human equivalents and their societies) and may certainly be compliant with natural laws (based on our current understanding of these laws) that apply to every system.

Interdependent evolutionary processes: In this section, we intend to show how simultaneously evolving systems, whether serially connected or connected in parallel, could speed up or slow down each other's evolutionary process. The hierarchy of living systems starts at the cellular level, and continues to the level of the global social organism, and perhaps beyond. These interdependent systems, which are connected in both serial and parallel fashion at all hierarchical levels, undergo their own evolutionary processes all at the same time, as their environments dynamically evolve. In such environments, every system imposes its own conditions upon surrounding systems while responding to conditions imposed upon it by other systems. Let us imagine a scenario in which societies on earth disregarded the early warnings of global warming and let accumulation of carbon dioxide and other pollutants in the air and water to rise beyond the tolerance levels of many species on our planet. As suggested by the theory of evolution "survival of the fittest," species with the lowest tolerance to these pollutants may become extinct, while new ones emerge and thrive in the polluted environment. With the emergence of a new organism in the ecosystem, new balances must be created among all living beings and organisms sharing the same environment, and as we know, there is always an unknown factor in these circumstances, such as emergence of new killer microbes and bacteria. We also know that a prolonged and sustained change in the environmental conditions of living organisms may trigger genetic mutations that would change the course of their biological evolution to make it easier for them to cope and survive in their new environment, and humans are not excluded from this process. But before this happens, living organisms will experience a period of tremendous crisis in health and functionality. When everyone is sick and unable to function, society becomes sick as well and loses its operational efficiency. As we can see, the course of evolution that a system (in this case, a society) chooses can affect the course of evolution of every parallel and serially connected system in relation with it. In this hypothetical example, we see how the operational efficiency of a society is affected when its members become dysfunctional and how careless environmental policies can tilt the balance in the ecosystem and result in the disappearance of some species and the emergence of new ones. This reminds us that no system is immune from the consequences of its own policies and actions, after they propagate throughout the entire chain of interacting systems that are operating in a closed-loop and interdependent fashion. In such an environment, the changes imposed by one system upon the others eventually results in others setting their own conditions and imposing them upon the first. In conclusion, the evolutionary process of any living system is the product of the simultaneous and interdependent evolution of parallel and serially connected systems. Since systems can influence the evolutionary processes of other systems, it is plausible to speed up or slow down their progress toward their intended goals. We will reconsider this subject in the next section, when we explore the dynamics of mental evolution in humans and its impact on social consciousness and social evolution.

The insensitivity of goal-seeking systems to the sequence of sub-processes contained in their evolutionary process: It is important to recognize that an enormous living system, such as a global social organism, has many levels of subsystems. For example, the subsystem immediately below the global social organism may be an alliance of nations with common religious or ideological values. Below that, it may be nations with different cultures, and one level down from that, may be economic institutions and corporations, and finally, humans at the bottom of this system hierarchy. Keep in mind that a subsystem's boundaries may not always be distinctly separated from other systems' boundaries, and in some other instances, they may even intersect. Take for example the branches of a multinational corporation each within a different society, or the alliance of a group of societies for economic reasons, and their alliance with others for their religious affiliation. Now imagine the chaos within the global social organism when all of these subsystems trying to attain their lowest possible state of internal energy and optimum stability, as they challenge each other.

In its evolutionary process and with the help of natural laws, the global social organism will eventually succeed in establishing harmony and equality among the members of every subsystem level within its hierarchy. But does it matter how or in what sequence these objectives have been achieved? Obviously, the global social organism does not mind. The evolutionary process of the global social organism may emphasize equalization on the societal or human level from time to time, or, it may proceed with both at the same time, also it may pause in one process for some time. If a pause occurs in the process of equalization at one system level (say, the human level), the process will be picked up at a later time to be completed when equalization in the societal level has progressed to a satisfactory level. Therefore, the course of the evolution of the global social organism may seem to take different paths, depending on the courses of the evolution of the connecting subsystems and evolving circumstances.

One of the disappointments of socialists after the end of the Cold War was that why such a progressive movement had suddenly lost momentum and seemed to be abandoned by all. In reality, the evolutionary course of the global social organism had reached a point where it needed to focus on equalization among societies (in terms of their prosperity) rather than continue to pursue equality among human beings in every individual society. After all, people can only be equal in their respective nations. They can be either equally poor or equally rich. The new evolutionary course of global society is meant to close the prosperity gap among societies, which is equalization of living standards among all nations. If it materializes, then an average person in every society will have similar life style. This process, however, will not bring along equality among members of one society.

This new tendency in the evolutionary process of the global social organism may take a long time before it matures and result in the system hopping back to human level for further refinement in equality among socioeconomic classes; this time on a global scale. These sequential processes, or hopping back and forth from one subsystem level to another, to enforce equality among the members of each subsystem level, are natural and must be embraced by everyone, particularly by socialists and other groups such as the anti-globalization movement. In the integration process of history where energy resources to support the growth of social organism are abundant, anti-globalization is an anti-history movement. Anti-globalization movement will never find sympathy among people as long as technological achievements of humanity has facilitated the openness of these societies to one another. In the world of anti-globalization, nations with poorer standard of life will remain poor and left behind, something totally opposite to the natural course of evolution of the global social organism. To follow the process of history, the focus of the anti-globalization movement must be on humane implementation of the globalization process, not opposition to it. In conclusion, it seems logical that goal-seeking systems may be insensitive to the sequence of the sub-processes leading them to their deterministic finality, as long as all of them are completed some time during the process. However, it does not seem that structural organization of the global social organism exhibits similar insensitivity to the sequence of the sub-processes leading to its formation. Every organism upon its formation needs to establish its central control system first, and then develop other functioning organs in a proper order to become a functional organism that is also operationally efficient. Therefore, the formation process of structural organization of the global social organism may remain deterministic and predictable, not only in its finality, but also for most part of its process.

Does the sequence of structural developments of the social organism map that of the human? It has taken millions of years of evolutionary process and trial-and-error for the human body to evolve into an operationally efficient and organizationally coherent system. The formation of human society as an organism started millions of years later in time than the evolution of human. As a result, the development of structural organization of the society lags far behind that of the human body. Despite striking similarities in the structural organization of these two organisms, we have not yet discussed whether the sequence of evolutionary processes that led to such similarities are indeed the same. In other words, would the social organism develop its sub-organisms in the same sequence as the human body? Would the relational bonds evolving between sub-organisms of the social organism be identical to those of humans? Would they be born in the same order? If so, then the social organism's evolutionary pattern is identical to that of human, which means that it follows the same pattern as human evolution. Furthermore, it may mean that the social organism's evolutionary pattern may be predicted by mapping it to the human evolutionary pattern. This may be a significant discovery in predicting what might emerge in the next stages of social evolution based on an advanced model that has currently transpired, i.e. human physiology.

Is it plausible that the entire history of the human evolution, starting from a single-cell organism to becoming a full-blown human, may be condensed in the nine months of a pregnancy? Could learning about the sequence of development of sub-organisms and their relational bonds during pregnancy provide a basis for predicting future developments in the evolutionary process of the social organism as it matures? If a scientist in the eighteenth century knew that the social organism would adopt a similar structural organization to that of human beings, then he could have predicted the emergence of society's nervous systems, the modern communication systems. If so, and using the same knowledge base, could we predict future developments in our social evolution? Most likely, we could. There is much to learn about the evolutionary process of the social organism and all of the relational bonds that will eventually evolve among its sub-organism and in particular, those among humans, by learning more about human physiology. Again, if there is any validity to this notion at all, it means that the evolutionary process of the structural organization of the social organism may be a deterministic process because it would be a duplication of a more advanced model currently in existence. The resemblance in structural organization of the two systems, and a comparative analysis of their evolutionary patterns may lead to an understanding of supportive technologies that need to be developed to assist the social organism to emerge with the next set of predicted properties that are bound to occur.

The dynamics of the evolutionary process of the social organism: So far, we have touched upon two of the main objectives that the social organism strives to accomplish. One is to evolve with a structural organization that resembles that of the human being. The second is to realize an equilibrium state (socio-economic equality) among humans as part of the implication of natural laws that apply to all systems. But one thing that we have not touched upon is; what controls and influences the momentum of this process? Can any parallel or serially connected system in the environment of social organism slow down, speed up or reverse its process, directing it to seek alternatives goals? The answer is yes. There are many factors that can result in one of the above-mentioned scenarios. The most powerful factor that might completely reverse the process of history and social evolution comes from the environment of the social organism, which provides all the life support systems that the organism needs to survive. We will discuss this in further detail later, but for now, let us assume that these life support systems are available in the environment of the social organism and that they are sufficient to support its structure for a continued growth and integration. Therefore, for the sake of this discussion, the intended goals of social evolution remain the same for the time being, namely, continued growth and integration. However, question still remains: *What factors would influence the dynamics of social evolution in attaining its structural and organizational goals?* Two factors that come to mind immediately will be discussed in this section. One is related to the fields of science and technology and the influence of these two on the dynamics of social evolution. The other is related to the dynamics of the mental evolution of human beings. With respect to the former, let us imagine a situation that has not yet been widely implemented or fully materialized in the structural evolution of the social organism. It is very likely that in the future, every human being wear a health monitor, like a wristwatch that we wear today, that would measure and report his/her health indicators to a central control system. Based on today's standards in regard to the notion of individual freedom and the right to privacy, this may seem to be a scary thought, but it is possible that it will find acceptance among people of the future generations and become a reality. Why? Because wearing a health monitor complies with the operation of a fully integrated living structure, in which all of its sub-organisms are closely monitored by the central control system. However, this should not come as a surprise to us because even at the present time, we are constantly being monitored in everything that we do. Our managers and supervisors monitor what we do at work. When we drive, we are monitored by the police or by street cameras. When we walk into a store or a bank, every activity of ours is monitored and recorded. Our e-mail correspondence, the books that we check out from the library, and the products we buy are all monitored. All of these surveillance activities are happening in the societies that their members are so proud to be part of, the so-called free societies. Therefore, the question of wearing a health monitor is not whether it would happen or not, but rather *when* it will happen, and the answer is when sufficient technological breakthroughs take place. In brief, it is technology that assists and drives social evolution and its structural organization to advance to the next level of complexity and integration. The faster these technologies emerge, the quicker the transition will be to the next stages of evolution.

Before we discuss the effects of the mental and physical evolution of humans and their impact on the speed of social evolution, let us review a few notions. As we know, characteristics of subsystems always transcend and manifest themselves into the high-level system and become a dominating factor in their behavioral patterns. But the characteristics of some living systems are dynamic and subject to change as they continually evolve, not only physically, but also mentally. Such changes in the subsystem (e.g., human) level may affect the evolutionary process of the social organism in a significant way. For the most part, in this discussion, we will focus on the mental evolution of human beings rather than their physical evolution simply because physical changes in human physiology do not take place very often, as compared to dynamics of mental evolution. The overall mental state of the humans is influenced by their survival instincts, emotional and rational states of their minds. If survival instincts take over, it could result in deceleration or reversal of the evolutionary process of the social organism in every aspect of its development. However, if rational behavior becomes a dominant factor in human conduct, then it could accelerate the process of social evolution toward its intended goals in integration process of history. Rational behavior is the result of improved knowledge in regard to the workings of the world, such as political and socioeconomic issues surrounding the life of the social organism and its connection with the life of individual human beings. Any further understanding in this respect at the human level might manifest itself in the consciousness of the social organism. Because human and social organisms are both self-regulating systems, any additional self-awareness may lead to major policy changes in the affairs of the social organism, which would speed up the process of social evolution in achieving its intended goals. The discussion of social consciousness will be elaborated further in the next chapter.

A brief summary of this chapter: In this chapter, we argued that the structural evolution of the social organism follows the same pattern as human structural organization. This is due to its proven operational efficiency and functionality. Based on this premise, we concluded that any process that strives to imitate another process becomes a deterministic process itself, simply because all of its future developmental stages can be predicted by mapping them to a known process. We also stated that the structural development of the social organism is closely tied to the advancement of science and technology, which are the key factors in pushing social evolution to attain states of higher complexity. In other discussions, we learned that the finality of social evolution on a global scale is an effort to achieve socioeconomic equality among all members at every subsystem level, though it appears that the social organism's evolutionary process remains insensitive to the sequence of sub-processes delivering these equalities to every subsystem level. Despite this insensitivity to the steps of the process, the social organism remains sensitive and resolute in accomplishing these equalities one way or another at the finality of its process. We provided examples of evolutionary processes pertaining to living systems that influence one another as they simultaneously evolve. We touched upon another factor that may influence the momentum of social evolution toward its intended goals (assuming the environment of the social organism does not pose a threat to its existence), which was related to the dynamics of human mental evolution, influenced by the progress of human knowledge in all arenas of sciences. Mental evolution at the human level would manifest itself in social consciousness (the mind of social organism), affect its behavioral pattern and change the course of its evolution.

CHAPTER 3

The effect of environment on the course of history and social evolution

Macroanalysis of history: In earlier arguments, we proposed that when a new set of boundary conditions are imposed upon a system, the system is forced to absorb or release some amount of mass or energy in order to adapt to this new set of conditions. This adaptation affects the relational bonds of the system's subsystems at all levels and alter system's properties as a whole. This is the behavior of every system, regardless of how large and complex or small and simple it may be. A social organism is a system that responds to its environment like any other system. Since social organism's survival is closely tied to the support of its environment, the environment becomes a major factor in setting the system's evolutionary course and determining its finality. If we accept the principles of evolution and adaptation process as they apply to all organisms and species, and likewise accept that a social organism is a living organism, then why should the social organism be excluded from those laws? Therefore, it would be realistic to suggest that the social organism's evolutionary process is, for the most part, a response to its changing environment and if it can thrive in a hospitable environment, then it can also become extinct in a hostile environment. As a result, when the social organism benefits from the support of its environment, it adopts an evolutionary process of growth and integration, and when it lacks that support, it adopts an opposite course of evolution, which leads to reduction and disintegration. Both these processes lead to deterministic finalities, one on the constructive path, and the other on the destructive path.

To better understand the processes of integration and disintegration, let us first discuss why a system that benefits from the support of its environment has a tendency to grow and integrate. As we remember, this goes back to the laws of nature and particularly, the second law of thermodynamics.

When two societies open up to each other, their integration demands a new level of infrastructure, such as, buildings, highways, airways and communication systems. This infrastructure is necessary to support their merger, and adds to the overall energy needs of the new integrated society. The energy needs of the integrated society comes from its environment, which needs to be converted to usable energy, and in the numerous conversion processes, a portion of the energy is dissipated into the universe.

As we know, the dissipated energy increases the level of disorder in nature; this is a natural tendency in the universe and is supported by the second law of thermodynamics. From this discussion, we like to conclude that the process of growth and integration of social organisms around the world seem to be deterministic because with each level of integration, the entropy in the environment proportionally rises. Consequently, if the integration of world societies into one social organism is a deterministic process supported by the laws of nature, it is necessary to know how this social organism is going to emerge at the end of its evolutionary process or its finality, when we add all other notions that we have discussed so far to its process. On a global scale, the social organism would probably emerge as a system with optimum stability and the least amount of tension among its subsystems (human beings). To minimize the tension among its subsystems, this social organism will demand socioeconomic equality, again, supported by the laws of nature. Other characteristics would be the emergence of a world government, centralization and regulation of the world economy and global financial planning, the promotion of harmony in every aspect of the social organism's life, and the evasion of all chaotic processes, such as the market economy. The global social organism will place a much greater importance on its security and stability than on uncontrolled growth. This society will also be environmentally sensitive. It will monitor its population growth closely and strive to improve its operational efficiency. It will have an international energy policy for the production and consumption of energy. It will have a universal culture built upon all the cultures of the world. In the integration process of history, all of the above-mentioned goals will be achieved at different stages of evolution. Completion of these stages may not have to be in the order given above and the process of evolution may shift from pursuing one goal to the other (depending on circumstances), but at the end, since all of these goals are deterministic, they will be achieved.

We can clarify the process of social evolution in attaining these goals by the following example. Suppose we leave home to visit a friend who lives on the other side of the town. On the way across the town, we will find tens or possibly hundreds of streets crisscrossing each other, providing a multitude of paths between our home and friend's residence. In this journey, nothing will stop us from choosing a specific path to get to our destination. The only difference between these paths might be in arrival time and the distance, depending which route we choose. The process of history is similar. The evolutionary process of a social organism gravitates toward a finality that is set by its environment and natural laws, but the process by which it would reach its finality is determined by circumstances. That is, even if we restart our history a million times, social evolution will remain focused on achieving the same set of goals, yet not a single process will match any other in its entirety. The fact that processes are different does not change the characteristics of the state of finality, only the duration of time that it takes for finality to be reached. Now let us assume that life support systems and energy resources in the environment fall short in supporting the social organism. Let us also assume that social organism's technological know-how lacks a solution for replenishing or finding substitutes for these resources. At this point, the environment will force the social organism to take a 180-degree turn and reverse its evolutionary course from integration to disintegration. Now the aim of the social organism is to shrink (minimize its size) to a point where the remaining energy resources in its environment are capable of supporting its reduced structure. With disintegration come negative growth, reduction, destruction of order, disharmony and inequality at every subsystem level. If the social organism cannot find a proper balance between its energy needs and the amount of energy available in its environment, it will continue to disintegrate until it becomes extinct. Like the process of integration, the process of disintegration of social evolution also remains circumstantial, yet focused on its finality.

To conclude this discussion, we proclaim that the evolutionary process of the social organism, whether integrating or disintegrating, is a goal seeking process and is insensitive to the sequences of the sub-processes, leading it to that finality. The supportive or non-supportive environment sets both finalities for the social evolution.

The deterministic goals of the social organism in building its structural organization, along with the development of a particular relational bonds among its constituents on the basis of natural laws, plus the interference of the environment in setting its finalities, lead us to believe that social evolution, or the process of history, is a scientific process. From this perspective, it is much easier to understand the history by understanding its intended goals and the state of its finality, rather than focusing on the details of its chaotic process in small cross sections of time in order to comprehend its entire process. Understanding the process of history from such detailed bits of information may be misleading from time to time, as they may not be part of the main historical trend. From this new perspective, which we call *macroanalysis of history*, it is much easier to predict the long-term goals of social evolution and determine the major trends of its process, and not to be fooled or deceived by minor turns that its process takes from time to time.

Microanalysis of history: We have a recorded history of our social evolution that could have been easily different from what it is today if circumstances were different. If, for example, an accident had prevented an individual from becoming a leader, this would have affected all subsequent historical events in which he would have been part of, and change the entire course of history subsequent to that accident. Most of us do not know where we are heading in our social evolution and how events are unfolding and for what reasons. Nor do we know how to control and alter those events. Imagine yourself in the passenger seat of a car that goes from one point to the other. The driver is the only person in control of the car and knows where the destination is. As he drives along the streets, you are wondering where he is taking you and when you are going to arrive at your destination. In other words, you are not in control of the journey and do not know where the destination is. All you can do is to write down the names of the streets and record everything you see as you ride in the car. The microanalysis of history is doing just that (recording historical events) and nothing more than the experience of the car passenger in one of the routes that takes him to the unknown destination, having absolutely no idea where he is heading and how else he could get there. Most historians write about the past and the present and try to analyze them from their own perspectives, which are biased viewpoints most of the time. Occasionally, they try to make predictions on future social developments based on the recorded information and if these predictions are based on information obtained from historical processes that are not part of the main historical trend, then all predictions pertaining to future developments of social evolution will be inaccurate and unfounded. Moreover, such predictions are usually limited to short-term developments, not long-term one. Like the passenger in the car, most of us, including our historians, have no idea where social evolution is taking us, and we are confused by its chaotic process and the turns that it makes in its journey toward its finality.

The macroanalysis of history will show us the finality of the social evolution, and make it easier for us to understand its main historical trends and attributes at a given stage, allowing us to determine what has been achieved up to the present time and what needs to be accomplished as we go forward. To make this clearer, assume that the passenger of the car has been given the coordinates of his or her destination. Now, he or she is no longer wondering where the car is headed. In fact, the passenger can direct the driver and correct him if he takes a wrong turn. Having a clear idea of the finality of social evolution, human beings can take part in driving the process along its correct path and avoid wrong turns that would only delay but not stop the social organism from reaching its destination. The responsibility of historians must not be limited to reporting and analyzing historical events, but to guide the social evolution to its destination in the shortest period of time possible. This goal is achievable through the science of history (macroanalysis of history) founded on the principles presented here and others yet to be found.

Macroanalysis and microanalysis of history as they apply to disintegration process of history: The macroanalysis of history, which is founded on the principles governing the behavior of systems and natural laws, allows us to predict both the finality and major trends of the social evolution, not only in integration process, but also in disintegration process of history. The macroanalysis of history, again, is not capable of predicting all the details of the process.

When the environment imposes threatening conditions upon the social organism and prevents it from acquiring the resources it needs to sustain its growth and maintain its structure, the social organism is forced to reverse its evolutionary course from the integration to disintegration process. The logical outcome of this process is that the social organism undergoes reductions in size until a new balance emerges between the resources available in its environment and those that it needs to sustain its new and reduced structure. Naturally, the most vulnerable part of the social organism (most subject to collapse to save energy) is the top-level infrastructure, which was the last formation of the social organism when it was integrating. With the collapse of this infrastructure, all of the relational bonds that had been established between the social organism's parallel subsystems at that level will either alter or vanish altogether, leaving its subsystems to survive on their own. If these now independent subsystems continue to fail extracting their energy needs from their surrounding systems and environment, the disintegration of systems and their infrastructure will proceed to the lower and lower subsystem levels until either the social organism with its entire subsystem levels vanish or, at some point, reach a new balance with its environment. Based on this argument, the macroanalysis of history will not only be able to predict the outcome, or finality, of the social organism in disintegration process of history, but also its major trends in achieving that state of balance. Other major trends and historical events in disintegration process can be predicted when one applies the notion of the lowest state of system's internal energy. When the top-level system collapses, it removes all the restrictions on its subsystems, particularly those directly under that infrastructure, setting them free to seek their own lowest state of internal energy in a fierce competition with each other. As we know, this was not the case in the integration process of history, where the high level system's state of internal energy took precedence over its subsystems, restricted their behavior, and enforced equality among them. Considering the characteristics and mindsets of human beings who have evolved in a hostile environment, we can imagine the level of chaos that would erupt in the life of the social organism in disintegration process of history. In general, the macroanalysis of history empower us to predict both the finality and the major trends of social evolution, regardless in what direction it evolves. The microanalysis of historical events in disintegration process will remain paralyzed as usual, and incapable of predicting the main historical trend and finality of the process. Theoretically, the disintegration process of history would remain circumstantial but deterministic in its finality and its main historical trend, as it was in integration process of history.

CHAPTER 4

Human nature and its influence on the course of history and social evolution

In the previous chapters, we discussed several influential factors that determine the trends of the social evolution and its finality. We talked about how the environment dominates the life of the social organism and sets its evolutionary course toward a process of either integration or disintegration. We discussed the authority of the laws of nature and, in particular, the second law of thermodynamics in determining the finality of social evolution and the relational bonds that would eventually evolve among the subsystems of social organism. We also argued that the structural organization of the social organism, which is in the infancy stages of its evolutionary process, attempts to duplicate the structural organization of human as a proven and operationally efficient structure. Moreover, the social organism itself faces the same challenges as its own subsystems (human beings), which is to survive in an environment with limited energy resources. This leaves the social organism with no other alternative but to become an operationally efficient organism. All of the above-mentioned factors, place a constraining effect on the evolutionary process of the social organism by restricting the range of processes that it can adopt, rather than leaving it totally open to adopt any process and any finality. As a result, any law that would further restrict social evolution to a narrower range of evolutionary processes would have a deterministic effect on its process.

In this chapter, we will introduce a new deterministic factor that might further restrict the social organism's evolutionary process. This new factor comes from within the social organism and pertains to the characteristics of its subsystems. In our earlier discussions, we argued that the characteristics of subsystems always transcend to the high-level system and become part of the characteristics of that system as well. One of these characteristics, which has a colossal impact on the process of history and the behavior of the social organism in everything that it does, is its *insecurity*, which is a human property. In this chapter, we will explore how the character of social organism, its evolutionary process, and in general our history has fallen victim to the evolutionary process of the human being himself. Some of the notions presented here in connection with this argument are well-founded scientific facts, whereas others are propositions derived from logical deductions.

The social organism's structural evolution and environmental connection:
Every detail of the structural organization of every living organism (animals, humans and their society) has been powerfully influenced by the history of evolving ecosystems that these organisms have evolved in. Environmental factors such as daylight and nighttime, ambient temperature, the intensity and wavelengths of light, gravity, atmospheric pressure, and air chemistry have had a predominant influence on the structural development of all living organisms. For example, the length of daylight on our planet has dictated the size and capacity of the part of our brain that engages in data processing activity for incoming information through the senses; similar to random access memory (RAM) in the computer systems. That is why, when night falls, this part of our memory is overloaded and it can hardly process the incoming information through our senses. At this point we fall asleep to shut down all of our senses, letting our brain to clean up this memory location, by filing or trashing the information. The speed of sorting through information and processing it is also influenced and determined by the nighttime hours. Once our memories are cleared and old information is filed away, we feel refreshed and ready to function again when the next day dawns. Restoring this data processing ability is probably one of the most important tasks of the brain while we are asleep because our survival depends on it. The healing and regulation of our bodily organs may be the next important functions of the brain during sleep. Additional examples of structural developments of humans in connection with their environment are; the formation of the rib cage to support the lungs from atmospheric pressure to make breathing possible. The location of the anus at the lowest part of the gastrointestinal system to allow the gravitational force to assist in the movement of digested material. These and numerous other examples are indications of how tight the connection between our structural development and environmental conditions has been and how delicate the balance may be to our survival.

Energy resources and their availability have also been enormously influential factors in a living organism's evolutionary process and its structural development. For example, as long as an organism in stationary position receives the energy it needs to survive, the organism will not evolve into a mobile organism to look for resources elsewhere, much less to develop a brain and senses to perceive its environment. Therefore, it is logical to assume that when a stationary organism can no longer find the resources it needs in its immediate vicinity, then, it will evolve with organs that will allow it to move around and find these resources elsewhere in its environment. If mobility was inadequate to locate the resources of the environment, then, the organism will evolve with a brain and sensory organs to assist the organism to perceive its environment better and find the hidden resources that could have not been found by having mobility alone. The structural development of animals on the basis of this theory makes perfect sense, as there are no animals evolved with brain and sensory devices that lack mobility, while the opposite holds true.

If our notion is accurate and the process of evolution of an organism is tied to searching for the resources of environment, then we will arrive at some interesting conclusions. If earth's environment was able to support the energy needs of a primitive living organism for millions of years without that organism needing to move from its site, this living organism probably would have not evolved into anything else, but to remain an elementary life form. This means that the lack of energy resources in the environment may have been responsible for the vast diversity and complexity of the life forms that have evolved on our planet. At the same time that this scarcity of resources has created enormously complex and magnificent organisms, it has also caused unavoidable violence among them as they compete for these scarce resources.

Now let us examine the behavior of a society from the viewpoint of an organism that searches for energy resources in order to survive. Early societies were similar to organisms with limited mobility, each society being able to find all of its energy needs locally. As societies grew larger and their needs for energy resources multiplied, so did their mobility to a point that today these societies can reach, with the help of their technology, to the other side of the world in search of these resources and compete with other societies to control them. Therefore, the evolution and structural complexity of a society is dominated by its environmental conditions, and its growth controlled by the availability of energy resource in its environment and the ability of society to exploit them. One day, human beings will be able to bring the energy resources of other planets to the earth, or build flying objects to take a small society to other planets where energy resources may be abundant. As we can see, the behaviors of social organisms—the patterns of their evolution and structural development—are quite similar to those of human beings, all driven by the availability of energy resources in their environment.

At this point, it seems logical to assert that the social organism's evolutionary process, its structural development, and its characteristics are all influenced by two of its surrounding systems: its inner systems (human beings), and its outer system (the environment). Human behavior controls the social organism's inner boundary, and any change in the attitude of human beings may well produce qualitative changes in the behavior of social organism. The outer boundary of social organism is controlled by its environment. Keep in mind that human beings are in direct communication with their environment, which means that any environmental change can affect human behavior and consequently the social organism itself. Figure 4-1 shows the inner and outer boundaries of a social organism.

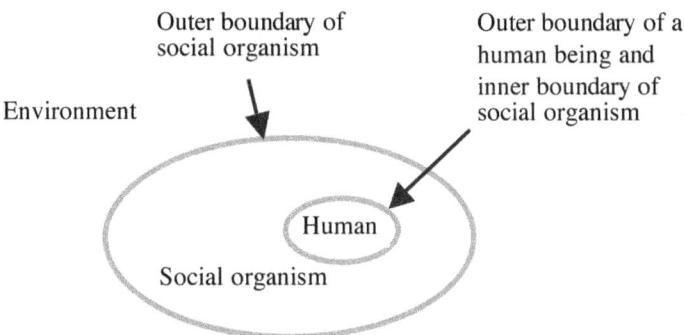

Figure 4-1 Boundaries of social organism

In conclusion, if the history of earth's environmental changes (evolution of ecosystem) has been responsible for the development of all physical and mental characteristics of humans, and if these characteristics transcend to social organism and influence its behavior, then by logical deduction the earth's past environmental changes have been ultimately responsible for setting the inner boundary conditions of social organism and dictate the type of social evolution and historical trends that we have today.

Exclusivity of the physical and mental development of an organism in connection with its environment: Is it possible that if our environment was not so hostile to our existence, our state of mind (attitude) would have been different today? Is it also true that such a change in our attitudes would have altered the attitude and behavior of social organisms themselves, making their interactions less violent than they are today? In this section, we will discuss the validity of these arguments.

There are two logical questions in this argument. First, could a human's physiological and psychological developments remain the same, evolving in different environments each with different characteristics, for example, evolving in a hostile or non-hostile environment? Second, could there have been a multitude of mindsets for humans evolved with the same physiological evolutionary process dictated by his environment?

According to the theory of evolution, life on earth began with the formation of a single cell that, in the process of evolution, diversified into millions of different life forms, each pursuing its own course of evolution, and diversifying again. For our argument, let us analyze the environment of a parasite. Most parasites attach to a host and feed themselves off the host or from the food that host acquires from his environment. These two different life forms, host and parasite, have two different environments, nature being the environment of the host and the host being the environment of the parasite. Obviously, the parasite's environment is friendlier to its existence than the host's environment, and if it were not for the ability of the host to acquire energy from his environment and support himself, the parasite would not survive. The question before us now is this: why have parasites not evolved with a brain and sensory organs to comprehend their friendly environment, and was there a necessity for this development. The answer is; there was no need for a parasite to evolve into a complex form in an environment that generously supports its energy needs. The host, however, has to evolve to a level of sophistication that allows him to go after the energy resources not easily obtainable in his environment. If the foregoing argument is true, then a hostile environment must be a prerequisite for the evolution of humans and other sophisticated animals, which is to evolve with a brain and sensory organs, and also develop a state of mind that is insecure and selfish. The evolution of species in a harsh or unfriendly environment cannot result in the development of mindsets that are secure and friendly to others. Based on this argument, we may make the following assertion, that the current physiological and psychological state of a species is the product of the history of evolving environment of that species. This also means that humans (or animals) could not have evolved both mentally and physically any different in the same environment.

If the earliest environment of the life forms from which we have evolved had been friendlier in terms of supporting their energy needs, and the early life forms had not had to struggle to survive, then those life forms would have never been evolved into organisms of greater complexity, such as animals and human beings. A hostile environment that leads to the development of sophisticated species, such as human beings, would also be responsible for the development of mind sets that are selfish and insecure and naturally affect the behaviors of larger systems, such as social organisms, that are composed of them.

If this argument is sufficient, we may then conclude that if we humans ever encounter an extraterrestrial species that possesses a complicated brain and sensory organs, then we can be certain that they, too, must have evolved in a hostile environment and have had a violent historical process, at least at some point in their social evolution. This would lead us to conclude that environmental history that has led to the formation of specific physical/mental states in humans is the primary reason for the violent trends in our historical processes. As we can see, one deterministic process, or trend, starting with environmental history has led to a chain of deterministic processes, such as our social evolution. This suggests that the social organism's evolutionary process (or our historical process and its trends) could have never been anything but violent, at least not until the social organism approaches its maturity. The predominant and deterministic trend to violent behavior will not change until the environment of every human on our planet has become safe and secure.

The foundation of instinctive, emotional, and rational behavior in the social organism: Like those of individual human beings, the behavioral patterns of a social organism can be categorized as instinctive, emotional, and rational. This should not come as a surprise to us, as human behavioral patterns, like other characteristics, transcends to social organism and dominate its behavior. Instinctive behavior in the social organism, which is a manifestation of human survival instincts, is as strong as the instinctive behavior of human being himself and supersedes emotional and rational behaviors when physical survival of the organism is threatened. Unlike instinctive behavior, the root cause of emotional behavior in a social organism is a more recent phenomenon that goes back only to a few thousand years, when humans started living in larger communities, generation after generation, forming customs and traditions unique to their societies. These traditions and belief systems, among other accomplishments of these societies, became a catalyst for the formation of bonds between generations, as well as among the members of each generation. These bonds formed independent and sovereign social entities that challenged and competed with other similar entities over survival matters. Therefore, emotional behavior in the social organism is generated by the collective attitude and behavior of all members of a society that share a similar culture, or identify with that culture and its history. Although emotional behavior is different from instinctive behavior, when the survival of the social organism is threatened, these two behaviors may become inseparable. In other instances, emotional behavior may exhibit itself in a placid form, as when societies cheer their sports teams competing for a title. Naturally, any commonality of culture, religion, or belief systems might become a catalyst for the formation of emotional bonds between social organisms, even if these organisms are geographically separated from each other. It seems that emotional bonds among members of a social organism or among social organisms themselves require the involvement of some sort of symbolic system, whether in the form of language, religion, or history.

The rational behavior of a social organism is associated with the communal knowledge within the organism, which is the collective knowledge of all individuals, for the sole purpose of exploring and understanding the behavior of all surrounding systems in its environment, including its own. It is interesting to note that as much as social organisms behave rationally and intelligently in exploration of their environment, they fail to behave in the same manner toward each other. This can be attributed to the lack of powerful theories concerning social evolution and the understanding of our historical process and the finality of the social evolution on our planet. In the absence of such theories, social organisms have no guidance to regulate their behavior and manage their integration scientifically. This leaves them with no other alternative but to resort to emotional and instinctive behaviors to resolve their differences. Such interactions between social organisms do not help the self-regulation of our historical process; therefore, the historical process remains violent by nature, moving slowly toward integration only by the sheer forces of necessity.

The effects of the environment on human beings and their social evolution: There is no doubt that our physiological structure and psychological state of mind are the products of millions of years of interaction between us and our environment, as we were both going through our own evolutionary processes. The earth's environment has never been friendly to any animal, including human beings. Earthquakes, wildfires, harsh weather conditions and disease made life unbearably difficult for every species and starvation led various species to look for opportunities to consume each other as sources of energy in order to survive. As a result, all species, including the human, have developed a strong sense of insecurity. Since human characteristics transcend to the level of the social organism, social organisms also exhibit insecurity in their behaviour. Therefore, as the earth's hostile environment has been responsible for the formation of a state of insecurity in the minds in human beings, it has also been ultimately responsible for the insecure behavior of social organisms and their behavior toward each other, which has shaped our historical process. Some behaviors of social organisms in this regard are their territorial behavior, the formation of armies and other defensive forces, and the storage of food and energy resources. Some of the major conflicts and wars waged in our history have been the result of the insecurity of the social organisms. Finally, most of the accomplishments in the areas of science and technology that have allowed us and our society to have a better control over our environment can also be largely attributed to the sense of insecurity. This argument may be convincing enough for us to conclude that a mere biological development within a subsystem may produce outcomes that will influence and control the evolutionary process of the system that contains it.

Hypothetically, if humans could have evolved in a non-hostile environment, neither their physiological structure and nor their psychological state of mind would have been those of contemporary human beings. For this human being, insecurity would have been an unknown phenomenon that would have also become an irrelevant characteristic of the social organism and its evolutionary process. Let us remind ourselves of the theory of history that Karl Marx put forward. The Marxist view of the evolution of society is founded on socioeconomic class struggle and the modification of production relations among human beings in the course of their historical evolution. This theory is valid for humans with a state of mind they have today, which is controlled mainly by their sense of insecurity. If they had evolved in a non-hostile environment and without development of their current state of mind, they would have become more generous and sharing humans and as a result, there would have been no socioeconomic classes much less to have a struggle among them. In this scenario, Marx's theory would have been unscientific, unfounded and not applicable to their historical evolution. In a sharing society, the transition to the finality of social evolution would have been quick and easy and without bloodshed. In other words, subsystems would have immediately submitted to the will of the high level system by adopting the rule of equality. Now, the questions are: Due to our current state of mind, are we forever doomed to resolve our differences through confrontational behavior? Would our sense of insecurity subside at any point in our history? The answer seems to be *yes*. Assuming that integration is the main historical process, our technological and scientific achievements would eventually help us to create a more secure environment for ourselves and over time alleviate our sense of insecurity, which would allow us to think more rationally rather than instinctively when trying to resolve our differences. Understanding and being aware of our weaknesses and how these weaknesses extend to the social organism to dominate its behavioral patterns and affect its relations with other social organisms will help the process of history to become less violent. Learning about the process of history and the inescapable finality that is awaiting all of the humanity would definitely make a difference in everyone's behavior. When human beings start to get involved in driving their social evolution towards that finality, social evolution, on a global scale, will become more of a self-regulated process, with minimum level of violence among its members.

A brief summary of this chapter: If a society is seen as a system that is surrounded by inner and outer boundaries, then changing the conditions of the boundaries can influence its behavior and its evolutionary process. As we have seen in the last few chapters, the conditions of the outer boundary of a social system is set by its current environment. The inner boundary is controlled by human behavior, which in itself is the product of history of environmental conditions up to the present time that humans have evolved in. This makes the environment the ultimate controlling factor of social evolution, as all the environmental conditions of the past continue to dominate the present and future historical events through human behavior. We have also discussed how a lack of energy resources in the environment of social organism can change the course of its evolutionary process from integration to disintegration, and set a new finality for the social organism to pursue. In this chapter, we stated that hostile environmental conditions are responsible for the development of sophisticated species with exclusivity in their physiological and psychological development in connection with those environments. Then, we argued that hostile environmental conditions would produce insecurity in humans' attitudes and behaviors that would then transcend to social organisms and become part of their attitudes as well. Finally, we concluded that the predominance of violence in historical trends and processes is rooted in the character of the human, reacting with a hostile environment. As a result, it would make sense to assert that the entire history of the earth's environmental conditions that has led to the development of the present-day human attitude has been indirectly but ultimately responsible for the social organism's current behavioral patterns. Consequently, all future environmental changes will not only affect the outer boundary of the social system, but through human behavior also indirectly affect the inner boundary conditions and have a compounding effect on its behavior and its evolutionary process. In this chapter, we also hypothesized that a non-hostile environment may not lead to the development of sophisticated species like humans, much less to the evolution of much larger and much more complicated organisms, such as social organisms. In conclusion, if evolving into a sophisticated species, such as human being required a hostile environment, it seems that we were doomed from the beginning to have a predominantly violent historical process, and any expectation to make this process non-violent, without first transforming the hostile environment of humans to a friendly environment is just irrational.

CHAPTER 5

The social organism and its behavioral characteristics in the integration process of history

Society is a multi-level ordered system that not only contains all of the characteristics of its subsystems in the hierarchy, but also possesses additional properties distinct to its structure that do not apply to any of its subsystems. In this chapter, we will discuss some of these properties and point out the importance of these properties in the behavioral pattern of society as a system. We will also compare some of the structural and operational similarities that resemble those of human beings, which continue to surface in the evolutionary process of the social organism. We have to keep in mind that any ordered system, regardless of its complexity, is always dependent on its environment for its energy needs so that it can grow and maintain its structural integrity while striving to keep the state of its internal energy at the minimum level as it interacts with other systems. Society as a system and a living organism has an evolutionary course or behavioral pattern that is strongly influenced by a number of factors, such as laws of nature, tendencies to evolve with a particular operational and structural organization, and the environmental conditions of the earth. These strong influences have set up particular trends and finalities in the evolutionary process of the social organism on earth that are deterministic despite the randomness that still may be present in its evolutionary process.

The importance of symbolic systems on the life of the social organism, its evolutionary process, and its consciousness: The human brain is composed of approximately 100 billion neurons that are highly interconnected. Communication among these neurons takes place through electrical pulses, and the speed of data processing is a function of the neural network, which consists of thousands and in some cases up to hundreds of thousands of connections for each neuron. This neural network allows parallel data processing and has many advantages over the traditional computing algorithms used by the computers we manufacture. A neural network is capable of learning. It can also sustain damage and continue to function and produce outputs. Society as an organism also has a brain that is in a distributed form that each individual carries a small part of it. From this point on, we will call the brain that every individual carries a "*brain segment*" and the distributed brain that composes all of these brain segments, the "*social brain*".

This social brain requires two conditions in order to function as an integrated organ, or network. First, there has to be a medium to connect the brain segments of the social brain. Second, there must be a *symbolic system* to produce meaningful communication among these brain segments. To create such a network, the brain waves (or electrical pulses generated by neurons) of one brain segment must somehow find their way into another brain segment. But how is this possible if the two brain segments are not part of the same organ? Humans and animals have evolved with sensory organs that are capable of transforming the neuron's electrical pulses into a different form of waves (sound waves and optical waves) that can easily propagate into their environment (a suitable communication medium), reaching other members of the society. When other members of the society, through their sensory organs, receive these waveforms, a reverse process takes place to transform these waveforms back to electrical pulses understood by neurons. The message is then recovered by comparison of these electrical pulses with those stored in the memory that has a cross reference with objects and thoughts processes, previously learned by the individual.

The sensory organs of the human body have made networking among them a possibility. However, due to the limitations of the range of operation of human sensory organs, the transformation of data sent or received is possible only in these ranges unless it is expanded by some means, usually through technology.

The next challenge to complete the working of the social brain (that is, creating meaningful communication among its brain segments) is to create the same combination of electrical pulses that generate a particular perception in each brain segment that is the result of a single visual effect or audio signal. It is only then that a full integration of brain segments can take place and form a higher level of cognitive entity in the hierarchy of living organic structures, with a much greater level of consciousness of itself and its environment. As the connectivity among the brain segments of the society continues to grow, assisted by communication technologies such as television and the Internet, so does the level of scientific achievement and technological breakthrough resulting from the enhanced calculation and creative power of the social brain. This is clearly visible from the accelerated pace of scientific and technological achievements of mankind in recent history as compared to earlier eras. Today, new political, philosophical, and scientific theories can immediately propagate around the world and result in an immediate and profound impact on the life of the social organism. If symbolic systems that represent objects, non-objects and thought processes, created by human beings, were not understood and recognized by other human beings, neither the social brain and nor the social organism would have existed in a meaningful way. What we mean by this is that there would have been no harmony or synchronization among its members, and so the social organism would have remained in a state of disorder and disarray. The collection of audio and visual symbols (language and art) used by humans to communicate with each other has created our symbolic systems that have been evolving since the creation of the very first human community, and it continues to evolve and become more sophisticated as we go forward. Language, art, and other symbolic systems need to be taught to every individual in a given society to make sure that all members of that society are able to connect and communicate with each other. As a result, educational institutions are created to take on that responsibility. Without symbolic systems, a social organism cannot organize itself in a meaningful way, and without a social organism and a social brain, advancements in science, technology, art and humanity would have not been possible. It is through these symbolic systems that humans have been able to convey their thoughts and philosophical viewpoints to other members of their society. Propagation of these ideas and viewpoints within the members of the society leads to the formation of higher levels of social consciousness within the social organism that will eventually modify not only the organism's relational bonds with its surrounding systems, but also those pertaining to its own subsystems. It is through knowledge, communicated via symbolic systems that the course of the evolution of individual human beings and their society is being set. In conclusion, without symbolic systems and a medium that allows human brains to connect and communicate, the social organism as an integrated organism will never exist.

Structural components and relational bonds in a society: Society (the social organism) is composed of living ordered systems (human beings) and non-living ordered systems (cities, infrastructure, houses, transportation systems, communications systems, etc.) designed and built by humans to facilitate their survival as a group. Interestingly, every human creation is an ordered system, and an ordered system (whether it is living or non-living) is dependent on energy from its environment to retain its structural integrity. But non-living ordered systems are incapable of extracting energy from their environment on their own in order to repair themselves, as a result, this task becomes human's responsibility. Factories, houses, bridges, and roads are all ordered systems (made by humans) that are part of the structural organization of social organism that need reconstruction from time to time and each holds a value in the society. As societies integrate and grow in size additional layers of subsystems in the hierarchy of the social organism, continue to emerge. These may push individual human beings, as a subsystem, further down in the hierarchy of the system. For example, a corporation that employs several thousand people is an entity that holds a greater value than a single individual; at the same time, it holds a lesser value than the society of which it is a part. Organizations like labor unions and political parties, which represent tens or even hundreds of thousands of individuals, hold a greater value than a corporation because they encompass and represent larger populations.

Based on these arguments, we can say that the structure of a society is composed of layers of subsystems, each with a different value attached to it. On this list, an individual human being occupies the lowest seat in the hierarchy of social organism in terms of his value, and the top-level infrastructure always holds the highest value. Like all other living organisms, the structure of social organism dynamically changes as it proceeds with its evolutionary process. The goal of its evolution is to achieve optimal stability and operational efficiency on a global scale, by creating harmony among all of its subsystems. Clearly, this is only possible if environmental conditions support the integration process of history.

One of the most important attributes of the social organism is the nature of the relational bonds among its subsystems, at all levels, that change dynamically as social organism proceeds with its evolutionary process. Although the laws of nature and thermodynamics have clearly defined the nature of these relational bonds at the finality of the process, in transitional periods, however, these relational bonds may be subject to change or be challenged by the subsystems that do not wish to give up their lowest state of internal energy. As a result, the challenge for social organism in the integration process of history is to overcome and win the battles that its own subsystems present to its process, preventing a smooth transition to a finality that is supported by the laws of nature and thermodynamics. Throughout history, brute force processes have won most of the battles the social organism has fought with its subsystems, though a few of these battles were also won through reasoning processes that require a higher state of social consciousness. When all of these battles have been fought and won by the social organism at the end of its evolutionary process, all living and non-living ordered structures will be harmoniously integrated into its structure and form an operationally efficient and optimally stable social organism.

Fundamental principles behind integration of the social organisms and the influence of technological breakthroughs in its process: In the integration process of history, there are two principles that apply. The first is that all systems and subsystems in the hierarchy struggle to maintain their lowest state of internal energy at all times. The second principle is that the high-level system's minimum state of internal energy takes precedence and priority over all of its subsystems' minimum states of energy, forcing them into an energy exchange and equalization process. In the disintegration process, however, the second principle is abolished due to the collapse of the high level system, which results in releasing all subsystems to search for and confiscate as much energy as they can from the remaining resources. As we saw in earlier chapters, the laws of physics and thermodynamics influence these two behaviors in living organisms on all hierarchical levels. The question is; how do these abstract laws apply to the living systems and manipulate their behavior?

To answer this question, we first need to translate some of the abstract physical concepts that are originally derived for non-living systems, such as *minimum state of internal energy*, to the behavior of living systems. The minimum state of internal energy for a living system, whether human or society, translates to system being safe and secure, has an abundance of energy resources or life support systems to sustain its structure and guarantee its survival, and also has maximum degree of freedom. It is in this state that the stress on the living system is at the lowest level and its stability at the highest level. The same outcome occurs when a non-living system maintains the lowest state of internal energy. Most of us would agree with this notion that the majority of living systems (human beings and social organisms) are seeking the lowest state of internal energy, if they find the opportunity to do so. We might ask how an upper-level system, such as a society, can impose its will on lower-level systems. After all, society is created by individual human beings and does not have a life of its own. This assumption is not quite true because when multiple living systems get together and build specific relational bonds among themselves, they create a new living system with its own evolutionary goals and objectives. The analogy is simple. When we compare trillions of living cells in our body with the defined relational bonds among them, they form the high-level living system that we know as the human being. In this case, we do not argue that a human being is not a living organism; why, then, should we argue that society is not a living organism? After all, just as human body is made up of living cells, so is the society. Society's living cells (sub-organisms) are human beings. In fact, the integration of living systems with defined relational bonds among them may create an even higher level of living organism that may extend beyond the global community. This is illustrated in Figure 5-1.

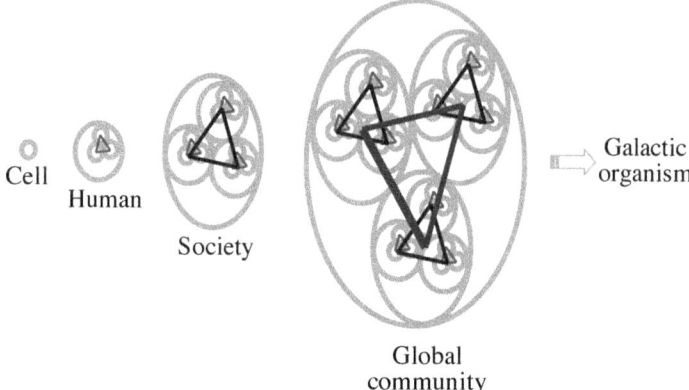

Figure 5-1 Integration of the living system

In Figure 5-1, the triangles represent relational bonds among lower level systems. To the right of the circle representing the human structure is a society composed of human organisms (people) with different types of relational bonds among them. Next comes a global community with societies as the building blocks of its structure, again with completely new sets of relational bonds. We have, of course, ignored the intervening layers of development, such as smaller groups and entities such as corporations, political parties, and international alliances.

Now if we believe that society and global community are, in fact, living organisms and that each really has its own evolutionary course toward stability, then these organisms can overcome opposition and impose their will on their subsystems. Again, the analogy is simple. Human cells have no freedom to separate themselves from the body. They cannot choose to perform a different function. By providing them with the nutrients to survive, the body treats them all equally. This is why the system called the human body survives and operates harmoniously. But compared to society as a whole, the human body is in a very advanced evolutionary stage, and it will take a long time before society evolves into an organism that can operate as efficiently as the human body and overcome the challenges of rebellious subsystems that do not want to submit to the will of the higher-level system.

It is the self-serving attitude of subsystems that opposes the will of the high-level system and makes the process of history the long and chaotic process it is. Not knowing that the historical process based on the laws of nature favors the high level system that eventually prevails by enforcing its conditions upon its subsystems. Although the availability of energy resources and dominance of the laws of nature are the controlling factors in the growth and integration of living systems, they are not sufficient alone for integration to take place. The other factor that makes the integration process of history possible is the overcoming the technological barriers that are in the way of integration, as integration in every particular system level requires a new level of technological advancements to make it a reality.

Without these technologies, integration would become impractical, despite availability of energy resources to support the integrated structure. For example, the formation of a galactic organism with other intelligent species around our galaxy would require new means of communication and speed of travel that we do not have today. How is it possible to integrate two civilizations that are four light years apart using today's technological know- how? Even a simple con-versation between earth and the distant alien planet, carried on at the speed of light, might require a human lifetime. Based on these notions, how can we then intelligently define the process of history? Is social evolution an unavoidable integration process of living systems, that is forced by the laws of nature, sup-ported by the environment, and made possible by technology, as these living systems come in contact with each other? Is finality of history the state that the high-level integrated living system eventually defines all the relational bonds among its subsystems and the state of energy that they may retain? Finally, are the science and technology that make integration process possible the catalysts and means that social organism invents and uses to construct its sophisticated structural organization?

Where does the hierarchy and growth of an ordered system stop? Open systems integrate starting with tense relationship and eventually homogenize and unify in their objectives. Theoretically, as long as a system can collect enough energy from its environment to support its subsystems and the infra-structure that connects them, it will continue to grow. The growth and inte-gration process can continue forever, as long as energy resources are available and the technological barriers are broken by scientific achievements. Just a few hundred years ago, for example, the notion of *globalization* was a dream. Today, thanks to advanced technology and availability of energy resources, globaliza-tion will become a reality that no one can stop. Likewise, colonization of space today seems an unreachable dream, but when technological barriers such as speed of travel and communication are broken and we are able to duplicate our environmental conditions on other planets, our growth process will continue. It is also possible that some time in the future we may encounter other intel-ligent species that possess the technologies that permit the integration of their civilization with ours and are not afraid to share those technologies with us.

The dissipation of energy in connection with social evolution and the process of history: Countless people have perished in our social evolution and in the integration process of history. More people are dying every day as the struggle for energy resources and life support systems between individual human beings and societies continues. As social organism evolves with the intent to self-organize itself, it would demand that all of its subsystems, exchange energy and find a state of equality among themselves. However, in most cases, subsystems with lower states of internal energy do not volunteer to take part in energy exchanges with other subsystems. This eventually leads to confrontation, followed by destruction of ordered structures, including humans. This loss, which is called dissipated energy, is essential in building equilibrium among subsystems and lowering the state of internal energy of the encompassing system, which is the global social organism. Subsystems with lower states of internal energy are those that control and confiscate resources, leaving very little or none for others. These subsystems could be wealthy individuals or prosperous societies. The dissipated energy resulting from such conflicts is part of the overall energy exchange between the subsystems. Based on the second law of thermodynamics, it seems that dissipation of energy is unavoidable and essential for achieving equilibrium at the subsystem level and stability and harmony in the encompassing system.

This rather pessimistic—but nonetheless realistic—view of the process of history may tarnish the reputation of humans, who are given too much credit for being the "animal with scruples that knows the difference between right and wrong" and are in charge of their own history. If we step back from the human perspective, however, we recognize the fact that human beings have very little control over their social evolution at this time. We have fallen victim to the laws of nature, the design of the systems, and even our own evolutionary process that has affected our behavior. Human history and social evolution are violent process, and for the most part, they will remain violent. As social evolution proceeds to its finality by enforcing equality in all subsystem levels, more people will become the casualties of history. Human beings can only be wise enough to lead the process to its destination by understanding it and managing to keep the dissipation losses at a minimum level. This can be done only by avoiding unwanted historical turns that are not part of the main trend of the integration process of history that would be responsible for an added level of dissipative losses. Unwanted turns in the historical process come from the subsystems of social organism having an inherent behavior of trying to manipulate as many resources as they can to retain the lowest state of internal energy, with little or no consideration for other parallel systems that may be starving for the same resources.

In the view of many, conflicts among peoples and societies rarely arise due to cultural, religious or ideological differences. Conflicts more often arise due to economic and survival matters and find ideology or religion as a mean to unify one group of people or a society against the others. The human race has enough violent history to see that to avoid conflict, it is crucial to maintain a state of equality among subsystems and keep losses due to dissipation at their minimum level. If people do not attempt to maintain a state of equality among themselves then the encompassing system, the social organism, will. This is due to the fact that the social organism is a self-organizing and self-regulating system that has power over its subsystems. To achieve its goals, the social organism can deploy its subsystems to advance its objectives or force its subsystems into a quagmire or a situation that leaves them no alternative but to submit to the will of the social organism and the forces of necessity. As history shows, this seems to be the common pattern.

Knowing this, we can still have some optimism about human wisdom and people's conscious involvement in their historical process. We may be able to control the dissipation losses and keep them at their minimum level, if we choose to leap to the finality of social evolution instead of fighting it. If we resist the intended goals of the social organism in organizing itself, then we have to take the long ride on the roller coaster of the historical process and pay a higher price for the destruction of order and human casualties, which are merely "dissipated energy."

Characteristics of human beings and their influence on the stability and evolutionary process of global social organisms: Top-level characteristics of social systems, such as economy, culture, and technology are the dominant characteristics of a social system and greatly influential in setting the system's behavioral patterns as it deals with similar systems. Large gaps in prosperity levels and technological know-how, along with cultural differences, are reasons for build-ups of tension among social systems. In the view of many, when the global social organism approaches its finality (a utopian society), its members will live in harmony, irrespective of their race or cultural background. Members of this society would more or less have an equal standing economically. They would also benefit equally from the services their society provides.

As we know, the current state of the global social organism is not even nearly close to such a harmonious social system whose subsystems are free from tension. For the global social organism to emerge as a harmonious and stable social system, according to the laws of nature, it is required that a great deal of its internal energy be released or dissipated; this would come from the energy exchanges between its subsystems, in all levels of hierarchy. Usually, the release of this energy takes place in a violent manner, as each subsystem struggles to maintain the lowest state of internal energy for itself. However, after the clash of subsystems followed by loss of lives and destruction of order, a much greater understanding and compassion may emerge among subsystems to equalize and unify themselves. If that is the case, what is the price that we have to pay, in terms of human lives and destruction of order, to unify the entire world into one community that is optimally stable and has established equality in all subsystem levels? Do we have any control over the total amount of energy that has to be released or dissipated from the structure of the global social organism so that it can reach its optimum stability? Even though there is a multitude of factors that set deterministic goals for the finality of social evolution, the process itself remains circumstantial and randomly guided or directed. This makes us wonder if there is a preferred process, among many, that would lead the global social organism to its finality with the least amount of dissipation losses. Finally, is the total loss due to dissipation between the current state of the global social organism and its historical finality independent of its process?

Let us use two hypothetical historical processes to clarify this notion. In the first scenario, if nuclear war erupts on a global scale, due to the build-up of excessive tension among nations, billions of lives would be lost and ordered structures would be destroyed within a very short period of time. This huge loss of energy from the structure of the global social organism, in such a short period of time (fast rate of dissipative losses), would instantly unify the remaining population of the world, if sufficient amount of life support systems still available for their survival. This is what World War II did in Europe, which initiated the unification process of European nations. In the second scenario, if subsystems of global social organism choose not to equalize, as they always do, then there would be frequent, smaller wars and battles among nations and peoples that may take a longer time before the whole system (the global social organism) achieves harmony and equality at all subsystem levels. Theoretically, if we add up all of the dissipative losses resulting from battles and small wars, (slow rate of dissipative losses but extended in time), would those losses be equal to the losses that were generated in the nuclear war in order to produce the same level of stability and harmony in the life of the global social organism? In the world of non-ordered systems, this (the initial and final states and not the process by which these states are attained) has a great deal of merit.

In mechanics, the loss or gain of potential energy stored in an object is a function of its past and present elevation and is independent of the path through which the object has changed its elevation. On the atomic level, jumping of the electrons from one orbit to another results in the release or gain of a certain amount of energy: the amount of the gain or loss is repeatable all the time. The question is; does this notion also holds true for the evolutionary process of social organism, meaning that, the dissipation losses are a function of the two states (initial and final) and independent of the path of the evolutionary process? If so, then all evolutionary paths leading to the same finality should produce the same level of dissipation losses, similar to the two historical scenarios we discussed earlier.

But this notion does not seem to hold true for the social evolution, because process of history can make turns that are not part of the main trend of integration process of history, and with every undesired turn the level of dissipative losses (destruction of order through violence) will increase. This is an indication that the dissipation losses are a function of the historical path. The undesired historical turns are the result of self-serving characteristics of the subsystems (a consequence of human biological evolution in a hostile environment and its manifestation in all upper-level systems) opposing the will of global social organism striving to self-organize itself. Therefore, as long as all of the subsystems within the global social organism behave in a selfish manner, it seems that for humanity to experience a non-violent historical process is just a dream. If we are to alter the violent historical processes, we must modify human beings' behaviors by securing their survival. Even if this happens and we manage to leap to the finality of social evolution and take the shortest historical path, we cannot avoid the dissipation losses altogether, but they will be the least level of dissipation losses compared to all other dissipation losses associated with other historical paths.

The question is; how can we change the characteristics of human beings and their behavior formed by millions of years of evolutionary process? We know the human being is a cybernetic system capable of studying his environment, learning and predicting the outcomes of the events before they actually take place. These qualities of human being assisted by knowledge system, gives us the ability to control our environment and probably our social evolution. If social evolution, or the process of history, ever becomes a science with convincing arguments in regard to the finality of history, it could affect the mentality of humans and consequently alter the violent trends of historical processes to peaceful and directed evolutionary processes. The science of history will teach us the finality of our relationship in an advanced and optimally stable global social organism. Through this knowledge, we would realize that our best and longest lasting security is linked to the security of all human beings, or there will be no lasting security. Science may also prove that the objectives of the higher-level system cannot be affected or halted by its subsystems, and one way or another, the top-level system will achieve its intended goals and self-organize itself, whether we cooperate or not. Understanding the process of history may result in much more active involvement of people who would want to assist the historical process, by electing leaders who would institute more humane policies that would start closing the gap between poor and rich nations. These leaders might also deviate from the confrontational policies exercised by their predecessors in dealing with other nations, which would minimize the number of casualties (dissipation losses) caused by those policies.

In summary, it is the behavior of human beings that influence the course of our social evolution, and only when human behavior is changed can we expect to see a different course of social evolution, i.e., one that is less violent. We could begin such changes by giving people a sense of security so that rational thinking can emerge. Afterward, we can show them that the process of history is not a meaningless and chaotic process, but follows certain rules and seeks predetermined goals that can be assisted by their active involvement in a positive way. If human behavioral patterns shift from instinctive to rational behavior, then it is possible to single out a process among other processes that would take the global social organism to its finality with minimum dissipative losses.

Factors contributing to the stability of the social organism: The necessary condition for the establishment of stability in the social organism occurs when a reasonable state of equality has been created among its subsystems in every level in the chain of hierarchy. While this may be a necessary condition, however, it is not sufficient. The sufficient condition is established when a harmonious and balanced relationship has also been evolved between that social organism and other external organisms, including the environment itself as a lifeline for all of those organisms. The environmental lifeline support of a system includes air, water, food, sunlight, energy resources, and all other elements that an organism needs to survive. For example, if the air or water is polluted or poisoned beyond repair, how would a living organism be able to survive? If our societies run out of oil and gas and have no replacement for these resources, how can these societies maintain their huge infrastructures and continue to stay stable?

But most natural resources that social organisms need are concentrated in certain parts of the world that are controlled by only a few while others are in desperate need of them. The struggle to control environmental resources that takes place among social organisms is analogous to the socioeconomic class struggle in an unjust economic system in which the wealth that is produced by all is owned and controlled by a few. In this analogy, human beings are subsystems of their societies as societies are subsystems of their own super-system, the global social organism. When an organism fails to support the energy needs of its sub-organisms, it will become unstable due to the deterioration of relational bonds of its subsystems that are struggling with each other to harness their own energy needs first. This instability propagates throughout the system organization at every level. Based on these arguments, stability of a system is tied to the stability of every surrounding system connected to it, whether in parallel or in a series. As a result, when subsystems in the hierarchy of a system receive the resources needed for their survival, that system becomes stable, though it may not be optimum stability. Optimum stability in a system can only be achieved when all subsystems have reached a state of equality. In the case of the social organism, this means socioeconomic justice not only at the human level but also at the social level, as measured by prosperity. The influence of the environment on the stability of the global social organism is immense and needs to be monitored with extreme care. If indicators of stability change suddenly for the worse, the social organism may quickly fall into instability. Since the environment of the social organism is dynamic, it is vital that global social organism watches environmental developments carefully and assess the need to react to them as early as possible.

Analysis of behavioral patterns of humans and social organisms: Human behavior is the result of a response generated by the brain and produced by interactions between stimuli and the brain's collective stored information. Information stored in the brain can be categorized into three sets: instinctive, emotional and abstract, which we called collected stored information. Instinctive information, which is hard coded, is composed of information gathered during the course of human evolution and is strictly related to matters of survival and it is not erasable from memory, at least not in a short period of time. Emotional information is related to personal experience and documented information regarding historical events of which the individual may be a part or feel having a connection with. This information can be replaced or modified much easier in comparison with instinctive information. In some cases, emotional behavior may be closely tied to an individual's well-being and survival. Abstract information has nothing to do with the individual's well-being and survival and is external to the body; it can include matters related to the individual's understanding of the world, including science, philosophy, art and music etc. Abstract information is easily replaced by convincing data or proof of concept and leads to logical or rational behavior. When a stimulus is generated in the environment of an individual human, it interacts with these three sets of stored information and produces three different outputs that are weighed against each other to generate the final output responsible for a particular behavior.

In an earlier chapter, we argued that all characteristics of lower-level systems are present in high-level systems. If that is the case, then social organisms must also behave instinctively, emotionally, and logically just as individual humans do. Unlike the case of the individual human being, where the physical location of the memory is centralized, in the case of social organisms, information is distributed in the minds of members of the society. The social organism also maintains more permanent, perhaps centralized, locations for information storage, such as libraries and universities. The function of these institutions is to transfer information from one generation to the next, just as genetic information is passed from one human to her offspring in the reproduction process. It is interesting that social organism's central banks for the collection and storage of information use materials (both paper and electronic storage) that outlast a typical individual's lifespan. This permanent storage allows social organisms to pass on the information to the next generation without erosion and help the social organisms preserve their character and sustain their operability on a continuous basis.

Social consciousness that depicts the mind of a society or a social organism is the sum of the instinctive, emotional, and rational states of mind of the members of a society. The behavior of social organisms that can be described by a statistical approach is the result of an interaction between a stimulus and the social consciousness. As we know, when the interaction of a stimulus with the stored information in the memory of a human being does not produce a life threatening or security related output, there is a greater probability that the power of logic will take control of the person's behavior. A society behaves in a very similar manner. When there are no life-threatening conditions, the social consciousness that determines the policies (behavior) of the state is more logical or rational than it is instinctive, which is the reflection of the general logical view of its members. This is rather obvious because when the social organism is not threatened, it means that its subsystems (human beings) are not threatened either, and it is the collective rational behavior of members of the society that produces the society's rational consciousness.

Using similar reasoning, rational behavior of a global consciousness cannot be expected unless societies (members of the global community) exhibit rational behavior. By logical deduction, we see that a rational global consciousness requires that all human beings that live in its hierarchy behave rationally. But human beings behave rationally only when their lives are secure. This suggests that unless hunger, disease, and hopelessness are eliminated from the lives of people around the globe, we cannot expect a rational behavior from them, which will become an obstacle to building a harmonious global social organism. If we ever choose to get involved actively in the historical process of building a harmonious global social organism, elimination of hunger, disease, and hopelessness should become priority number one. After that, everything else will fall in place automatically.

Influential factors shaping social consciousness: One major factor that influences social consciousness leading to a particular social behavior, arises from the need of the social organism for life-support systems provided by its environment or other surrounding systems. When these life-support needs are adequate, social organism's behavior, influenced by the social consciousness, becomes more rational than instinctive or emotional. However, when support systems fall short to support the needs of the social organism, social consciousness may tilt toward instinctive and emotional states. Aside from the life-support systems that have enormous influence in shaping social consciousness, other factors can also influence social consciousness. The personal experiences and the recorded history of humanity have a significant impact on social consciousness. Contemporary policies, ideas, technological breakthroughs, and philosophical views are also important factors that shape the social consciousness. Misinformation and the misrepresentation of reality (techniques used by the forces that control a society) may generate a temporary state of social consciousness so that the society may be driven along a desired evolutionary path. Whatever shapes the social consciousness also shapes the process of social evolution, because social consciousness is the ultimate force behind any change in social evolution.

Elements essential to the survival of humans and social organisms and their influence on the evolutionary processes of these systems: Karl Marx's economic theory, with its implications for the social evolution and process of history, is only a special case of a general theory of history. A more general theory should encompass all elements that are equally important for the survival of human beings and their societies. People cannot survive without air, water, and food, and if we are denied from these vital elements, our societies will not survive, either. In addition to these elements, a society needs other natural energy resources, such as fossil and nuclear fuels, to support its infrastructure. Since our planet provides an abundance of air and water to everyone, historical events so far have not been dominated by the struggle over manipulation of these elements. However, this does not mean that there will not be future struggles over air and water. The scarcity of the food and the difficulty of acquiring it have caused major competitions among humans to secure these resources for their own use that has led to major historical events. Marx's theory of history of modern society mainly applies to this element of survival (food), which manifests itself in the production relation of humans in their economic systems. We can also observe that some historical events have been influenced by nations competing for natural resources such as oil and gas, which are scarce and needed by nations to survive. We can thus consider these resources as elements of life that larger systems (societies) need to maintain their infrastructures and operations. To emphasize the importance of other life elements, such as air, in historical events, we may appeal to a hypothetical situation that may become a reality in the future to show that any of these survival elements may play a major role in the theory of history. Suppose that fifty years from now, the entire world is heavily industrialized and air pollution, which is the primary reason for the formation of acid rain and global warming, is basically wiping out the rain forests, melting the polar ice and changing the climate so drastically that the entire ecosystem and all life on earth is threatened. Also, suppose that with exception of few nations the rest of the world community is trying very hard to reduce the emission of pollutants into the atmosphere to reverse this dangerous process, which is alteration of ecosystem. If the uncooperative nations continue to be insensitive to this life threatening issue, could this trigger an economic sanction by the rest of the world upon those nations, or in the worst case could it trigger a war to topple their governments? Similar tensions could easily build up between nations when one nation's irresponsible policies regarding water resources affect the lives of people and animals in other nations. These tensions between nations could lead to war or set off a different course of political action that would change the course of our history, even though they have very little to do with socioeconomic issues. As we have demonstrated, theory of history is not only about economics and production relations, but also about other life-support systems upon which human life depends.

Cellular activity, a structural characteristic of human physiology applied to the social organism: Most of the trillions of cells that make up the human body are stationary and remain in their proper locations in the body. These cells must function and cooperate with each other harmoniously so that human being can survive. Given these circumstances, the degree of freedom of human body, assuming that it has no relational bonds or connections with other similar systems, is greater than the freedom of any of its individual cells, which have relational bonds with each other within the body. This notion points to a mathematical and mechanical reality that the degree of freedom of a system diminishes with every additional connection or restriction imposed on that system. When humans create relational bonds with each other to form societies, they accept some loss of their individual freedoms. Likewise, when societies decide to cooperate on an international level, they, too, agree to relinquish some of their individual freedoms to the world community or global society. Therefore, theoretically it would make sense that as a living system starts to drop to the lower ranks in the system hierarchy, its freedom (in the context of our perception of freedom) decreases because a larger number of relational bonds between that system and all other parallel and serially connected systems with it are formed. Systems in the higher ranks in the hierarchy, however, retain greater freedom because restrictive relational bonds with other systems are limited. As we mentioned earlier, the structural organization of the social organism would eventually resemble that of the human at its maturity, and if this organism expanded further to become a global organism, that, too, would evolve to resemble the structural organization of human. Since organisms of this size would require greater stability to be operationally efficient, they may force their subsystems into something like cellular activity with little individual freedom. The definition of a cell in a society is not necessarily a fixed point within its structure, but rather a domain in which a single human being operates (works and lives) within its perimeter, distinctly different from the other cells.

With the advancement of technology, new realities are emerging to suggest that the sizes of operating cell may shrink even further in the future. For example, we are already witnessing the ability of people to work and exercise in their homes, and shop on-line and have what they bought delivered to their homes. This trend brings some concerns regarding the inability of people to control their freedom, as they start turning into functional cells trapped in the structure of their society. There is no doubt that we will have to take a responsible role in our societies if we want to keep our societies stable and functional, but it would be a frightening thought to learn that we have been enslaved by our society. This conflict between social and individual freedom may, at the end of our social evolution, settle in favor of the high-level organism, just as it has in the case of human body in relation to its organs and cells. In that progressive stage of social evolution, human beings may arrive at a different interpretation of freedom (different from temporary interpretations) and live more comfortably with the fact that they have become functional cells in the structural organization of the global social organism.

Regeneration and structural replacement, another characteristic of human physiology ascended to the social organism: As we know, cells in human and animal bodies are naturally replaced on a continuous basis to rejuvenate the structure of the human or animal. The new cells take on the responsibility of the aging cells and continue to support the operation of the organism as a whole. Regeneration is another characteristic of living systems that allows them to repair or replace a lost organ or member of their structure and continue their operation. The operation of a society is no different from that of the individual human being. Consider humans as cells in the structure of the society each having certain responsibilities, for which they are trained. As these individuals become weak and dysfunctional due to the aging process, the system takes them out of circulation by retiring them and replacing them with newly trained and more energetic human beings. The elderly will eventually die and flush out of the system, just as the human body does with its dead cells. Just as regeneration in human level, social organisms also rebuild and repair damages inflicted upon their infrastructure to resume their operation. The importance of these similarities and replications of evolutionary patterns between human structural organization and that of the social organism may assist us in predicting the process of social evolution.

The social organism and the development of its immune system: As we know, there are many sub-processes that need to be completed in the evolutionary process of the social organism before it reaches its finality. These sub-processes resemble the human structural organization and satisfy the applicable laws of nature and systems. Since the collapse of the Soviet Union, the focus of social evolution on a global scale has shifted from equality among people in every society toward the equalization of prosperity levels among societies, particularly between the North and the South blocs. The metaphoric expression of North and South blocs were first used in 1970s, to separate the wealthy states such as US, Japan, European states and the Soviet States from underdeveloped and poor nations, which happened to be separated by their geographical locations. Most of the advanced nations were in the Northern Hemisphere and poor in the Southern Hemisphere. This geographical separation may no longer apply to every state in the North and South, as some of the Southern states such as Brazil and Taiwan have joined the wealthy states of the North and some Soviet States experienced economic decline that puts them in the ranks of the Southern states. Despite these changes, we will continue to use these metaphoric expressions to separate the poor from the rich disregarding their geographical locations. The current gap of the prosperity level among rich and poor nations has created so much tension among them that a clash between these blocs is unavoidable, and it has, in fact, already started. This clash does not differ from the socioeconomic class struggle in a society, but this time it is taking place at a different level of social hierarchy, among societies themselves. In recent years, the South has declared war on the North through terrorism since those who engage in terrorist acts are aware of the technological superiority of the North that leaves them with no chance of winning in a direct confrontation. The Southern bloc societies are relatively immune to terrorism because their societies are not as integrated as those of the North and infrastructure damages can be tolerated with minimum effect on their daily lives. However, any sabotage to the infrastructure of the social organisms of the North may bring about tremendous blow to their economy and their way of life, and that vulnerability makes them extremely nervous. The armies of the North have been designed with such sophistication and capability to counter any detectable enemy, but even with all of their capabilities, these armies are powerless when they do not know where, when and how the enemy may strike. In this clash, which may last for a few decades, several processes will be completed from the perspective of the social organism's evolutionary process on a global scale. First, societies of the North will find new grounds for cooperation to defeat international terrorism. This cooperation will strengthen their ties as a unified and single social organism. At the same time, terrorist organizations of the South will expand and gain sympathy among their populations and invite them to join the fight against "infidels," but in reality, the battle is against occupiers and imperialists of the North. In this process, the societies of the South will also find more common grounds for their cooperation and unification. The result of this clash, which will be extremely expensive for both North and South, would result in the development of new policies toward the South in the form of economic assistance to close the prosperity gap between the two blocs, hoping that it will minimize the influence of terrorist organizations recruiting new soldiers from those populations. In the meantime, as the North continues its fight against terrorism, it will invent new technologies of surveillance, monitoring, and detection to make those societies more proactive in detecting their enemies and removing them surgically before they get a chance to initiate their own attacks. These various technologies, added to the current military, police, and intelligence forces, will become the social organism's immune system; an immune system that is built to stay even after the conflict between the North and South is ended and these societies have been united. During the next few decades, the main focus of the social evolution on a global scale would be to develop immune systems that can intrude into the privacy of citizens and further restrict their freedom in order to improve the security of the global social organism, and the catalyst for this development is "war on terror". We might wonder if the global social organism plans all of these and set us against certain realities so that it can build its structural organization (as planned in its evolutionary process) with little resistance on our part in losing our freedom, as most of us will trade additional restriction in our freedom with greater security and stability.

Surveillance, tracking, and monitoring devices as means to secure the operation of the social organism: Human society as an organism is no different from any other organism in which its operation is closely monitored by a central control system. The thought that one day human society might evolve in such a way that every activity of every individual is closely monitored is terrifying because we are not used to the idea of being monitored. In the long run, however, we may accept that reality as a way of life. It is unimaginable that a highly sophisticated organism (society) whose survival and security are so highly dependent upon the operation of its subsystems (humans) would leave them unchecked and in total freedom. In this developmental process, the activities of individuals would not be the only thing to be monitored. The social organism would also monitor its environment. An example of a monitoring device would be a health monitor worn by every individual, particularly after people reach a certain age, to report their critical health parameters to a medical center on a continuous basis without the interference of the person wearing it. This device might even act as a personal medical advisor and remind the individual of his or her inadequate physical activity and/or improper diet. We have already seen such monitory systems becoming a reality of our lives, such as what we read, what we buy, and maybe in the future, what we think. The global social organism, with its huge economy and population, would have no other alternative but to monitor and control its environment for air, water, and soil quality. It will have no choice but to monitor the environment to prevent or minimize the destructive forces of nature. This will be achieved through an array of sensory devices equipped with transceivers, providing early warnings to central control systems so that counter measures are taken to either prevent or minimize destructive impacts on the global social organism. In general, the stability of the global social organism, with its huge structure for continuous operation, can only be maintained through prevention, which means having sufficient feedback from every constituent of the social organism, including its environment, to forestall any crisis before it gets out of control. Such preventive measures would require that the whole planet be equipped with sensory devices that transmit data to local or central control systems and receive instructions in real time.

The structural organization of society in its advanced evolutionary stage: In human body, there is not a single cell that is not connected, controlled, or monitored by the central control system. Human society is composed of humans and non-living ordered systems built by humans for a particular purpose that is important to the operation and well being of the society. If the structural evolution of a society follows the same pattern as that of the individual human being, then these ordered systems within the society will eventually be connected to ensure that they are operational and in harmony to enhance the society's overall operational efficiency. In its evolutionary process, the social organism continues to build its nervous system using communication technology to bring living and non-living ordered systems under one structural organization, in which each subsystem is connected to other subsystems or monitored by either the local or central nervous system. This state requires that all non-living ordered structures be equipped with sensory devices to report their status and receive orders. As a result, we will soon witness the integration of sensory devices with communication technologies into the design of every non-living ordered structure. This means that each human being will be able to control his personal equipment and devices remotely, which will start a new era of communication between humans and objects. This process will further include communication between objects. If the non-living ordered structures built by humans assume such an important role in the well-being of the society and its operation as an organism, then their inclusion into society's structural organization will become inevitable and deterministic. One day, we may sit in our cars and type in our destination and our car will join the flood of cars in the web of traffic, moving toward different destinations, all controlled by computers and satellite systems with no possibility for collision.

Government: Government is the social organism's central control system. It controls and regulates its operation. Whether a government is elected or not, its role as a central control system or coordinator of the organism's operation is essential. Without it, the social organism would fall into chaos and experience paralysis. In the past, a government was composed of a powerful individual or a select few who imposed their will upon their people and conducted the operations of their society based on what they believed was good for that society. In most cases, the self-serving and suppressive policies of these leaders put them in a comfort zone that was beyond the imagination of the members of their society, most of whom were living in poverty and starving to death. The members of these societies were not allowed to have any participation in setting the policies of their government, which means that they had no control over their own fate.

In modern times, the concept of government, at least in theory, has changed. Now members of the society can participate in the election process of the government of their choosing, based on their best judgment that the elected government is able to tackle all challenging issues related to domestic and foreign affairs. In theory, when members of a society replace their government through election process, they expect that the policies of the new government reflect the current state of social consciousness and address all unfulfilled promises that the previous government failed to deliver. Therefore, social consciousness becomes a key factor in deciding which political party will take charge of the affairs of the society. This is why politicians work so hard to gain the public trust and turn public opinion (social consciousness) on their side. When social consciousness, which is the state of mind of the social organism, influences the policies and operations of the government, this is an indication that the social organism has started to take charge of its own evolutionary process. Because social consciousness plays a major role in the election of modern governments, it has led to the development of techniques and strategies that can influence the popular opinion in favor of policies that a select few would benefit from. This is done through falsification of truth, manufacture of new realities, and misinformation provided to the public through mass media, particularly during the election process.

In integration process of history, social consciousness will eventually prevail, take charge of the social organism's evolutionary process and guide it to its deterministic finality. At that time, the government, or the central control system, will become inherently democratic, even without direct participation of the people in the political process, analogous to the operation of human body, which treats every constituent in its organization equally. In the stage of finality, the major part of the government (but not all) will be composed of gargantuan computer systems and an army of mathematicians and software engineers whose jobs will be to improve the operational efficiency of the organism by monitoring the distribution of goods and services throughout the world. They will also monitor all environmental activities that might affect the global social organism's well-being as part of their numerous other tasks.

Whatever the case, the prerequisite for the existence of a social organism (or any other organism) is that it has a central control system or government capable of coordinating its operations. This requires harmonization of its constituents' activities and attending to their survival needs, whether this is achieved by their direct participation in the government or not. Because the concepts of government and governing philosophy are as dynamic as anything else in our social evolution, let us not be surprised if one-day computers become major players in our governments and make critical decisions in leading our social evolution. Probably the best part about having a computer as a government official is that it would be immune to corruption.

Harmony and system efficiency: Aside from the will to survive, which is a dominant factor in the behavior of every organism, in the case of human beings, behavior is also influenced by belief systems, thoughts, customs, and traditions that form the emotional part of their brains. A person may carry emotions that are not part of his/her own life experiences, but are events that occurred to his/her parents or ancestors. Adding individual personal experience, each human being develops a unique personality. Such vast variety of personalities within a society may result in disharmony among them and affect the functionality and operational efficiency of the society. To improve operational efficiency, societies impose common goals, forcing one set of belief or value system on their people, or create mutual understanding among them, all to create harmony within their societies. Whether these sets of belief systems are right or wrong is not important, as long as they serve the purpose. In most cases, creating social unity becomes the responsibility of the government, which is the society's central control system. The government is fully aware of the fact that without harmony and unity among members of the society, the operation of that society will become highly inefficient and ineffective in dealing with other societies. As a result, a society will resort to any policy to create harmony among its people.

As social evolution proceeds in the integration process of history and societies merge, expansion of harmony throughout the enlarged social organism becomes both inevitable and deterministic. With every integration process, either in a society or on a global scale, a greater degree of harmony also starts to emerge to make the operation of the expanded organism more efficient. During the past several decades, advanced nations have signed numerous treaties that are meant to coordinate their policies and, at the same time, restrain their behavior. These treaties apply to almost every part of the social organism's life, from trade (the World Trade Organization) to military affairs (the North Atlantic Treaty Organization) to environmental agreements (the KYOTO protocol). In summary, living organisms strive to improve their operational efficiency as a deterministic process, due to limitation of natural resources in their environment, which necessitates establishment of harmony among all of the living and non-living ordered structures within the hierarchy of their systems.

What are the elements that create harmony? Before we start identifying the elements of harmony that might lead to the creation of common objectives among people, let us declare that if people do not receive their basic survival needs from their society, achieving harmony among them becomes an impossible task. Without life support systems, there is no chance that members of a society will come together and live in a harmonious way with each other (at least not for a long period of time), let alone set high-level objectives to attain as a group. In modern societies, economy is the lifeline of the people and probably the most important contributor in establishing harmonious relationships among them. Without an economy that is capable of supporting every member of the society, other elements, such as culture, religion, and ideology that might further contribute to harmony would not work effectively. In fact, when the economic factor that is the foundation of harmony is present, members with a variety of cultures, religions, and ideologies may live in harmony with each other and form common objectives, despite their diversity. The establishment of order could also improve the operational efficiency of a society. Although harmony always accompanies order in a society, but having order does not always equate to having harmonious relationship among the members of a society. This is because order can be established through fear and punishment as a consequence of disobedience and misbehavior. This is why societies have systems of law to keep their members in line with the society's objectives. However order is established, (through fear, compassion or mutual understanding) the net result is more or less the same and the society becomes more efficient when order is enforced.

Another way to create harmony among the members of a society is to control and manipulate their minds through sources of information, usually controlled by the government. Information is particularly important in modern societies where social consciousness plays a major role in setting the objectives of the society and its future domestic and foreign policies. When the mind of every individual is manipulated in favor of certain policies (altering social consciousness), harmony and unity among the members of the society will improve, allowing the government to exercise its policies with little resistance from its members. This makes the government and the society more efficient in dealing with problems arising both domestically and internationally. Harmony among members of a society is created by all of the aforementioned elements and it is not one or the other. However, depending on the governing philosophy in a society, one element may play a more dominant role than the others.

Element of culture in establishing harmony in a society: *Culture* is one of the characteristics of a social organism that plays a major role in the behavior of the organism. In the process of evolution, and for survival reasons, some animals, including humans, chose to live in groups to protect themselves from other animals looking for opportunity to consume them as sources of energy for their survival. Living in groups gave people and animals several benefits, including mutual protection and cooperation in hunting and food gathering. Living in groups, necessitated communication among members, which started with sounds and noises that led to the creation of language and, eventually, the development of writing. However, language is not the only product of group living. Other products, such as rituals, customs, and diet, also became elements of culture that connected the members of one group and differentiated them from others. The dependency of groups on their environment to survive, forced them to mark and guard their territory and protect its energy resources from being exploited or consumed by others. As groups merged and grew, so did their territories. Despite the fact that culture has become a distinctive characteristic of human society, in reality, it is nothing but a byproduct of a cooperative/collective effort by the members of a group to manage their survival in a hostile environment. This means that culture alone would never be able to hold a group together if the group's survival were threatened by a lack of life support systems and energy resources. This is why culture, religion, and ideology are secondary to economy in the creation of harmony among the members of a society.

Religion and rule-of-law and their influence in establishing order and harmony in a society: Even at the earliest stages of social life adopted by human beings, the need for a set of rules to limit behaviors within the group was felt very strongly. Whether any set of rules helped all the members equally or served only a few depended on who controlled the group and enforced the rules. In the earliest times, aggressive individuals who provided leadership to their groups benefited most from the group's activities. These rulers set harsh punishments for disobedience and crushed all opposition to their control. In the process, the fearful but united society under the leader's control became stronger, as a result of harmony. The fear factor and fear of punishment has always been the key element of control of the behavior of individuals in a society, even in modern times.

In later stages of our history, other systems of laws began to appear, starting with religion, which was meant to protect and support all members of the society equally, at least at the beginning, and to create harmony within the society. Aside from the philosophical aspect of God in a religion, all other implications of religious beliefs were human and designed to bring man's behavior under control to create harmony within the society. For example, the concepts of judgment day and punishment after death of those who violated the religious laws during their lifetime are based on fear. The genius of this concept is its inaccessibility; once we believe in life after death and the severity of punishment in the next life (in hell), our behavior will come under control. For centuries, fear of divine punishment has been an efficient way to overcome man's natural behavior, shaped by his evolutionary process in a hostile environment that turned him into a selfish creature. Despite the fact that religion brought a great deal of harmony and stability to human society, it had its limitations and disadvantages. Limitations, because it could not convince every one of its notions, and misbehavior continued to be a civil issue. Disadvantages, because it created non-progressive and stagnated societies with humans under religious hypnosis. To overcome these shortcomings, man himself stepped in more aggressively, set his own rules for civil disobedience to protect members of the society, and extended the punishment of the misbehaved to the current world as well. As a result, he enhanced the harmony and stability in his society and became capable in breaking loose from the stagnation and dogmatism that religious beliefs brought upon him. There is no doubt that the combination of religious beliefs (a set of man made divine laws) as well as civil laws (man made earthly laws) have helped to harmonize and stabilize modern societies around the world. But the big question is this: is our engagement in the harmonization process of our society our own idea, or is it imposed upon us by the social organism itself, as part of its endeavor to self-organize itself and become a fully functional and efficient organism?

Ideology and its role in the dynamics of social evolution and harmony: Earlier, we argued that religion served the social organism in its evolutionary process by controlling the behavior of its members using fear, and produced a somewhat harmonious relationship among members of the society. The complexity of modern societies, however, have created many new relationships among its members that are not clearly defined or guided by the religious laws, such as how should the affairs of a society be conducted? What should be the relationship between employee and employer and how should a society conduct itself when dealing with other societies?

In the process of social evolution, humans have discovered or invented new methodologies to deal with their social issues that most of the time they were in disagreement with the old methods, and in disparity with moral and ethical principles of their time. These methodologies that were guided by an ideology, upon implementation altered all the existing relational bonds among humans and moved the social organism to the next stage of its evolutionary process. Therefore, *ideology* as it applies to social evolution, is a system of thought that dynamically evolves to assist and guide the process of social evolution to its finality, by examining the relational bonds among humans in every stage of their historical process. However, not every ideology has always assisted the social organism along its path to a more advanced stage of its evolutionary process; some ideologies, in fact, have had a regressive effect on social evolution.

A progressive ideology is an ideology that conforms to the predetermined finality that the laws of physics and thermodynamics have set for social evolution in the integration process of history. A regressive ideology opposes that finality. Regressive ideologies whose contents oppose the natural laws of systems, their integration, and their evolution into their predetermined natural and stable states, delay historical processes but do not alter them, as it is beyond human ability to change natural laws. This means that ideologies that are mainly designed to protect and support the interests of a small segment of the society will remain transitional and fail to derail social evolution. In every epoch of human history and social evolution, progressive ideologies have helped social evolution to proceed to the next level by improving equality among people (in relative terms) and enhancing the stability and operational efficiency of the social organism.

However, from time to time, regressive ideologies have arisen to derail social evolution from its natural path and reverse positive steps that social evolution has taken toward its finality. We have to recognize that this is the natural course of change in social evolution. Conflict that arises from ideological differences may create a temporary disturbance and disharmony in the affairs of the social organism, but eventually, progressive ideologies will prevail and will lead the organism to the next stage of its evolutionary process. Consequently, at the same time that an ideology can create harmony among people, it can also create a temporary state of disharmony. As we know, millions of lives have been lost in the violent struggles to move societies from slavery to feudalism, from feudalism to capitalism and from capitalism to socialism. The struggle for greater justice among members of a society and nations has always been accompanied by an ideology whose purpose is to unify oppressed people and exhort them to rise up against those in control of power and resources. Progressive ideologies have always succeeded in the end, as they have taken the system one step closer to the intended goal of social evolution. As new progressive ideologies replace the old ones, this process will continue to assist the global social organism to achieve its goals.

The role of information in the harmonization of a society: As we know, throughout history and particularly in modern times, controlled stimulus and misinformation have been used to manipulate and control the population of a society, in terms of their collective behavior. All governments without exception have used these methods to achieve unity of opinion and harmony among their people and to facilitate the implementation of certain policies for political purposes. An example is the indoctrination of people during the Cold War against communist or capitalist ideologies. In the Western hemisphere, particularly in the United States, the majority of people, who did not even know what communism stood for, distrusted it and used the word to insult anyone who had a different political opinion. The same was true in the Soviet bloc, calling non-communists a "*bourgeois*", meant as an insult. Misinformation policies exercised by both camps during this period kept the majorities of their populations in the dark and unified them against the enemy.

With the advancement of knowledge in the area of behavioral sciences, the techniques of mind control have become so sophisticated that even well informed citizens have a hard time knowing to what extent their judgment has been impaired by false information. Information is the foundation of knowledge that can produce judgment leading to a specific behavior, and to manipulate behavior, information needs to be controlled. From a government's perspective, or from central control system's point of view, working efficiently towards one goal requires cooperation and harmonization of all members, and that can only be achieved when they all think and behave alike.

After World War II, some of Western countries, primarily Britain and the United States started to invest heavily in the development of techniques used to control social behavior. The application of such techniques is not limited to the creation of harmony among the members of one society, but also creation of disharmony among them if necessary. The later techniques have been used exclusively against hostile societies to drive them into chaos and instability for political gains. Because non-prosperous and undereducated nations are far more vulnerable to misinformation, the use of censorship and the control of information by their governments is far greater than in prosperous and well-educated nations. This is rather obvious, because the foundation of harmony among the people in prosperous nations, regardless of their governing philosophy, lies in the strength of their economy, which cannot be easily shaken by misinformation.

After all of these arguments, it seems that the element of harmony in a society, irrespective of how it has been achieved, is a necessity, not only for the existence of the society as an organism but also to improve its operational efficiency. In some cases, harmony among the members of a society is achieved through the strength of the economy, whereas in others through fear, ideologies, culture and finally manipulation of the mind. In most societies, all of these elements play a role in harmonizing their members, but with different degrees of intensity. This notion proposes that a living organism, such as a society, that is a self-organizing organism will find mechanisms to impose harmony among its constituents. Otherwise, it will cease to exist as a functioning organism.

The role of science and technology in the evolutionary process of the social organism: One of the most influential elements defining the course of social evolution is scientific and technological achievement. Probably one of the very first tools that a human ever made was a weapon to kill and to protect himself against other animals, which means that the earliest technology evolved around making weapons to protect humans from their hostile environment and facilitate hunting and food gathering. Humans continue to develop tools to further improve their safety and their productivity and bring convenience into their lives. Science and technology have helped humans study their environment with greater details, and have allowed them to understand and predict their environment to become more proactive in protecting themselves and expanding their control over its resources. Today, science and technology are not only the tools we use to control and exploit our environment, but are also means we use to explore our environment and nature to satisfy our curiosity regarding underlying questions, such as why we are here. Science and technology play a crucial role in the process of history and social evolution, and two of the critical technologies that have had significant impact on the course of social evolution are communication and transportation technologies. Although primitive forms of transportation and communication have always existed among societies, but the twentieth century technological breakthroughs have expanded their connectivity and accelerated their integration process. This means that formation of global social organism without these technologies would have been impossible. Integration process has brought numerous challenges with it, such as management and maintenance of the colossal infrastructures of the integrated communities and societies that require sanitation, health care, electric power and housing. Once again, science and technology have resolved these issues. Automation has helped to increase industrial output and has allowed more people to enjoy more material things than at any other time in human history. At the same time, it has sent a large percentage of workers to new frontiers and accelerated the process of innovation and discovery.

However, as much as science and technology have been responsible for making our lives more secure and integrating diverse societies, they have also brought some unfavorable consequences with them. Science and technology have had many negative impacts on social evolution, such as the development of weapons that serve no purpose but to destroy life and the infrastructure of our societies. Medical discoveries have prolonged the lives of people, with both negative and positive effects that we will discuss in later chapters. The dissemination of industrial byproducts into the environment has poisoned the air and the water to dangerous levels, and this trend seems to grow as more nations join the club of industrial nations. When industrial nations pollute their environment, the pollution does not stop at their borders; it travels across the planet and affects the life of every human and every species on the planet. This irresponsible behavior should give every living being a legal right to protest against polluters.

Social evolution on a global scale has reached a stage of self-awareness that needs to revisit its early operational procedures and replace them with new and internationally approved ones. For those who believe in globalization, they must know that without strong global policies, a social organism on a global scale would never survive. Fortunately, science and technology can provide solutions to all issues surrounding the integration process of societies and to environmental problems. In fact, science and technology are directly responsible for the level of integration on the global scale that has taken place among societies up to this moment. With every advancement in the field of science and technology, the global social organism acquires a new level of sophistication in its operation and structural organization to the point that it will evolve into an organism that would have all the operational complexities of human body and more.

Economy: In an economic system, each member of the society becomes responsible for a particular task that he/she is best at. The products or services produced by these members are then shared with other members of the society to fulfill the multiple needs of each member of the society. This is a much more efficient way of production than having each member of the society produce products that meet all of his needs on his own. However, this system of production has created a great deal of dependency among its members to produce for the needs of others. For example, only a small percentage of the population in an economic system may be responsible for the supply and distribution of food. Another small percentage of the population may be responsible to provide housing and shelter for the society. In modern societies, automation has enhanced productivity and created a great deal of wealth for those who own means of production. This has led to the division of the society, whose members fall into different socioeconomic classes. Those who own the means of production and wealth also control the power and policies of the state, which further consolidates their socioeconomic position. Economy and social welfare are the lifelines of all members of the society, and when policies of the state are designed to benefit only a minority, it creates resentment and tension among the socioeconomic classes. When tension builds up among the classes, it results in the violent overthrow of the governments by the masses, followed by the dissolusion of the upper socioeconomic class and confiscation of the means of production for the benefit of all. There are numerous examples of socioeconomic revolution in history—the French, Russian, and Chinese revolutions.

Economy and production relations among the members of a society are the most influential factors in the evolutionary process of the social organism. When these relations are strained due to unfair distribution of the resources among the members of a society, it is likely that a socioeconomic revolution take place to correct the shortcomings of the current economic system. There are major differences of opinion among philosophers, economists, and social scientists as to which economic system would best fit human nature and at the same time keep the society in a reasonable state of stability (with the least level of tension among its members) and dynamism for its growth and operational efficiency. Our economic philosophies can generally be divided into two different camps. On one side, we have capitalism, which emphasizes individualism and puts it above the society, and on the other side, we have socialism, which puts the society above the individual. The philosophical question remains, however, which of these economic systems would eventually prevail at the end of our social evolution?

To answer this question, let us examine capitalism in action. As we know, in a capitalistic system, there is no central economic planning. It is believed that if there is a demand for a service or a product, that demand will eventually be met by a supplier. In this economic system, competition and adversarial relationships among businesses and individuals are favored, and there is minimal regulation so that competition, which is the key to product improvement, cost reduction, and innovation, is promoted. Clearly, there is very little harmony and cooperation in this economic system, particularly at the macroeconomic level, because companies competing for market share are trying to put each other out of business so that they can manipulate the entire market and increase their profit margins. However, if we closely look at the operation of an economic institution (corporation), we notice that its operation is centrally controlled and harmonized by the board of directors. The board of directors provides leadership, optimizes corporation's performance and is responsible for strategic and financial planning. The directors and executives use every technique possible to improve productivity and efficiency within the economic institution and preach cooperation, teamwork, and harmony to their employees.

Surprisingly, the same philosophy fails on a larger scale, as at the national level capitalism operates in the absence of leadership and in complete disharmony and chaos. Does this mean there is a great opportunity to further optimize a capitalistic economy by harmonizing it from the top? Most of us are probably aware of this fact that when a system is optimized at the subsystem level, it does not necessarily imply that it is optimally efficient in the system level. To the contrary, when a system is optimally efficient at the system level, this necessitates that all of its subsystems also operate with optimum efficiency. The design of capitalist economy is based on the insecurity of both economic institutions and individuals; moreover, it is designed to be competitive and adversarial; an environment that simulates the hostile environment that humans have evolved in and adapted to. It is in these insecure environments that humans become more productive. In modern days, the capitalist economic model has been responsible for the prosperity of Western societies and the accumulation of personal and national wealth within these societies. This economic system has also been responsible for almost every war, revolution, and civil unrest, when some individuals or nations went too far in exploiting the others. The fact is that in a capitalist economy there is a fine line between partial stability of the system and its transition to chaos and conflict among its socioeconomic classes; this is due to injustices inherent in this economic system. Knowing that capitalism on the macroeconomic scale is inefficient leads us to believe that in the process of socioeconomic evolution, this shortcoming will be gradually corrected to further optimize the entire economy at the system level, which is the adoption of centrally controlled economy.

This finality correlates well with the notions we have discussed so far in regard to laws governing the behavior of systems. As global social organism harmonizes itself in its evolutionary process, it will also harmonize its economy, which is to replace hostility with cooperation, insecurity with security and instability with stability in economic environment: all the characteristics that capitalist economic system lacks. As the world economy becomes integrated and reaches maturity, its stability would become a major challenge that would require harmonization, not only for the benefit of economic institutions but also for the working people. Fierce competition on the global level will enslave the working classes, who will eventually become physically and mentally ill trying to keep up with the demands of the institutions that pay them wages. Continuing on this path will force the tired and exhausted working class of the world that is forced into an endless cycle of competition, to rise against the system, demand its abolishment and adopt a socialist way of life. It is also possible that this economic transition may take place by the sheer force of necessity, meaning that economic reforms are initiated at the top-level system and not forced upon the top-level system by its subsystems. At the end, and regardless how this transition is made, centralization, increased levels of regulation, and global planning of the world economy will become the deterministic outcomes of the global socioeconomic evolution in order to enhance its stability, efficiency, harmony, and security at all subsystem levels and to allow the global organism to operate as a true living organism. As socioeconomic evolution gets closer to its finality, it will terminate all of the adversarial relationships among economic institutions and replace them with harmonious relationships and cooperation. At the same time, it will distribute more equally the wealth of the society among its members. The global social organism, with its gigantic economy, cannot survive as an organism with stress and disharmony trapped within its organization.

Politics: Behavioral science is the study of the brain's logical outputs resulting from an interaction between a stimulus and all three sets of information in the human brain, which are vastly different among individuals. In fact, when a large and varied number of stimuli are applied to the brain of a human being, it produces a set of logical outputs that are unique to that individual and can be characterized as his personality. Like a living organism, society has a personality, which is defined by its traditions, language, culture, and in general its history. Similar to any living organism, society has survival instincts and will defend itself when its survival is threatened. Survival instincts are characteristic of its subsystems (humans) that have transcended to the system level. Societies also engage in rational discussions and debates regarding environmental issues and scientific activities, and in general, exhibit behavioral patterns that are as distinct as those of individual humans. Like other organisms, societies try to survive in a competitive environment beside other societies while striving to preserve their identities, which differentiate them from the others. The collective behavioral patterns that maintain the survival, security, and identity of a society in a challenging environment where many societies are competing to manipulate and control the scarce resources in their shared environment are referred to as *politics*.

Politics is the art of surviving in a competitive environment without engaging in conflicts that may lead to destructive processes. The political process is a long-term action plan adopted by the leadership of a society in response to a stimulus generated either internally or externally. In democratic societies, the state of mind of the members of the society (the social consciousness) greatly influences the political processes chosen by the leadership of the society. It is obvious that not every society will adopt the same political processes in reaction to a particular stimulus, first, because not every society's state of mind is identical and, second, because the stimulus may not produce the same level of insecurity in every society. In this way, societies are like individual human beings. However, when security and the flow of energy to a society are threatened, societies behave in the same manner and use political processes to form alliances and compete for resources. Like other characteristics of a society, its political process is also in a dynamic state. As societies around the world merge and economically integrate to form larger societies, their political processes will merge and integrate as well. At the end, when the global social organism reaches its finality, the only challenge the global community will face will be the challenge of its environment. All political processes then will be aimed at securing the society and maintaining a constant flow of energy to its structure.

Government and its leaders in the evolving social organism: When multiple organisms, such as human beings, form a society, their immediate need for a central control system to harmonize the activities of the larger organism becomes obvious. In the past, when societies were not as complicated as they are today, such central control systems were composed of a single leader and his associates. As societies grew and technology advanced, the role of the leader became more complicated. He could no longer manage the activities of his society with only a few people helping him. As a result, *government* was born. Government consists of individuals and leaders who have different areas of expertise, yet all work together to harmonize the operation of their society. Government is the central control system of a society that supports the supply lines of energy and communication systems and manages security, defense, and other matters. This is why society cannot operate without government, just as the human body cannot operate without a brain. The size of a government is directly proportional to the size of society in terms of its population and the sophistication of its operation, which is measured by its technology and economy. In recent history, we have witnessed the creation of the United Nations as a central control system of the global social organism. The U.N. is still primitive in its evolutionary process, but it is maturing as a world government. At its maturity, the U.N. will manage and harmonize the activities of global social organism at the macro level while leaving the local governments to manage the micro tasks at the lower levels, namely societies and smaller communities. Let us keep in mind that with every level of integration and the formation of larger agglomerate of societies, governance becomes increasingly more difficult that will require a more intelligent central control system equipped with highly sophisticated technology to conduct its operation.

Why global governance is a necessity: As globalization proceeds and economic ties among nations strengthen, economic stability becomes extremely important. Economic or political instability in any part of the globe could immediately propagate throughout the world economy. This alone would dictate the necessity of having international economic laws and financial policies that would immunize the world economy against being taken hostage by economic policies of rebellious local governments or international financial institutions. In the future, the global economy will be centrally controlled and regulated to achieve stability, efficiency and harmony. This will have a negative impact on the dynamism of innovations and productivity of today's Western economic institutions, which need to be maintained by providing incentives and rewards to those who achieve higher standards in their performance. The issue of energy and its distribution will become the most important aspect of the international laws and policies of an integrated world economy, to prevent the blackmail of the world economy by those who possess and control the energy resources. International standards for clean air and water and other environmental issues will be dictated to the entire world community, and all societies will be held accountable. For these and numerous other reasons, the governing body of the international community will become increasingly dominant and will become involved in setting up standards and policies for every community around the world to a point where local governments might lose their self-governing power and begin to merge into the world governing body. At this point, the functionality of local governments will be reduced to mayoral status and a country will become a province on the world map, where borders are drawn for formality only. Today, stronger nations control the policies of United Nations, but economic integration and globalization will change that as multinational corporations and economic institutions will be present everywhere and will not differentiate among peoples and territories for the sake of stability, security, and profitability. As a result, superpowers will no longer dominate the globe and weaker nations will gain a voice in the international community. Of course, this is only a short-term view of social evolution. A long-term view shows that social evolution will continue to be dominated by the laws of nature that will define all the relational bonds among parallel living systems in every subsystem level on the basis of equality.

The codependency of societies and their merger mechanism: As societies interact with each other through cultural exchange, economic development, or cooperation in science and technology, they become codependent. If these interactions expand into every arena of social life, this codependency would become even stronger until it reaches a point where two societies are forced into a structural reorganization to form a single organism and merge their governing bodies. This should not come as a surprise, as we have witnessed the gradual merger of societies around the world, such as the European Union the old Soviet Union or current Russian Federation.

When societies have been codependent for a long time, their separation becomes extremely difficult and painful from every aspect of social life. The separation of peoples who have already assimilated and adapted to one another's way of life would be equally difficult. A good example of this was the collapse of the Soviet Union, which threw every member of the union into economic chaos. However, the breakup of the Soviet Union was not a reversal of the historical process (disintegration), as most of the formerly soviet nations (Eastern European nations) were absorbed into the European Union, which is another bloc that continues to grow. As globalization proceeds and trade agreements expand among the blocs and societies, so would their codependency. This would lead to further expansion and merger of the blocs until every society on earth is included. This process is deterministic and non-stoppable as long as energy resources of the environment are sufficient to support the growth and integration of these societies.

Historical trends in social evolution: We have presented many arguments regarding the finality of history and how it is controlled by the laws of nature, its structural organization, and its relation to the energy resources and life support systems in its environment. We have also argued that this finality is deterministic and process independent, which means that any historical process characterized by its own circumstantial situation and process randomness would be able to lead social evolution to its finality. When we talk about process randomness, what do we really mean by that? Is the domain of randomness unlimitedly wide, or there are limitations to this randomness? These questions give rise to a new hypothesis that there may be other influential parameters related to the randomness of historical processes that are part of setting up these trends. If so, what are the parameters?

Looking back at our recorded world history, we find few peaceful mergers of groups and societies in any part of the world. Most mergers and integrations began with violent confrontations between peoples or groups or societies. Competition, control, manipulation of life support systems, and (in the modern world) money and power have been the controlling mechanisms that set historical trends in our social evolution. But where are the underlying causes of such violent behaviors and how were they acquired at different system levels? To answer these questions, we need to emphasize once more that in a system hierarchy all of the characteristics of the lower-level systems transcend and manifest themselves in the high-level system and influence its behavior, which in this case would be the characteristics of human that manifest in the larger society. Therefore, it would suffice to analyze the root causes of violence in human behavior to understand the violent behavior of society and finally, how historical trends are being set. Looking carefully at human behavior, we can relate it to insecurity. Human insecurity is a product of the evolutionary process for millions of years in an unfriendly environment. As a result, insecurity has become a psychological state that controls human behavior. This controlling factor then manifests itself in behaviors such as the accumulation of life support systems, competition, seeking control and power and being territorial. Naturally, these behaviors lead to confrontation with others who are seeking the same things. We can see similar behaviors in higher level systems, such as corporations and societies. Competition for resources naturally creates conflicts at both the human and social levels and sets violent trends for historical development. Therefore, it would be logical to assert that today's historical trends, which are mainly violent, have been set by the history of environmental conditions during human's evolutionary process. Since it is hard to erase human's instinctive memory, the trends in our social evolution and historical events will continue to remain violent as long as the feeling of insecurity in the minds of humans have not been moderated. To change these historical trends, we need to work on humans first and provide a safe and secure environment for their survival. Our science and technology have been key elements in altering our environment and making it more secure for us, and they will continue to do so in the future. We no longer are afraid of predators and we can shelter ourselves from harsh weather conditions in our air-conditioned homes. Our technology has also assisted us to produce more food per person than at any other time in our history, despite having hunger in many regions of the world. Chances are that our technological advancements will further improve our sense of safety and security in the future, thus changing our historical trends from violent to peaceful processes, as we get closer to our historical finality.

This means that even random historical events could fall into a specific historical trend that is dictated by the level of security of both individuals and societies. A strong sense of insecurity would obviously lead to violent historical trends, and a strong sense of security to peaceful trends. Consequently, we may have a chance to transition from violent historical processes of our past and present, to peaceful processes in the later part of our social evolution, as human security improves with the help of science and technology. The science of history that gives a meaning and a sense of purpose to historical processes can not only change the perception of history among individuals, but also affect social consciousness. This would result in a drift of policies from violent trends to peaceful trends in resolving the differences among all subsystem levels in the hierarchy of global organism.

Harmoniously directed and randomly directed social evolution: Before we start our discussion on this subject, let us conduct two experiments. In the first experiment, while connecting one end of a conductor to a high voltage and the other to ground, we will heat the conductor to a high temperature. In the second experiment, we will cool the conductor to a temperature near zero degrees Kelvin. Let us study what happens to the movement of the electrons in the conductor. In the first case, where the elevated temperatures cause thermal vibration of the atoms, electrons will have a hard time managing their journey from one end of the conductor to the other due to collisions with the fields of vibrating atoms. This results in a zigzagging but forward movement of the electrons along the conductor. In the second case, atoms are no longer in vibration, allowing superconductivity to emerge in the conductor. This allows the free electrons to transit smoothly along the length of the conductor, virtually without collision with atomic fields.

Now let us compare these two experiments with conditions that apply to social evolution. In both experiments, the electrons were forced by the voltage difference to travel from one end of the conductor to the other; this is analogous to transitioning toward a finality in social evolution. The finality acts like a magnet, or attractor, pulling all historical processes in its direction. In spite of the higher or lower degree of randomness in the paths of the electrons in our two experiments, randomness continues to be bounded within the volume of conductor, which means that restriction applies to the randomness of electron's path. This is analogous to social evolution, which allows a limited number of circumstantial situations to interfere with its course of evolution while continuing to pursue its intended finality. In other words, when there is an intended goal to be met, neither these experiments nor the process of social evolution is open to unlimited randomness or circumstantial situations in their evolutionary processes. As we know, social evolution has been guided from time to time by progressive ideologies (which are in line with the laws of nature) that have assisted the social organism to achieve new states, few steps closer to its finality. Obviously, all of these ideologies have come from humans themselves and have inspired others to join forces and take social evolution to its next stage of evolutionary process. We are not in contradiction with ourselves as to who is driving the social organism's evolutionary process—individual human beings or the social organism itself. In the next section, we will discuss how the social organism's evolutionary goals can inspire us and how inspiration surfaces as progressive ideologies that can help the social organism to achieve its intended goals.

In the meantime, let us go back to the definitions of harmoniously directed and randomly directed evolutionary processes. There is no doubt that in these processes, inspired human beings are the initiators of progressive ideologies. But the problem is this: if people do not know what the finality of social evolution is, or where it is headed, how they can judge whether a new ideology is progressive or not? Ideology thus becomes a matter of personal belief and creates a great deal of contradiction among different groups of people, particularly among nonbelievers who see the new ideology putting them in an undesirable state of energy, or state of comfort.

This sets the entire process of social evolution into a state of chaos and makes it a random yet directed process where it takes a longer time for progressive ideologies to find acceptance among the majority of people. Acceptance of progressive ideologies among people often comes through forces of necessity. In this historical process, the forces assisting the social evolution are limited and less organized, like the movement of the electrons in the heated conductor. However, when people agree on the finality of social evolution on the basis of science, they can benchmark any new ideology against the characteristics of social organism at its finality and immediately determine whether or not that ideology is progressive and deserves attention. This would then harmonizes the larger population in a much shorter time to rally behind the progressive ideologies, while limiting the obstacles in the way of its implementation. Obviously, this social evolution will become more self-regulated and organized, as compared to the previous one. We like to call this process of social evolution a harmoniously directed or harmoniously guided process, as a universal self-awareness conducts its process.

Guardians and defenders of the social organism in advancing its objectives: In earlier arguments, we stated that all systems and their subsystems, including living organisms, tend to minimize the state of their internal energy as much as possible or act as selfish systems. However, occasionally we observe some behaviors exhibited by living organisms that contradict this theory. For example, how would a suicide attack on enemy lines by a kamikaze or suicide bomber, where the attacker loses his life, fit in this theory? To understand this contradictory behavior better, let us refer to the human body's operation once more. White cells in human blood are cells that are ready to fight and defend the body from any intrusion that is perceived to be harmful or fatal to the body. In the process of defending the body, these cells die so that the body can survive. In the case of the social organism, soldiers and police officers are analogous to the white cells. These volunteers choose to become the guardians of the social organism in case other social organisms, individuals, or the environment threatened its survival. A kamikaze or suicide bomber does exactly the same thing. He/she is a volunteer soldier who is ready to die by inflicting the utmost damage to those who threaten the social organism they are affiliated with. These examples show that these defenders have one thing in common: their strong connectivity with the high-level organism, which has a higher purpose than theirs. Hopefully, by now we have established that systems at a higher level in the hierarchy of living organisms, can inspire their sub-organisms (which are their instruments or guardians) to achieve their evolutionary goals and objectives with the assistance of those who are well connected with these objectives, and have formed strong alliances among themselves to defend them.

Let us now go one step further and expand the idea of connectivity to the global social organism, which has an even higher purpose than those of the societies and individuals in its hierarchy. The global social organism makes no distinction in its evolutionary process between humans with different cultural backgrounds or their races, unlike societies that are identified by their culture, economic system, race, or political ideology. In the integration process of history, where globalization becomes a deterministic outcome of its process, the global social organism will inspire subsystems at every system level to become instruments for realization of its objectives. These inspired subsystems (individuals and societies) will be able to see a greater purpose in global social evolution than their own, as a process that would lead to the formation of a community of peoples who have overcome their differences and live side by side in peace, harmony, and justice. These inspired subsystems will oppose all self-serving policies adopted by any government or individual that would create an obstacle to achieving these global objectives, even if these policies benefit them or their own societies in the short term. Obviously, not everyone who is connected with the objectives of the high-level organism has a similar or accurate understanding of global organism's true evolutionary objectives. Some people may believe that achieving unity and harmony on the global scale, is in the promotion of religious views, whereas others may promote economic ties and trade among nations.

The real question is this: what do we know about the objectives of the evolutionary process of a higher order organism? Is our interpretation of these objectives real and accurate, or is it merely our personal views based on our own cultural and economic ties? For centuries, Christian and Muslim missionaries, and others, have traveled throughout the world to preach their faith and try to unify the world under one ideological belief system, which they believed served a higher purpose. In the twentieth century, capitalism and socialism did the same thing, although from a socioeconomic point of view. It is possible that in the twenty-first century theories in sociobiology, history, and social evolution will give us a better understanding of social evolution and its objectives and guide us to organize ourselves to achieve these objectives and become the defenders and guardians of the global social organism. This may seem like an odd concept, but when we look at the operation of human body and its sophisticated organization, we see that every cell in its organization is connected with the objectives of the body as a whole, although they have limited understanding of their role as operatives of the larger organism.

Is the grand plan of self-organization of an organism drawn at the system level, or does it happen at the subsystem level? Each individual's consciousness is shaped by his knowledge of the world, his life experiences, and his sense of appreciation that there are relational bonds between him and other surrounding serial and parallel systems, whether or not these relational bonds mean anything to him/her. This consciousness then becomes the underlying foundation of the individual's behavior. Social consciousness, the sum of consciousness of all individuals results in the exhibition of a specific social behavior, which may be unique to each social organism. It is important to note that social consciousness can be manipulated when the consciousness of every individual in the society is altered. This can be done when individuals are subjected to new information or exposed to new realities. Both of these can change the behavior of the individual and if it expands throughout the population, it would change the social consciousness, leading to the alteration of social behavior and finally affecting the course of social evolution. The question now is: if the social organism is a self-organizing system, how and to what extent does it influence our minds to create a social consciousness that is favorable to its desired course of evolution? Obviously, the social organism cannot directly influence our minds, but it can expose us to new realities and force new necessities upon us, in order to influence our consciousness and change our behavior. When new realities arise in our daily lives, they affect many of us, but not everyone, as every individual may interpret them differently, ignore them, or work against them because they may be in conflict with his self-interest. Naturally, this would create a social consciousness that is not quite uniform and in conflict with itself. Those who accurately interpret and acknowledge the new realities become the instruments of the social organism by influencing the social consciousness and changing the course of social evolution.

To better understand what we mean by "becoming the instrument of the social organism," let us discuss the role of the activist in the social evolution. Those who have lived in an underdeveloped society and/or monitored the political processes of such a society, particularly during the Cold War, will appreciate the following discussion. But before we go further, let us remind ourselves of the very basic theory that we proposed earlier, which determines the behavior of every system. In that theory, we suggested that systems are selfish by nature and look for opportunities to minimize the state of their internal energy in all times. Nevertheless, this does not seem to be the case with revolutionaries who have sacrificed their lives fighting the corrupt and puppet governments that rule most of the underdeveloped societies to help the suppressed population and bring about justice to their political system. Among these revolutionaries, we can find doctors, engineers, economists, writers, and others. Although this group of educated individuals had the opportunity to do well for themselves under the same corrupt governments, they chose not to work with those governments and put their lives at risk by joining the revolution. This behavior certainly defies the principal law of systems that suggests that every system is looking after itself. It also defies the laws of evolution pertaining to self-preservation. It is quite understandable when a poor man rebels against his government because he is hungry and fighting for his survival, but when a doctor rebels, there must be a different explanation for his behavior.

The predicament in this discussion is to explain the behavior of these educated people and place it somewhere within the framework of systems theory. When ordered structures are destroyed and lives are lost (dissipated energy) in a socioeconomic class struggle, the outcome always serves the larger organism because it brings about greater equality and harmony among the remaining subsystems and minimizes the internal state of the energy of the organism itself. The question is: what makes an individual knowingly put his life in danger and defy the laws of systems and his evolutionary instincts? In his mind, is he helping the suppressed people of his society, or he is serving the evolutionary goals of the larger system (society)? Is it possible that individuals in this category possess a higher level of consciousness that connects them with the evolutionary goals of the larger organism? Do they become catalysts or instruments of the social organism and take social evolution to the next level by their sacrifice? Is it possible that the larger organisms inspire their members and individuals with greater level of consciousness so that they can assist them in execution of their grand plan? Finally, is the grand plan of social evolution drawn at the top-level system and suggested in an indirect way to the individuals by putting them against inescapable necessities and realities, or all of these happen in subsystem level, as we tend to believe?

Let us remind ourselves that any time two non-living systems form a relational bond or become open to one another, a larger system is immediately born, and with it, a plan for its evolutionary process. Are living organisms any different from non-living systems, and do these laws change when it comes to living systems? If not, then there must be a plan drawn at the top-level system, and those of us with greater consciousness and fidelity to that system level become its instrument and carry out the objectives of its evolutionary process. If this is the case, can we then reason that social consciousness may be a product of social organism, and well connected with its evolutionary goals? Can we also reason that this product is imposed upon its members and individuals by exposing them to a series of inescapable realities? If so, then social organism's evolutionary goals will take precedence over the goals of its subsystems, down to the very individual level. Today, the world societies are connected and a global social organism is in the process of formation, with it, there is a grand evolutionary plan that would include all of us. This global social organism may recruit many of us to become its instruments and assist it in achieving its evolutionary goals. Obviously, this group of individuals (internationalists) would have a higher degree of consciousness in comparison with nationalists, which in most cases their interests are in conflict, because what may be good for the global social organism may not be good for a particular society, which is consistent with the behavior of systems; pursuing self-interest. Globalization of economy with socioeconomic justice for all, internationalism, environmentalism and humanitarianism are all imbedded in the social consciousness and evolutionary plan of the global social organism.

Figure 5-2 shows the fidelity of subsystems to higher system levels within the hierarchy of the system, as driven by their consciousness in a cross section of historical process. It is through this fidelity that the top-level systems find an opportunity to achieve lower states of internal energy among all other competing systems and drive their evolutionary plan forward.

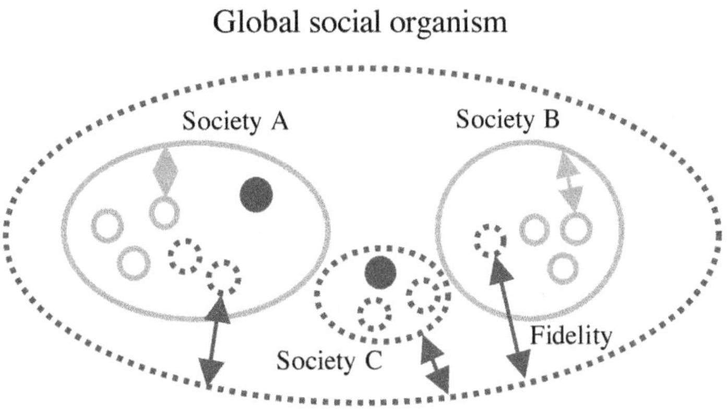

Global social organism

Figure 5-2
The fidelity of subsystems to higher-level systems

In Figure 5-2, we have shown the global social organism encompassing first level subsystems called Society A, Society B, and Society C. Within these societies, there are individuals with different fidelities or affiliations to higher system levels. Individuals shown with solid line circles within the larger solid line circles have greater fidelity to their society with nationalistic attitudes and little or no fidelity to global society. These individuals, who are the instruments of the Societies A and B, assist these societies in seeking their lowest state of internal energy in competition with other systems. As shown, the predominant social consciousness in these societies is nationalism and those with fidelity to the global social organism, shown with dotted line circles, are in minority. In contrary, in Society C, the majority of individuals with fidelity to the global social organism have formed a society that is committed to the goals of the global society, meaning that the predominant social consciousness in this society is internationalism. This society, along with individuals in other societies with fidelity to internationalism, promote a social consciousness throughout the world that assists the global social organism to achieve its intended goals, which may be in conflict with the goals of Societies A and B and may be even Society C itself. But Society C, is willing to make those sacrifices for the benefit of the larger community, which would include all the societies and all individuals. Naturally, we can always find individuals in any society who have no fidelity to any system but themselves. These individuals are selfish and driven by their instincts in everything that they do. The solid dots in our graphical illustration, represents these individuals. In reality, fidelity or affiliation of subsystems to high-level systems is much more complicated when we add other affiliations with intermediate systems, that we skipped in order to simplify our system hierarchy and our argument.

Self-regulating social evolution: In its early stages of evolution, society was not self-regulating as it is today. Our weather channels continually update us by predicting future weather patterns in our neighborhoods and warning us to take shelter in severe weather conditions. Our healthcare system has started focusing more on proactive medicine rather than reactive, which could go even beyond that level with the help of genetic engineering. There are numerous advances of this kind in every aspect of our lives. This trend indicates that not only every individual, but also society as a whole, aims to predict its own process and react to forces that impact its evolutionary process, when they are in early stages of their development. When an individual or a society becomes capable of such predictions, it becomes a self-regulating system. In this situation, the system can interfere in its own evolutionary process early enough to divert its process from a path that may be destructive or damaging to its structural integrity.

As a result, self-regulation provides a new level of security and survivability for the organism as it becomes capable of predicting and avoiding harmful interactions with other systems in the path of its evolutionary process. Nevertheless, the organism would not be able to make these predictions, unless it were equipped with a certain level of knowledge regarding its environment, which may comprise of both living and non-living entities. It is clear that if a system had a greater level of knowledge, its ability to make predictions would improve and self-regulation would extend to cover the events more distant in the future.

Actions taken by an organism to avoid unwanted interactions with other systems may be divided into two categories. The first is to interfere with the evolutionary process of interacting systems, and the second is to divert its own evolutionary process from the current path to avoid or minimize the severity of those interactions. In the end, these actions result not only in the diversion of the evolutionary process of the organism, but also the outcome of its interaction with predicted forces. For example, our knowledge of astronomy, coupled with the help of computers, enables us to accurately predict the path of objects that may be on a collision course with the earth, decades ahead of time. With this level of knowledge, society may have enough time to react to such an event, save part of its population, and not be annihilated by such an event. Suppose that in the future mankind develops technologies to destroy terrestrial objects, on a collision course with the earth, far into the space before they get too close to the earth, which in this case, the entire population of earth will be saved. However, the course of action needed to encounter such a threat may put the entire planet on a different course of socio-political development and unify all the nations against such a threat that otherwise would have not happened in such a short period of time. There is no doubt that both humans and societies are in the process of learning to control and self-regulate their own course of evolution and as knowledge continues to grow, so would the level of self-regulation. With the help of knowledge and self-regulation, our historical trends may also change and become less violent as we start to appreciate the role of natural laws that define our relational bonds in social evolution.

Globalization versus imperialism: There is a major difference between imperialism practiced by imperial powers early in the twentieth century and the globalization process being conducted by them and other advanced nations today. Imperialists used to install puppet governments in their colonies that were protected by a small army from the colonizing nation, and through the support of this government, they were able to exploit the people and their land for profit. The imperialists made sure that a master-and-slave relationship was established between themselves and their colonies. The master-and-slave relationship was not only emphasized in economic life, but also extended into issues of race and culture to humiliate the people living in the colony. At the same time, these imperialists were writing a glorifying history for themselves that was filled with tales of aggression, occupation, enslavement, and exploitation of other nations and peoples. The colonies were undeveloped for decades (or even as long as a full century) so that they would remain dependent on their masters "forever." Most colonies had only one or a few industries, whether oil refineries, tea processing plants or another, depending on the type of natural resource found in their territory. The element of race and nationalism during the era of imperialism was of great importance. In today's world, racism and the idea of the master-and-slave relationship between nations and peoples are no longer acceptable. Economic development, expansion of trade, and increased level of cultural exchange among nations have weakened nationalism. In the United States, for example, people with different national origins have been working side by side for decades to develop new products and provide services to others. Today, corporations that are larger than governments are dictating the global policies. For these multinational corporations, nationalism is irrelevant; what is important is increased levels of profitability and growth. This change of focus has led to globalization. These corporations do not recognize borders. They want to be present in every corner of this planet to gain a greater share of the market. As we can see, there is significant difference between imperialism and globalization. In globalization, underdeveloped nations will eventually be developed, which would have not been possible during the era of imperialism. Today, corporations move their assets, knowledge, and people to offshore territories, to maximize their profitability, disregarding national interests and prejudices. It is true that at the beginning of this process, the corporations might profit from lower labor wages by keeping a much larger portion of the workers' productive power as surplus value to themselves. However, in the long run and through a deterministic process, their profits will begin to shrink as they start competing for skilled labor by paying workers higher wages. The demand for skilled labor may result in an improved educational system that would bring literacy to a nation, leading to a demand for yet higher wages and a higher standard of life that would be comparable to advanced nations. We also know from Marx's economic theory that labor value as an exchange commodity is the basis for the value of every commodity, and if labor needs for survival in these economies (the people's standard of life) gradually equalizes with those of the advanced nations, so would their wages and the value of products that they produce. It is at this stage that corporations would start feeling the pressure of competition—when their profit margins start dropping and they begin to think of moving their businesses to other parts of the world to once again benefit from cheaper labor. As this process continues, eventually there will be no place on earth that is not developed by the invasions of these corporations.

Looking at this process from another perspective, it is very possible that the global social organism's inherent intelligence and its evolutionary process toward self-organization and stability might have been using the greed of these corporations as a force to equalize the prosperity level of underdeveloped economies and advanced nations. Obviously, something that was not the main intension of these corporations when they entered new markets. It seems that, in the long run, the globalization process will eliminate the prosperity gap among nations and bring about equality among them, which is one of the intended goals of the global social organism in its evolutionary process. However, we must know that achieving equality at this subsystem level does not necessitate achievement of equality at other subsystem levels, such as the human level. Closing the equality gap among other subsystem levels will take place through sub-processes already in the working or through others initiated in the future.

Flawed globalization policies of advanced nations: According to the leaders of the West, globalization is the wave of the future. It's the new world order that attracts everyone's attention. Nevertheless, we wonder if they really understand what is involved in the globalization process. For the Western leaders, globalization means free trade and the exploitation of cheap labor. But there is a much broader concept in globalization that will eventually emerge, whether these leaders understand it or not. This broader concept is: *to have a set of laws that apply to every aspect of life in the global community that is accepted and respected by every nation.* In this kind of globalization, no nation can have special status with a veto power over the rest of the world. If disagreement arises over global policy issues that may result in taking votes, the vote of each nation should be scaled according to its population, with no right of veto if one nation's interest comes into conflict with the interests of other nations. The current system serves the interests of only a few nations and ignores all others. In a true global community, nations must share their technology with each other and advanced nations must help those that are behind to catch up with the rest of the world community. Regardless of their geographical locations, the natural resources of the world must be shared by all nations, particularly when it comes to energy resources. In a true global community, all activities, particularly in regard to economy, must be harmonized among nations for common goals and objectives. This will eliminate tension among nations. Every human being on earth must be treated with dignity and provided with basic survival needs so that he or she can become a productive member of the global community.

These are only few examples of how nations should conduct themselves and their policies to achieve a desirable harmonious state leading to the building of a true global community. However, none of these has been exercised by the advanced nations, who have been advertising the globalization concept for years now. These nations are using the word "globalization" as an opportunity to expand their economies into other territories and use the cheap labor to maximize their profitability. They also create hostility instead of friendship among nations in order to sell billions of dollars of armaments and provoke them into war to destroy each other's infrastructure and economies, so that they depend on the advanced nations forever. After these economies are destroyed, the advanced nations walk in, rebuild it and of course either own it or become a major partner. The same objectives have also been achieved through monetary policies, imposed upon small but growing economies without firing a gun. Unfortunately, this is the initiation phase of globalization and as brutal and hopeless as it may sound, it leads to the same desired state that was proposed at the beginning of this section. Living organisms such as the global social organism are systems with intelligence. One way or another, they can manipulate and tilt the process to their favor and achieve their intended evolutionary goals, regardless how hard their subsystems try to avoid it.

Some of the characteristics of the global society: The characteristics of a global society can be defined by culture, race, and ethnic mixture, as well as economy, technology, government, and political system. In the mature global society, borderlines separating the nations will become meaningless and nonexistent, as the populations of nations spread all over the world and form a homogeneous mix of peoples with different backgrounds. With the relocation of people to new territories, their culture will be relocated with them, which in the long run will blend with other cultures and form a uniform culture around the world. With the exception of a few prominent languages that will gain global acceptance and survive as universal languages, the rest will slowly vanish and become part of the history.

Global society will have a global government, which will devise the top-level policies and hand them over to the local governments for execution in their territories. These territories will not be economically and technologically self-sufficient, but will be highly dependent upon each other for energy and material needs. The interdependency of these territories with each other will not be considered a weakness but rather a strength, unlike today's societies that strive to become self-sufficient. After all, none of the organs in the human body are self-sufficient. Adversarial relationships among competing economic institutions and systems that are considered healthy in today's economic philosophy will be replaced by cooperative relationships among these institutions on a global scale, and, for the sake of economic stability, there will be international regulatory laws. The world government will play a central role in socioeconomic development on a global scale. Like any other living organism, the global society will be highly dependent upon energy resources to maintain its structure, continue its operation, and prevent instability. To achieve these goals, it will need to globalize all of the energy resources around the world, including their technology and systems that distribute them. To minimize environmental damage, the global society will regulate the type of energy that each nation or territory (depending on its climate) will be allowed to use. Research and development in the area of energy technology will be internationalized and intensified to find replacement resources if current resources diminish. Making sure that the flow of energy to the global organism's territories is not disrupted, will be one of the major activities of the global society. Because the disruption of energy flow to territories can result in economic instability and, in the worst case, dissolution of the global society, the energy industry will become one of the most heavily regulated industries. Next in line for regulatory laws will be the telecommunications industry, which forms the nervous system of the global society. Finally, other important matters, such as education, health care and employment, will become the rights of every global citizen. Eventually, members of the global society will come to recognize that it is the stability and efficiency of the operation of the social organism that matters most and that this goal cannot be met by unhappy, stressed-out, frustrated citizens. In the global society, no nation or territory will have an independent army. These armies will be dissolved so that they no longer pose a threat to other nations or their neighbors. Instead, there will be an army under the command of the United Nations that acts as a security force throughout the world. Space exploration will also intensify and an international defense force will be established to develop weapon systems to counter possible threats from outer space, such as asteroids that could wipe out human civilization.

These are some characteristics of the mature global society that will materialize as time goes by. However, these processes are not going to take place smoothly and without conflict between nations and individuals. The process may create an enormous level of violence and casualties along the way before the global society, or global social organism, starts to emerge as the outcome of this process.

Emerging signs of globalization: There are many indications that we are on our way to the formation of a global community. Some of these signs are listed below.

- Formation of larger economic, political and security blocs among nations, such as the European Union, which has been expanding and adding new members.

- Facilitation of economic integration and trade among nations through advancements in communication and transportation technologies.

- Immigration of larger populations from one country to the other for the purposes of business, education and employment that would further assist the assimilation of cultures.

- Formation of the United Nations as a central control system to resolve world problems that one nation alone cannot solve.

- Development and expansion of communication technologies that form the nervous system of the global social organism.

- Development of transportation systems that form the arteries of the global social organism to supply the energy and material needs of each nation or territory.

- International cooperation to tackle environmental, legal, and health related issues.

- International cooperation to prevent the proliferation of weapons of mass destruction.

- Human rights organizations.

Non-harmonized and uncoordinated global economy based on the free market economy: When a corporation moves offshore, its main incentive is greater profitability. Greater profitability can only be achieved by greater surplus value generated by labor and through the invention of methodologies to improve the operational efficiency of a business. In the process of competition, sooner or later, all competing companies will learn, either on their own or from outside consultants, how to improve the efficiency of their operation and stay competitive. As a result, competition will put the corporations on an equal footing, and competitive winners will be those whose labor force generates more value in a given time or works longer hours without pay. In reality, as technology travels to other parts of the world, skilled labor in underdeveloped societies eventually learn how to build identical products. Thus, they will break from the mother company and start competing with it, first in the same market and later expanding to other markets. The fierce competition to gain larger market share will force corporations to demand greater productivity from their employees for their mutual survival. In this process, employees will work longer hours (which is the beginning of modern slavery) to keep their jobs and support their families. This generation of human beings will suffer tremendous health problems, to a point where the average life expectancy will start dropping due to stress-related diseases and ailments. Long working hours will also create numerous problems in the lives of families, as parents are not able to spend enough time with their children and spouses. Due to the instability inherent in this economic system and the immense connectivity of the world economy, any economic depression that begins in one corner of the world will immediately propagate throughout the world, and before that depression is contained, another is likely to arise somewhere else. The ever-increasing dynamics of technological advancement, along with economic turbulence, will create an environment that is extremely hostile to the survival of economic institutions with limited resources. They will become extinct, leaving economies and markets to be monopolized by the larger institutions that possess greater resources to sustain themselves in such an environment. The market economy will leave every subsystem in the hierarchy of the system in a state of instability and uncertainty that will make the system to some extent dysfunctional on the global level. It will be then that a shift in thinking would evolve suggesting that central control of the economy might not have been such a bad idea after all, because it provides greater stability at every system level and makes the economic system more efficient at the macro level. If this reform does not take place on time, there will be political consequences, such as worldwide uprisings of the working classes against the market economy.

In the meantime, market economy will offer some advantages to the social evolution before it is abandoned. First, it will allow nations to join in free trade that enhances their levels of communication and interdependency and produces greater economic and cultural ties among them. This will further unify the nations as one community, which means that, it will serve as a catalyst for integration of societies into one global community. In this community, there will be socioeconomic classes, as usual, but individuals will be respected for their talents, contribution, and productivity and not by their race or country of origin. Second, despite of all the shortcomings of this economic system at the macro system level, it will help to close the existing prosperity gap between societies (particularly between the North and South blocs), not because it has the intention to do so, but because it will surrender to economic forces. In brief, market economy will be a transitional economic system moving toward a harmonized and centrally controlled economy that will assist in integration process of history.

Efficiency of economic systems: Living organisms (both individual human beings and the societies they live in), including all other non-living ordered structures, such as machinery, cannot function, be productive, or grow without receiving energy from their environment. Following up from our earlier discussion of the laws of thermodynamics, none of these systems, regardless of how efficiently they are designed, are capable of transforming 100 percent of the energy they receive into growth or productive work without raising the entropy of their environment. Raising entropy can be seen as increasing the disorder or pollution in the environment surrounding the system. The efficiency of a system, which is measured by its ability to transform or convert its received energy to work, growth, or a useful function, is calculated by the following equation:

$$Efficiency = \frac{E_2}{E_1} \times 100$$

where E_1 is the input energy received by the system and E_2 the output energy in the form of work or a desired output produced by the system. For example, if a system is calculated to be 70 percent efficient, that means only 70 percent of its received energy has been effectively transformed into a useful purpose and the rest has been wasted, which raises the entropy of its environment.

Except for its complexity, the economic system is no different from any other system. In the economic system, input energy is transformed into growth and structural maintenance, including products and services it produces. Most of the economic indicators, such as the gross national product (GNP) or gross domestic product (GDP), look at the output results of the economic system without relating those results to the input energies. It is unfortunate that indicators do not exist to show the efficiency of an economic system, the potential for its improvement, or its contribution to the pollution of the environment. In the United States today, the majority of people drive their cars to work. The cars need gasoline to run and produce no value beyond taking people to their workplaces, not to mention the wear and tear on the cars that require maintenance and replacement more often than if the cars were driven for personal use only. Let us assume, temporarily, that public transportation is abundantly available so everyone can get to work and use his/her car only for personal needs. We can all agree that with higher fuel economy cars the energy our economic system needs would be significantly lower and as a result, our economy would be more efficient. With a lower level of input energy, that is, we would be able to produce the same products and services and create less pollution in the environment. According to statistics, approximately 90 percent of all newly established businesses file for bankruptcy within the first two or three years from the date of their establishment. What value do these companies add to the overall output of the economic system? Obviously, not very much. Can we make arrangements so that these businesses survive before they run out of money? Can we prevent them from getting into product lines that markets are already saturated with? Can we encourage these businesses right from the start to move into new frontiers by assisting them with the expertise and financial support to succeed? Aside from stabilizing inflation in an economic system that is far from perfect, what value will the four to six percent unemployment rate bring to the economy, other than to elevate the level of crime to the point where a larger police force will be needed to protect the rest of the citizens from this minority, desperate to survive, who commit crime by resorting to drug dealing and robbery? To deal with this minority the society also needs a larger group of judges and lawyers, followed by prisons (and their guards) built to hold the criminals and keep the rest of the population safe. If we had an economic system that could employ all the unemployed, there would have been less need for the police force, which would have let them to engage in more productive work than watching the behavior of this unfortunate minority, or victims of social injustice. There are hundreds of such examples that, even in the most advanced nations, are not properly addressed when it comes to putting the entire economy (at the macro level) into a system that needs to be optimized and made efficient similar to a corporation. Imagine what could be achieved if the economy were optimized from the top.

In theory and practice, if the subsystems of a system are operating efficiently, that does not necessarily mean that the system as a whole is optimized and efficient. However, if a system is optimized from the top, it is necessary that all of its subsystems be optimized and made efficient down to the last subsystem level in the hierarchy, or system is not optimized yet.

On the global scale, the economy is even less efficient than at the national level. As we know, one of the most lucrative businesses for advanced nations is the sale of weapon systems. Some of the most brilliant scientists of the world are engaged in research and development projects pertaining to weapon systems with greater and greater destructive power, instead of getting involved in development of technologies that will help humanity by terminating hunger, healing diseases such as AIDS, developing clean energy resources, etc. The destructive power of the weapons these scientists develop can wipe out infrastructures, kill human beings' and animals, and pollute the environment beyond repair. When there is war, all of the efforts put into construction of ordered structures, including human life, go to waste. Weapons thus add a negative value to the world economy and its overall efficiency because their function is to destroy. What if the military budgets of the whole world were combined to develop the world instead of destroying it? What level of efficiency the global economy would have achieved if these budgets were allocated for construction purposes rather than destruction? Do weapons systems add to our security? In contrary, with every advancement in development of new weapon systems our security becomes more marginalized than ever before. But we do not understand this until it is too late. Unfortunately, human beings' as well as social organisms' behavior is strongly influenced by their insecurity, and despite understanding logical arguments, they will continue to fight and destroy one another to find more security. This will slow down the process of integration and make it more chaotic, and, from an economic point of view, inefficient, not only on the national level but also on the global level.

Ideal socioeconomic model based on human body's organization and operation: From the systems point of view, maximum operational efficiency can only be attained when optimization is applied to the highest level of the system. Most economic studies conducted in the West have focused on the development of methods and techniques that make an institution more productive and more competitive in the world market. The economic culture of competitive systems has both positive and negative consequences. The positive consequences are abundant products and services of good quality available at reasonable prices. The negative consequences are far worse for both economic institutions and the people who work for them. In competitive environment, economic institutions and their employees are engaged in a fierce Darwinian competition with their rivals that allows only the fittest to survive. When economic institutions feel financial pressure, they pass it down to their employees by cutting their wages and benefits while expecting them to work harder. This translates into a new level of exploitation and reduction of workers' purchasing power that offsets any positive benefits these workers may have gained from the competitive economic model. The hostile and non-harmonious relationship among economic institutions reflects the inefficiency of the economy as a whole. Hostile environments force companies into bankruptcy and loss of their assets, which is a waste of resources, not to mention the negative impact on people's lives when they lose their jobs. In this economic system, employees are overworked, stressed out, and exhausted; factors that become the cause of many illnesses, plus social and family related issues. But these issues are irrelevant in this economic system, and in fact, they are seen by corporate leaders and venture capitalists as new opportunities for new enterprises to be launched. The competitive economic model does not look at the efficiency of the economy at the macro level but focuses on the efficiency of the micro level systems, and as long as everyone is busy doing something (basically anything) and someone is making money of their productive work everything is fine. The competitive economic model is smart enough to come up with solutions to all the inefficiencies that it creates at the macro economic level. To control crime (which is the result of unemployment) and socioeconomic classes produced by this economic model, it employs a larger police force. For overstressed and sick people, it builds larger health care systems and invents more pharmaceuticals and the list goes on and on. In this economic system, everyone seems to be working very hard, but is this economic system efficient? In brief, competitive economies are not efficient when they are analyzed in light of a larger economic scale.

The human body's organization and operation are the results of millions of years of evolutionary refinement. The body has now reached a level of efficiency that is unmatched by anything that man has ever created. Why shouldn't we be wise enough to apply this model to our socioeconomic system, where all the organs work harmoniously and not competitively? After all, the social organism in its evolutionary process is bound to organize itself similar to human structure, and adopt most, if not all, of its operational procedures.

Ethics, moral values, and social evolution: The rule of law, ethical and moral values, are part of human and social consciousness and are strongly connected to circumstances arising from the dynamics of the processes related to the evolution of humans, their society and their environment. These circumstances contribute to the formation of human and social consciousness and their behaviors. In religious laws, behavioral patterns defined as "bad" and "good" are not subject to change under any given circumstances; and they referred to as moral values. An analysis of the moral values of different religions reveals contradictory values. For example, polygamy is banned in most denominations of Christianity and considered immoral, but it is allowed by Islamic and Mormon fundamentalists. Such contradictory moral values may never change from the religious point of view, and we may rightfully raise the question of their validity as "divine" laws. The fact is that moral values themselves are nothing but products of circumstances, but after they are declared to be divine laws, they become stagnant and unchangeable.

To differentiate moral values from values dictated by circumstances, we have created another term, *ethical values*. Ethical values are subject to change based on our best judgment of what is right and what is wrong at any given time and situation. To make our point, let us compose some hypothetical situations. Suppose that in the decades to come, after humans have tried everything to stop population explosion, we reach a consensus that the only way to stop this phenomenon is to sterilize men and women after having two children and enforce it by law. As much as this policy seems morally wrong from almost any religion's perspective, it may seem ethically right due to inability of societies to deal with the environmental and socioeconomic consequences of overpopulation. Let us now imagine another scenario where most of the population of earth has perished in an epidemic caused by a virus and only a small number of people have survived due to their immunity to this killer virus. In this case, it seems to be ethically right to abandon sterilization and abortion and encourage the population to reproduce more freely in order to populate the world. As seen in these two scenarios, two opposing ethical values were adopted to deal with two unique circumstances. In the first scenario, moral and ethical values were contradicting while in the second scenario they were in agreement.

Let us assume a third scenario in which history is in disintegration process. Societies are disintegrating and the food supply is in shortage, to the point that survival instincts of humans have started to kick in and replace their rational behavior. We may wonder how moral values may sustain themselves in these circumstances and continue to dominate human consciousness and his behavior. The fact is that all human values, moral or ethical, are subject to change as the circumstances dictate. Divine laws are no exception in these conditions; they, too, are subject to reinterpretation to fit new circumstances and justify human and social behavior.

Summary of social evolution and its deterministic finality: Based on our discussion so far, we can summarize our thoughts as follows. Human beings and their societies are living systems, that part of their behavioral patterns are influenced and controlled by the laws of nature, such as physics and thermodynamics, which are the same laws that govern the behaviors of the non-living systems. Every system has relational bonds with its surrounding parallel and serial systems in the hierarchy of the system. For example, a society has relational bonds with other societies, with its subsystems (human beings), and with its environment. Living systems have negative entropy; to survive and maintain their structural organization they need to consume energy, which comes from their environment. Consumption of energy raises the entropy of the environment and creates pollution and disorder while it lowers the entropy of living systems, which is an increased level of order within their structural organization. When life support systems and energy resources are abundant in the environment of an organism, that organism tends to grow, expand, and integrate; when these resources are scarce, the organism tends to have negative growth, contraction, and adopt a disintegration process. Such relational bonds between a social organism and its environment result in setting two deterministic finalities and historical processes for its evolutionary course; we called these processes integration and disintegration processes. We argued earlier that a social organism, upon formation, pursues its own evolutionary course and includes all of its subsystems, as part of its structural organization. In a multi-level system such as a social organism, its subsystems at every level of the hierarchy are in search of their own lowest state of internal energy and stability, as laws of systems dictate. However, in the integration process of history, the lowest state of internal energy and stability of the high-level system takes precedence over the subsystem's desired state of internal energy by forcing them to exchange energy and reach a state of equilibrium or equality in all subsystem levels. This is one of the areas where natural laws dominate the behavior of living organisms. If society is in disintegration process, then the subsystem's optimal stability takes precedence over the system itself, as the larger system gives up its structural integrity and releases its subsystems as independent systems. In terms of its structural and organizational evolution, society follows the human evolutionary pattern and structural organization. We showed many similarities between human structural organization and that of the social organism. When societies integrate, given enough time, similar components of their structural organization will merge to form larger components and the system as a whole emerges as a single organism with the same structural organization and the same components. In the disintegration process, when the larger system's infrastructure collapses, the opposite takes place. Smaller systems emerge from the larger system as independent organisms and struggle for their own survival.

We have also discussed how history is a goal seeking process that its finality is set by the laws of nature and that society's structural organization and operation pursues a predictable evolutionary process with maximum efficiency. Obviously, the finality of our history and social evolution must be achieved through a process composed of a multitude of sub-processes, each responsible for achieving one of the characteristics of the social organism at its maturity, including all relational bonds between its subsystems. All of these sub-processes need to be completed by the time social evolution reaches its finality to construct a global social organism that is harmonious, stable and operationally efficient. We have also argued that despite having a predictable finality in our historical process, the process itself remains circumstantial and unpredictable, as sub-processes can be completed in any random sequence. They may be interrupted and resume later, after another sub-process is completed, or they may all be progressing in parallel with different rates of completion. We have concluded that the process of history will never repeat itself, even if it restarts a million times. However, if a sufficient amount of time is provided to every historical process, social organism will always end up with the same characteristics when it reaches its finality. We mentioned that earth's hostile environment has created a sense of insecurity in the human race that has transcended to the social organism, dominating its behavior and resulting in certain types of interactions with other social organisms that are, for the most part, violent. To change these violent historical trends, we have argued, that human environment needs to be changed, so that he feels secure in this new environment. In these circumstances, humans will become more rational, and the social organism will follow and become rational in dealing with other social organisms, which would lead to non-violent historical trends.

In the previous chapter, we also mentioned that human beings and their societies are self-regulating (cybernetic) systems that can interfere in their own evolutionary process by acquiring knowledge regarding their environment, themselves, and other surrounding systems. Human knowledge and ideas can propagate throughout the social system and, in time, create a social conscious-ness so powerful that will influence the course of social evolution through a col-lective effort. We have also argued that in the presence of abundant life support systems and energy resources, social evolution takes the direction of integration and none of the policies of self-serving subsystems or individuals are able to halt or reverse its process forever. In fact, if it is diverted, the intelligence of the system will find a different evolutionary path to achieve its goals. This is also true in the reverse process (disintegration process), where no harmony and stability can be created permanently when resources are vanishing and systems are collapsing.

At the end, understanding the process of history on the basis of science will generate a positive social consciousness among all subsystem levels in the hi-erarchy of the global social organism, which in turn will lead to a shortcut in attaining the finality of social evolution by adoption of correct policies and behaviors. A "shortcut" is a historical process that is a straight line between the current state of the social evolution and its finality, which results in limited dissipative losses by avoiding unnecessary self-inflicted ones. All of the above discussions are illustrated in Figure 5-3.

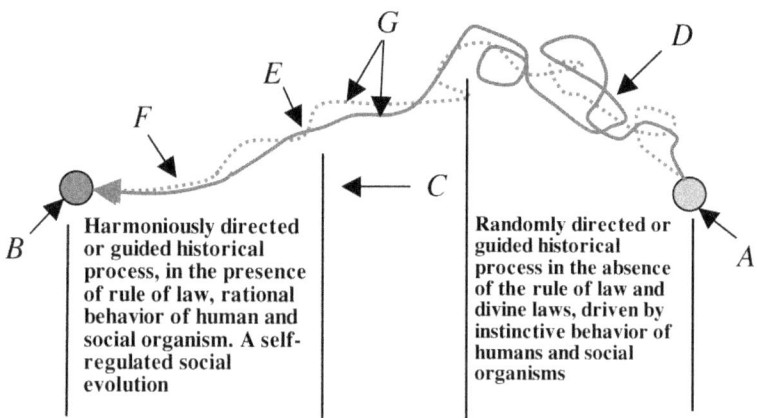

Figure 5-3 The Evolutionary Process of the Social Organism

A. Birth of the social organism.

B. Finality of social evolution, as dictated by the laws of physics, ther-modynamics, and systems theory. Highly stable, efficient, and harmonized social organism in its operation. It has a structural organization analogous to the human structure.

C. Direction of the historical process (integration) set by the availability of energy resources and life support systems in the environment of the social organism. These processes are reversible at any time due to the changes taking place in the environment of the organism in terms of the availability of these resources.

D. Trend of historical process, in this case, violent, set by the effects of hostile environmental conditions on the state of mind of humans during their evolutionary process, and its manifestation in the behavior of social organisms. At this stage, social evolution is a randomly directed process.

E. Continuation of process D, where the social organism and its subsystems start taking control over their environment and start controlling their own evolutionary process as self-regulating systems. A highly intelligent organism with advanced technological and scientific achievements. A reduced state of insecurity at this stage of evolutionary process would provide a less violent transition to the finality of social evolution.

F. A much smoother and non-violent process of social evolution, assuming human beings are in charge of their environment and have been freed from the insecurities that once controlled their behavior and influenced the behavior of social organism as well. It is at this stage that social evolution will become a harmoniously directed process.

G. Two historical processes shown with dotted and solid lines, as an indication that historical processes never repeat, only at birth and finality, assuming environmental conditions remain the same for both processes.

Violent historical processes take a much longer time to achieve their finality due to randomness, and self-inflicted losses associated with their process (similar to the right side of the plot). A peaceful historical process is a shortcut and generates minimum dissipative loss when compared to all other processes when they achieve their finalities (similar to the left side of the plot).

Painting a picture of the finality of social evolution in the integration process of history: The finality of social evolution on earth will encompass the entire population of the earth under one sophisticated central control system that oversees its high level operation, with regional and local central control systems overseeing their regions and reporting to the next higher level of leadership. In this society, the economy will be centrally planned, although individuals will be recognized and rewarded both financially and by other means for their hard and creative work, giving a hint of capitalism in a society that uses the ideals and principles of socialism as its governing principles. In this society, people will have the right to free health care and free education and can rise to their fullest potential. People will be able to retire with dignity and without fear of unemployment.

This seems unrealistic, but if we look at the human body and its operation, we do not find any cells being denied nourishment because the health of the human body depends on the health of every single cell in the body, and so does the social organism. In the state of finality, most ordered structures, living or non-living, will be integrated into the structure of the social organism, where they will be monitored for security purposes. Naturally, this will limit some of the notions traditionally associated with human freedom, particularly freedom of privacy, but central control will be necessary for the security of the social organism. Freedom of speech and an open environment for constructive debate and activities will remain the characteristics of this social organism, notions borrowed from both the ideals of today's democratic societies and the ideals of communism founded on the basis of dialectical materialism. Assuming that the social organism continues to remain optimally stable and support all of its members equally, modification of the governing principles and the operational efficiency of the organism will be made through logical, mathematical, and computational methodologies rather than by political ideologies. At this stage, all human beings will communicate with a single language and most cultures will have blended into one single culture. For the sake of stability and security, all members of the society will be provided with basic survival needs, which will force the central government to globalize all natural resources and the means of production. This will be done to improve the fair distribution of these resources among all people. In this society, a much larger number of humans will be engaged in research and development activities when compared to those engaged in similar activities in today's advanced societies. New discoveries in the fields of science will continue to shake the foundation of the various branches of religion and reduce them to glorified stories of human history with no connection to divinity. This will further pave the way for the integration of nationalities that are so divided today by religious and cultural differences. However, the concept of a creator, or God, will remain unchallenged and unanswered long after the social organism reaches its finality. The social organism's environment will remain a focal point in all of its policies, particularly in connection with the use of its resources, consumption of energy, and issues related to pollution and security. Policies regarding population growth or reduction will be tied directly to environmental and energy policies. This will ensure that the social organism will resume its optimal state of stability in its evolutionary course as it transitions through challenging environmental conditions. The job of science in this society will be, partly, to predict emerging environmental conditions that will affect the survival, security, and stability of the social organism, and to predict these things far in advance so to allow sufficient time for the social organism to respond and make proper adjustments to avoid undesired consequences. In other words, the social organism at this stage will become a self-regulating system that will design its own evolutionary course, limited only by its scientific and technological capacity.

CHAPTER 6

The social organism and its behavioral characteristics in the disintegration process of history

As we declared earlier, the process of history is reversible. Everything that man has achieved in his long struggle with the forces of nature and among his own kind to get to present state of social evolution can be reversed. Rational behavior can easily be dominated by instinctive behavior in organisms at all hierarchical levels. Starting from the top-level system and proceeding the bottom, order would turn into chaos, moral and ethical values would be transformed, and processes of expansion and integration would reverse to processes of contraction and disintegration. These are feasible scenarios when the environment stops supporting the social organism with the energy resources or life support systems it needs to grow and sustain its structural integrity at all hierarchical levels. We must also understand that the two main trends of social evolution—integration and disintegration—can revert to the other at any stage of their evolutionary process when the main cause that sets their direction reverts.

In this chapter, we will try to explore these possibilities and predict some of the outcomes and consequences of the processes involved in the disintegration process. This chapter will serve two purposes. First, we will analyze the logic and validity of the theoretical assumptions we have set forth in this book. Second, we will warn humanity of the dangers ahead in our social evolution so that we may choose wisdom over foolishness in conducting our affairs.

What constitutes the disintegration process of social evolution? There are numerous things that can threaten the life of the social organism and every living subsystem in its hierarchy. Some of these threats can be avoided by planning and using rational judgment, whereas others cannot be avoided. The lives of the social organism and all life forms on earth can be wiped out in a matter of a few months if a large asteroid collides with the earth; merely an uncontrollable accident by social organism based on its current technological know how. Others could be depletion of our resources followed by a full-blown world war with the application of nuclear weapons.

In this discussion, we will focus on the environmental factor in the course of social evolution and how lack of environmental support can reverse the process of history, either temporarily or permanently. The reversal of historical process would be accompanied by the destruction of order. In fact, the destruction process makes perfect sense, since it reduces the sizes of ordered structures to minimize their dependence on energy resources that are depleting or have run out. Nevertheless, let us be more accurate in our definition, because we may ask: If our history is in integration process, then how can we explain the wars we are conducting and the damages we are inflicting upon our ordered structures and ourselves? This is a legitimate question and to answer it, we propose that in either historical process there will always be a mix of destructive and constructive processes. However, when an environment with abundance of energy resources sets the trend of social evolution, the trend would be predominantly integrative. In that case, the construction of order would surpass the destruction, whereas, in the disintegration process, the destructive processes would overwhelm the constructive processes. The level of destruction heretofore seen in integration process has been relatively mild and as a result of placid competition among living organisms. In the disintegration process, destructive processes may be colossal and far more brutal. The increased threat level posed by a hostile or depleted environment would intensify organisms' competition for the remaining natural resources. This competition would result in a size reduction of all ordered structures on the global scale. Sporadic destructive processes within predominantly integrating process, however, would in time revert to constructive processes when the sub-organisms start to merge and integrate. This would likewise be true for sporadic constructive processes in a predominantly disintegrating historical process. In such a case, the constructive processes would become temporary and then revert to destructive processes as the larger organisms start to fall apart and disintegrate. Thus, as social evolution starts to approach its finality in the integration process of history, violent trends and destructive processes will start to subside under the influence of rational behavior of organisms in a safe and secure environment. In the disintegration process of history, where the environment can no longer support any organism, the level of destruction and violence would dominate the entire process, under the influence of instinctive behaviors of organisms fighting for their survival.

The root causes of self-inflicted disintegration processes within the predominantly integrative process of history: In a predominantly integrative process of history, disintegration takes on a milder form of destruction on a global scale caused by regional wars, dysfunctional economies, poor planning, or corruption at the highest level of the social organism. We will refer to these destructive processes as self-inflicted because most of the time the environment of the organisms has not initiated these processes. Let us further clarify this assertion by stating that all societies in the world belong to a larger organism, which we call the global social organism. Societies are the subsystems of the global social organism. As the global social organism evolves, it tames all of its insubordinate and selfish subsystems at all levels and emerges as a stable and organized system. In this process, the competition among subsystems, in all levels, to gain a more favorable and secure position still creates sporadic conflicts and destructive processes. As a result, from the viewpoint of the global social organism and its top-level process, these destructive processes are self-inflicted phenomena that are not triggered by the environment. The root cause of self-inflicted destruction in the historical process lies in human nature and his hunger to manipulate and control as many resources as he can to feel secure. As this characteristic of humans transcends to higher system levels, such as social organisms, they, too, exhibit the same levels of insecurity and attempt to manipulate the resources of their environment. In doing so, they clash with similar systems trying to do the same. Most of the time, the destruction resulting from these conflicts over resources, whether between human beings or social organisms, has little to do with deficiency of resources in the environments of these organisms. This means that these conflicts are not triggered by the environment itself, but rather by the unwillingness of organisms to share environmental resources. Although these conflicts can cause a significant level of destruction and inflict damage to the infrastructure of the global social organism, they are temporary and reversible when the parties involved reach a consensus to share resources and integrate. Another reason that forces the social organisms into confrontation is unequal distribution of natural resources around the world that are considered vital to the survival of the social organisms. For example, some parts of northern Africa lack adequate water resources and receive insufficient rainfall for agricultural activity. Other regions may have an abundance of water resources, but lack other resources such as oil, gas and minerals needed to run their industries, and as we know, industry is a crucial element in the survival of advanced societies. This unequal distribution of vital resources around the world has created an environment of either competition or cooperation, whichever works better for the survival of the organisms involved. Cooperation among social organisms for mutual survival manifests itself in the form of international agreements, such as those for free trade. But from time to time, when one social organism decides to deny others the resources it controls, in order to gain control over their political life, it is almost certain that it would create conflict among them, if these resources cannot be found elsewhere. Consequently, disintegration and destruction may follow. Afghanistan is a good example in this case, where this country became the battleground among the superpowers for geopolitical advances and the control of energy resources of the Caspian Sea and the Middle East. Thanks to foreign intervention, Afghan society disintegrated, and as a result, millions of people were displaced, infrastructure was destroyed, chaos and lawlessness reigned throughout the country and within a short period of time, Afghan society regressed in every aspect of social life. Another example is the war that United States declared against Iraq. The claim was that Iraq possessed weapons of mass destruction (WMD); this pretence covered up one of the main reasons for the U.S. invasion, which was to gain control and secure Iraq's abundant oil resources. Not only to secure United States future energy needs but also as a strategic initiative to control the entire region's energy resources, that is the bloodline of most European and Asian economies. Controlling these resources would also give U.S. an upper hand in efforts to subdue rivals, such as China and India, which will be emerging as superpowers in the next couple of decades. The attack on Iraq was also the result of political insecurity of U.S. and the wish of the government to emerge as the controlling organism on a global scale. This war has destroyed most Iraqi cities and their infrastructure. It has taken the lives of hundreds of thousands of Iraqi people and at least thirty thousand of Americans who have been killed and wounded in this war; all of this due to human insecurity and the manifestation of this human characteristic in the attitudes and policies of social organisms.

Self-inflicted disintegration caused by overpopulation: Another factor that may lead a social organism to exhibit destructive behavior in certain regions of the world is overpopulation, where economic growth and development in these regions cannot keep pace with population growth. What this means is that every man's share of resources shrinks over time to a point where survival becomes extremely difficult for everyone. These conditions could trigger civil unrest, revolution and heighten the level of tension between the poor and the rich, not only at the individual human level but also at the societal level. The level of tension found between prosperous and non-prosperous nations correlates directly with the prosperity gap, which seems to be widening daily, not only because the prosperity of advanced nations grows but also because the poor nations become poorer due to their population growth. As we know, this tension has manifested itself in the form of organized conflict called *terrorism*. In fact, terrorism is nothing but unconventional warfare waged upon prosperous nations by non-prosperous nations. Terrorism produces a great level of destruction, not only in the territories of the prosperous nations but also in the poorer nations when the prosperous nations retaliate. Since overpopulation is a contributing factor in the phenomenon of terrorism, we cannot afford to ignore population growth anywhere in the world. At the end, everyone will suffer equally from the consequences of overpopulation. International terrorism, which is a phenomenon that troubles most prosperous nations today, is feeding itself in societies that have faltering economies.

If people and their societies are capable of predicting the destructive power of overpopulation and refuse to take action to control it, then all subsequent destructive processes associated with overpopulation will become self-inflicted. If we also know that the prosperity gap leads to tension and conflict and choose to do nothing about it, the subsequent destructive processes, which are part of our social evolution, will also be self-inflicted. To avoid these self-inflicted destructive processes, the international community must get involved in both controlling population growth throughout the planet and equalizing prosperity levels among nations.

Disintegration processes caused by natural disasters: Social organisms, along with other species living on our planet, are powerless to protect themselves against the awesome powers of nature that strike from time to time. Every time an earthquake, tsunami, flood, hurricane, or tornado strikes a human community, it wipes out not only the people but also their cities. We call these episodes "natural disasters" and try to cope with them by rebuilding. Some natural disasters may even change the course of social and biological evolution of species on our planet. For example, it has been theorized that the extinction of dinosaurs on earth has occurred subsequent to a powerful collision between an asteroid and the earth. This event changed the course of evolution of species on earth and allowed other species to populate the world. For example, millions of years after this event *homo sapiens* followed by modern human beings succeeded in taking charge of the planet and populate it with their societies.

Epidemic diseases might also destroy large populations, and some species that may be unfit to survive will die off through the process Charles Darwin called natural selection. In the mid fourteenth century, plague epidemic hit Europe and killed large number of Europeans with no natural immunity against this disease. Today, African societies are suffering from AIDS epidemic and large number of their population dying every year, and their societies disintegrating. In the past few decades, particularly in the Northern Africa, we have also witnessed the disintegration of societies and the deaths of millions of people from starvation caused by uncooperative nature.

These forms of disintegration inflicted upon the social organism by natural forces are not in the category of self-inflicted destructive processes, as the environment has initiated them. Humans have little or no control over these forces and most of the time cannot avoid them. These destructive episodes are, however, in most cases localized and do not derail social evolution on the planet from its predominantly integrating process. Nevertheless, destructive forces create a great deal of pain for humans and their societies and can lead to possible interference in their evolutionary processes.

In this discussion, we have assumed thus far that earthquakes, tsunamis, hurricanes, and other environmental disasters were created by natural forces. Recently, however, the superpowers have shown the capability of creating these natural phenomena using electromagnetic weapons systems. Such weapons have already been tested and used for political gain. These weapons are capable of inflicting tremendous structural damages to the infrastructure of cities and destroy lives. For an ordinary person, it is almost impossible to distinguish between a man-made earthquake and a natural one, unless he/she is expert in the field. Nevertheless, the losses created by man-made weather conditions and earthquakes would all fall into the category of self-inflicted or self-imposed destructive processes.

How to avoid self-inflicted disintegration processes: Future mistakes can be prevented if we can predict the consequences of today's actions and policies. While it is true that not all historical events can be predicted up to the last detail, but every set of details comes only with certain trends in historical processes. Therefore, if our policy-makers followed proper historical trends, which are predictable, we could avoid some of the unwanted or unpredictable details associated with unwanted trends. Let us clarify this with a simple example. If we choose to be friendly with everyone in our neighborhood, it is likely that the neighbors would be nice to us, too. We may not be able to predict all the details or actions of our neighbors' kindness or the favors they do, but it would be very unlikely that a neighbor would break our window or dump garbage on our driveway. The chosen trend avoids these unwanted details and produces others, which maybe for example, invitations to their homes for dinner or having a picnic together.

We can now argue that it is up to individual people and their societies to choose what details of historical events they prefer, and pick a historical trend with appropriate policies that would generate those details. We know that the root causes of self-inflicted destructive processes lie in the characteristics of living systems, whether they are individuals or the societies, which are willing to do anything to be secure and survive. We have no choice but to work with these characteristics and design our policies and behaviors in such a way that the security and survival of every individual and society are guaranteed and respected by other members of the global community. If we fail to properly design our policies, we may face the undesirable consequences of our inappropriate and selfish policies. Social evolution has reached a state of self-consciousness that is capable of not only understanding its own evolutionary process but also predicting its own future and finality as a single organism forming the global community in which every single human being would have a responsible role with respected and protected rights in that community. If this is so, why should we not assume conscious control over our historical process and harmoniously direct it to its finality, rather than leaving it to random (yet directed) processes that always accompany unwanted disintegration processes? What is the point of building more weapons that can be countered by other weapons yet never buys anyone any extra security? If this trend were reversed and military budgets of the world were dedicated to developing third-world nations, such activity would give everyone a level of security that no weapon can ever provide.

Disintegration of the social organism due to an unsupportive environment: Now let us discuss a couple of hypothetical situations to show how disintegration can become a predominant course of social evolution with deterministic trends and finality. First, let us imagine that one day a large asteroid collides with earth, causing the entire atmosphere of the planet to fill up with poisonous gases and clouds that block the sunlight. Such an event would alter the quality of the life support systems, such as air, water and temperature on our planet on which every living organism depends. Most of the plant life would die, which would destroy the food chain, thus starving most species to death. All social organisms and living subsystems in their hierarchies, including the human race, would disintegrate. The disintegration that the social organism would endure after the immediate destruction of its structure will extend into the future for decades before environmental conditions reverse back to normal and allow the remaining life forms to start over. Second, let us imagine that one day the sun starts to die. It would be only a matter of time before all life forms on our planet disintegrate and die.

Life on earth is so delicately balanced that the smallest change in current settings can trigger the disintegration process of social organisms and humans and wipe out our civilization from this planet. When the disintegration process becomes a predominant historical process, the social organism will continue to downsize until it finds a new balance between its survival needs and those provided by its environment. At that point, the disintegration process slows down and eventually stops. Downsizing of the social organism starts with elimination of top-level infrastructure and, if necessary, proceeds to subsystem and sub-infrastructure levels within the hierarchy, including people. The destroyed ordered structures no longer need life support systems to maintain their order, therefore, size reduction makes perfect sense in disintegration process. Likewise, when we study the impact of an economic recession on the life of a society, once again, size reduction becomes the dominant process. The first victims of an economic recession are roads, bridges, and buildings that make up a society's infrastructure. If recovery does not come in time, these structures will continue to erode until they collapse and break the system into pieces. Similarly, how many times have we witnessed the downsizing of corporations (as living organisms) when their earnings (energy resources) shrink, sometimes to the point of laying off all of their employees and filing for bankruptcy (extinction)?

At this point, we can analyze the behavior of an advanced social organism on a global scale as it falls victim to uncontrollable environmental conditions and slides into a historical process that is primarily disintegrating. Suppose this process reversion takes place sometime in the future, when societies have been united by the formation of bigger blocs, or maybe even a single bloc called the global social organism. The first response of the global social organism to this crisis would be a rational response. It would try to address the problem and find solutions without changing the operational or governing principles of the global society or altering existing socioeconomic relations among its sub-organisms. After these solutions fail, however, emotional and/or instinctive responses of the sub-organisms will become stronger and force the global social organism to reform its operational and governing philosophy by resorting to political ideologies that would best serve the fair distribution of limited life support systems that are quickly vanishing from the environment. Such a socioeconomic transition in the governing philosophy of the social organism would be the last attempt by its sub-organisms to preserve the structural integrity of the global social organism and prevent it from disintegration. It is only logical to believe that in such circumstances, political ideologies such as socialism, would prevail and gain overwhelming support, if these ideologies have not yet been strengthened in the operation of the global social organism by being near its finality. If a qualitative change in the global social organism's governing principles and socioeconomic relations becomes a necessity, then there will be a period of chaos and temporary disintegration (perhaps also self-inflicted) that would be tolerable, as long as this political transition holds the global social organism together and prolong its life.

Now let us assume that shortages of life support systems continue to be felt strongly in the global social organism, even after the most appropriate and most just socioeconomic policies have been adopted in the operation of social organism. It would be at this stage that the rational and emotional responses of the sub-organisms start to disappear and instinctive responses begin to take over. The global social organism is now broken into smaller blocs that form alliances against each other, followed by confrontation and violence, in efforts to control and manipulate the remaining life support systems. In these circumstances, confrontation may mean annihilation of an entire bloc if necessary. If the shortage of resources continues, the constituents of the surviving bloc will start breaking down into smaller and smaller blocs, dismantling other top-level infrastructures, and forming new alliances to control what is left of resources. This breakdown of the social organism and its downsizing will continue until a point of balance is reached between what is left of the global social organism and the remaining life support systems that can support its structure. Under these circumstances, violence will subside, and once again, rational behavior will start influencing the attitudes of the social organisms and their subsystems toward each other. If this balance is not attained, however, the disintegration process will continue to the point of complete disintegration of the global social organism, releasing all of its subsystems (individual human beings) to survive on their own or in small groups. At subsequent stages, the remaining individuals would perish from starvation, disease, and other natural causes. In disintegration process of history, as described here, the "Darwinian law" or "rule of jungle" would be the only rule that would dominate the behavior of individuals and their societies. In this process, only the strongest and the most brutal will survive.

The picture we have painted here suggests that in the disintegration process of history, the social organism collapses at the highest system level first and then proceeds down to the next system level, and so on. This process is the opposite of the integration process of social evolution where individuals and societies integrate to form the global social organism. The level of chaos and destruction in the disintegration process is almost unimaginable for those of us who live in the integration process of history. Even though the global social organism has not yet been threatened by the shortages of life support systems (such as energy resources), the question remains: can we foresee the future and prepare ourselves in advance to avoid our disintegration?

The state of law and order in the disintegration process: When the global socail organism starts to break up, the first set of laws that fall victim to this process are those pertaining to the international system; this is the same system level whose infrastructure is threatened. At this stage of the disintegration process, nations or communities of nations that have formed smaller blocs to protect themselves from other blocs begin to assemble their own sets of internal and international laws that best fit their needs and interests, rather than those of the world community as a whole. These laws would allow a nation to wage an unprovoked war against another bloc or other nations that may happen to have more resources in their territory. In this stage of the disintegration process, the principle of sovereign nations, once respected and protected by the international community, will be abolished. Wars will be fought with the intent to wipe out and annihilate a bloc or a nation in its entirety, leading to total devastation. As disintegration proceeds and catches up with individual societies, the next level of laws and regulation that will be subject to break down will be those of state. This process will start with the formation of smaller groups within a society, disobeying its laws and claiming they are ineffective to protect them or meet their needs.

In summary, when systems break down in any level, it means that the laws that govern and restrain the behavior of subsystems at that system level are already weakened or broken altogether, throwing the system into chaos and disharmony in that system level. This process is the opposite of the integration process, where merger of societies and their cooperation results in the creation of new laws and regulations.

Morality and ethics in the disintegration process: Under the name of God and the leadership of European popes and kings, Crusaders massacred Jews and Muslims by tens of thousands in their quest to regain rule over Jerusalem, the birthplace of Jesus. Thus, warfare was justified by medieval moral values. But God's command is "Thou shalt not kill". How can the religious leaders commit such crimes in the name of God, yet preach morality to others? At first glance, the rationale behind these religious wars, provoked by the champions of morality, seems too weak, but when we add the economic factor to these historical events, then everything starts to make more sense. For example, the Crusades were encouraged by the European merchant community, which had close ties with the church and needed a military presence in the Mediterranean to open and secure the doors of trade between those nations and European societies. Other reasons for initiating this religious war were the greed of popes for money, land and revenge against infidels. To accomplish these goals, they created moral grounds to wage war against non-Christians living in the birthplace of Jesus.

What this means is that morality can be easily exploited to become an instrument of control used to pacify a population in peacetime and unify the people during wartime. This control is done by powerful minorities, which are constantly seeking political and economic gains. In more recent history, during Ronald Reagan's presidency, when the Cold War between the West and the Soviet Union was at its peak, it was Reagan who labeled the Soviet Union the "Evil Empire." His idea was to set the moral grounds for the American people for possible confrontation with the Soviets. When Muslim fundamentalists seized power in Iran in 1979, they called United States the "great Satan," again to set the moral ground and to unify their nation for possible confrontation with U.S. More recently, President George W. Bush declared an "Axis of Evil" that was in part a preparation of his moral grounds for war with Iraq and possibly the entire Middle East. Interestingly, the Vatican opposed this new war as being immoral, while the Christian Zionists and evangelical churches in the U.S. supported it. Is it not ironic that the followers of Jesus in two different denominations have two different sets of moral values regarding war on Iraq? Or could there be other factors, mostly economic gains and political ties and affiliations, that dictated the position of fundamentalist Protestant churches in U.S., but not the Roman Catholic church, led by the Vatican in Europe?

As we can see, moral values are subject to interpretation. They are influenced by economic, political and environmental conditions, and it is highly unlikely that these values remain unaffected by changing circumstances. Political or religious leaders can use, reinterpret, or even exploit moral values to unify the masses, if this will help to save the life of the social organism or advance the goals of a minority in a changing environment. In the disintegration process, where resources continue to dwindle and endanger the life of all organisms, renewed interpretations of moral values, reinforced by the survival instincts of the social organisms and their dependent sub-organisms, will justify the brutality of wars by organisms against each other. In such circumstances, crime and genocide will have God's blessings. In these circumstances, ethical values will not be an exception to the rule and will follow the same path as moral values.

A brief summary of this chapter: In this chapter we have explained that the current process of history is primarily an integrating process, although it can swing to a disintegrating process if life support systems in the environment start to diminish or vanish altogether. We stressed that as much as the laws of nature and the environment dominate the finality of social evolution in the integration process of history, in the absence of environmental support, these same laws determine a new faith in social evolution and its historical process. We indicated that destructive processes can simultaneously exist in either historical process, with a ratio of constructive over destructive processes larger in the integration process and smaller in the disintegration process. We argued that the destructive processes taking place in a predominantly disintegrating historical process sustain themselves until a new balance between the remaining environmental resources and what remains of the social organism has been attained. We also mentioned that the root cause of all destructive behaviors in our social evolution, regardless of the direction in which the historical process evolves, can be found in human nature, with his insecure behavior and a strong will to survive. We indicated that an overpopulated world can be as dangerous as any weapon of mass destruction that would promote destructive processes in our historical process. Manipulation and control of energy resources by a few can be as dangerous as population explosion and also lead to destructive processes when societies who need those resources resort to force to obtain them. The Iraq War was the beginning of such a process. The U.S. flouted international law and invaded a sovereign country to seize control of its resources. In cases like this, moral and ethical values can be molded to circumstances to justify unlawful, immoral, and unethical behaviors that are driven by survival instincts. We stated that in a predominantly disintegrating historical process, the social organism collapses first at the highest level, along with all the laws and regulations pertaining to that system level, and proceeds to the lower system levels if necessary. For example, the breakup of international law is the precursor to the breakup of the international community.

We conclude this chapter by stating that human beings and social organisms are capable of influencing the path of their social evolution by being wise and setting aside their insecurities, by working together to create a safe and secure environment for all of humanity. They can cooperate to minimize the self-inflicted part of destructive processes in their historical evolution and harmoniously guide it to its finality. This work requires population control, globalization of energy resources, and efficient use of these resources. They need to work together to eliminate hunger and disease from underdeveloped nations and give them the means to catch up with developed nations. More importantly, they must abandon weapons development whose sole purpose is to find new and more efficient ways of destroying larger bodies of ordered structures.

CHAPTER 7

Misrepresentation and misconceptions of our social evolution in recent history and issues of concern as we go forward

Stages of historical evolution: Marx, Engels, and Lenin, among others, had an accurate view of historical processes driven by economic forces, which are strongly tied to the survival of living organisms. In their view, a utopian society could be created through the implementation of socioeconomic justice throughout the world that put an end to exploitation and the struggle of man against man. This view is not far from our theory of systems governed by the laws of nature, which requires equality in the state of internal energy of the subsystems to produce optimum stability at the system level, which is a natural course of evolution for any system. In our discussion, the word "system" applies to society, or the social organism.

After the Russian Revolution and establishment of the Soviet proletarian government, Marxist ideology started to spread all over the world, particularly among industrialized nations where exploitation of labor was unprecedented. It was during the Cold War that intellectuals and the working classes of the industrialized societies, influenced by Marxist ideology and Soviet Union's accomplishments, started to penetrate into their governments and transform their socioeconomic systems by introducing socialist concepts. In Europe, the upper socioeconomic class that used to control governments had no alternative but to blend capitalist economies with socialism in order to survive both politically and economically. By the end of the Cold War in 1989 and after decades of reform and social transformation, Europe had turned pink in the spectrum of political colors. Clearly, socialism had an enormous impact on the course of the social evolution of most industrialized nations and in particular the European nations. Achieving such levels of socioeconomic reforms in industrialized societies, and alteration of social consciousness throughout the world took many decades and with huge sacrifices on behalf of the intellectuals and working classes of the world, but the course of history and social evolution as it was conducted during the Cold War had to be interrupted for many reasons. First, the arms race between Soviet Union and West was reaching a level of sophistication that was becoming increasingly dangerous and out of control, threatening civilization as a whole. Second, the economic pressure of the arms race had paralyzed both camps, particularly the communist bloc due to a poorly managed economy and the funding of progressive movements throughout the world. Third, the large ideological gap between socialist and capitalist economic systems had already been closed, in terms of the popular desire in the East for individual freedom and in the West for the better treatment of the working class.

It was then that the two camps decided to change the course of history and end the Cold War. One of the wrong conclusions regarding the termination of the Cold War reached by historians and others is the victory of the West over the Soviet Union because they came out of it economically stronger. At the same time, when the founders of socialism abandoned their cause, this left a vague impression in the popular mind regarding its validity. The Russian Revolution and the subsequent expansion of the Marxist ideology made a huge impact on the entire world as the ideology that promoted equality, consistent with systems theory, as a way of life before it temporarily left the stage to other historical developments. Therefore, it is fair to say that there was no clear winner in the Cold War, as each camp partially succeeded in promoting its ideals throughout the world. After the Cold War ended, historical evolution switched from an equalization process among people within societies to equalization among societies under the name of globalization.

Globalization is another process (desired by the North but not necessarily accepted by the South) by which the societies actively engage in economic relations to pave the path for the integration of their societies into one global community, driven by capitalists and the notion of market economy. Theoretically, in this process and over time, economic forces will gradually close the large prosperity gap that has been in existence among these societies for decades due to political and economic suppression of the underdeveloped nations by the imperial powers. As always, the societies of the South perceive globalization as another example of the economic aggression of the North against them and their cultural and religious heritage. These undeveloped societies will resist the process of globalization that will result in a clash between North and South societies, with millions of casualties before it settles. The process of history, which is the evolutionary process of global social organism, is a complicated process that switches from one course of development to another from time to time, or it may progress in all fronts simultaneously, while it has its destination in mind as systems theory dictates. Any economic injustice or inequality on the subsystem (human) level that was not corrected in previous historical processes will be corrected through other processes at a later time, either in parallel with or subsequent to the globalization process. In other words, socialism will rise again, and this time it will take over the world.

As we can see, different processes that achieve equality at different system levels represent different historical stages, and we should not be concerned about the sequence of these processes because they are all relevant to the state of finality. As long as historical process proceeds in integration mode, any unconcluded historical stage, due to hopping of the social system from one historical stage to another, will be attended again for the completion of its process because without its completion the global social organism would not be at its optimum state of stability. Historical evolution moving toward an integrated and stable global community may comprise a multitude of sub-processes, each responsible for bringing about equality at a particular subsystem level in the hierarchy of the system. We have called each of these processes a historical stage. These stages do not have to occur in any particular sequence and may take place in parallel, in series, overlapping, or be interrupted and continued at a later time. There is no determinism in the sequence of events in the historical evolution of our global society. Historical determinism pertains only to the finality of social evolution and the development of particular relational bonds among subsystems and operational principles, not to the process by which it attains that state. This means that these historical stages, or the sub-processes associated with them, are interchangeable and never the same, no matter how many times we start our history over again. However, the outcome of these processes is a single finality, assuming a sufficient amount of time is given to the entire process.

The struggle of man against man and man against nature: Theoretically, when the social organism reaches its optimum stability on global level, the tensions among its subsystems will reach their minimum level, which indicates that the struggle of man against man has ended. Perhaps by that time, there will be no divisions between societies, as they would be assimilated into one society called the global community. In this state, all human beings will accept their state of internal energy, which would be more or less equal, after a long history of struggle and violence against each other. Those of us who believe in the finality of social evolution and its inevitability, will conduct themselves in such a way as to assist the process, unlike those who fight the process, believing that they are capable of changing that finality. No one can change the finality of history and social evolution, but we can accelerate or decelerate its process.

Observing some historical events will show us how foolishly some leaders of the past have conducted policies that disregarded our historical finality. Before and during the World Wars I and II, European nations were divided economically, culturally, and racially. Today, these nations are united but the price they paid for their unification was the destruction of their cities and infrastructures, not to mention human casualties of over fifty million people. American wars in Japan, Korea and Vietnam, which resulted in the loss of millions of lives and the destruction of property and infrastructures, did not change the finality of their intended relationship as constituents of global community. Today, the United States is allied with its former enemies. The Cold War, between West and East, which lasted about seventy years, (started as early as 1919 with the establishment of communist international organization) ended after countless lives were lost in the ideological wars that were fought around the world. Today, Europeans and Americans are investing heavily in Russia, China and all Eastern European nations, trying to absorb them into a larger economic sphere to avoid future conflicts among them.

Isn't it time that we ask ourselves, *why go to war with a nation we will eventually become allies with?* Isn't it time to elect leaders who believe in the deterministic finality of our social evolution (dictated by natural laws) that can lead us to our destiny with minimum level of destruction and human casualties? The most dangerous leaders are those who believe that they can control the process of history and drive it to the destination of their choice. It is time to vote these leaders out of power in every community and elect new leaders with humanitarian vision not only for a select group of people but for all peoples of the world. It is time to share our knowledge with each other to shape a powerful social consciousness throughout the world and bring about necessary changes that can put an end to the struggle of man against man.

The struggle of man against nature however, will never come to an end because without the exploitation of nature no ordered structure would ever exist. Human beings will continue to explore their environment to understand its mysteries, tap into its resources, and learn how to control it in order to survive. Theoretically, there is no end to the discovery of nature's mysteries, and for man to have full control over his environment, he must continue to unveil the mysteries of nature, which may take him an eternity. Therefore, man's struggle with his environment will be forever.

Root causes of violence in the historical processes: If violence can take different forms, they are all the extension of one another with different degrees of frustration in the minds of the oppressed against their perpetrators. In violent acts between classes of people as between nations, both parties may feel victimized by the other, but in reality, there is only one victim and one perpetrator.

In the past, justification to invade and conquer other societies and territories was not needed, and the last thing in the mind of a conqueror was whether or not public opinion would support him. In the modern world however, public opinion is powerful and important, and usually does not support aggression against other nations without proper justification, which is a positive sign of progress in our social evolution. But today's leaders have also become smarter. They manufacture justifications to reshape the public opinion and win the support of their citizens for their aggressive policies. Unfortunately, like all other systems, living systems have evolved in such a way as to seek their lowest state of internal energy and fight to keep it that way. This is why our historical process has been so violent. But there is a controlling factor in this process that does not allow the violent behavior of subsystems to go on forever. This factor comes from the encompassing (high level) system. Since the encompassing system also seeks its lowest state of internal energy, it exerts its power upon its subsystems at all levels and force them to adopt equal states of internal energy. Global social organism as the encompassing system will eventually subdue the selfish behavior of all of its subsystems (societies, economic institutions, and individuals) and gradually emerge as a stable system or organism with little or no violence among its constituents. For the foreseeable future, however, violence will remain as a major force driving our social evolution and a key factor in settling the differences between the subsystems within the global social organism. We may ask, if violence is presented as the key factor in settling differences between human beings and societies, before they can proceed to the next stage of social evolution, then violence would become a law and a necessity to drive the social evolution, which means that it will be around for the entire process. This is not quite true. Self-awareness and consciousness in human beings and their societies dynamically change. Human beings are systems that continually explore their environment and improve their knowledge in every field of science, including their own biological and social evolution. Therefore, it is possible that one day, we may reach a level of knowledge and understanding regarding our social evolution to accept and submit to its inevitable finality. Knowing that this finality will happen one way or another, and it would make no sense fighting it. Through this wisdom, we may finally realize that the root cause of violent behavior in our social evolution that takes place in every subsystem level is due to inequality in that system level and closing these gaps can accelerate the process of social evolution on a global scale to its finality, which will bring lasting stability to our societies and to human life on our planet. Therefore, it is realistic to believe that peaceful reforms and social transformations will eventually replace violence as social evolution approaches its finality.

Marx's economic theory as it applies to closed and open systems: Marx's theory of history, which is based on political economic theory, did not actually materialize in capitalist economy as he predicted. This has produced some doubt in the validity of his theory in setting the course of history and the role that it plays in altering the relational bonds of human beings who are socioeconomically connected in their society. Marx's theory generally indicates that the accumulation of surplus value (generated by the working class) in the hands of capitalists tends to widen the economic gap between the rich and the poor, which will eventually result in a revolution of the working class that will overthrow the capitalist system and replace it with a socialist system. In this revolution, the working class will confiscate and own all the means of production, which will alter socioeconomic relations among people. Marx's economic theory, which predicts socioeconomic equality among members of a society, is in agreement with the proposed theory of history, which is driven by natural laws and systems theory. Critiques of Marx's economic theory state that most revolutions in third world societies, particularly during the Cold War, were premature and occurred prior to implementation of a capitalist and entrepreneurial system in their economy. At the same time, the working classes in capitalist societies have not been revolting against their economic system, as Marx predicted they would. Therefore, his economic theory must have been invalid.

But critiques of this theory have disregarded its true implications, which was meant to apply to closed economic systems, not the open ones. In an open economic system, external economic and political forces can become substantial factors that can easily derail the system from its natural course of evolution and produce a completely new set of outcomes. Subsequent to the Russian Revolution and the polarization of the world following World War II, both the Soviet Union and the West manipulated left and right wing revolutions in third world countries for geopolitical reasons, even though at the core, wars were being waged between economic systems. Despite the growing popularity of socialism among intellectuals and working classes in the capitalist societies, there were several reasons why capitalism survived, and avoided revolutions in capitalist societies. The two most important reasons were the adaptability of capitalism to the changing political environment and the realization of capitalist governments that if human rights abuses continue in their societies, revolution might follow. This adaptation came from continuous concession of the upper socioeconomic class to the demands of the working classes and resulted in reform policies that improved the working conditions and benefits of the working classes. This allowed the capitalist to stay in control of their societies a little longer. There is no need to mention that this historical move was predicted by the notion of dialectical materialism, inherent in the Marx's theory of history. The third reason why capitalism survived is becasue of the technological advances in automation that increases productivity and allows cheaper products to be available to the majority of the working class, improving their standard of life. Let us not forget that the insecure economic environment of capitalist system has also been partly responsible for the increased productivity, because workers have to work very hard to keep their jobs and wages. The fourth reason for the survival of capitalism is that most of the capitalist systems in the West were imperial powers that controlled a multitude of colonies that had valuable natural resources that generated a tremendous amount of wealth for the colonizers. This wealth was transported back to the imperialist societies and elevated their economies while leaving the colonies with very little to survive on. The pouring of wealth from colonies to imperialist societies and distribution of that imported wealth among the people made the working class of these societies, to some extent, content with their lives and prevented revolutions, despite an ever-increasing disparity between the rich and the average worker in these societies. In the meantime, the environment of the poverty-stricken colonies became ripe for left-wing intellectuals to organize the masses against their puppet governments who were collaborating with imperial powers in the diversion of their national wealth abroad, leaving their own population in poverty. To these intellectuals, who were inspired by Marx's teachings, capitalism was only a transitional stage toward socialism, and, therefore, it made no sense not to skip that stage and adopt socialism as the desired socioeconomic system.

The Soviet Union, which was pursuing its own goal of international communism, was a main sponsor and supporter of these revolutions around the world. Soviet leaders knew very well that by helping these colonies to liberate themselves, they would cut off the flow of wealth into imperialist societies that eventually would drive them into instability due to economic difficulties. Imperial powers who knew the Soviet plans, reacted vigorously in confronting these movements by installing brutal dictators in every one of their colonies to destroy every opposition to the state of the affairs in those colonies. Obviously, most of the historical events that took place in the world, particularly in third-world countries, at the time of Cold War were not directly related to the economic issues, but rather the political battle between the believers of two opposing economic systems that were trying to achieve world domination. The political battle between the capitalists and socialists during the Cold War led to major concessions on both sides and a shift of policies towards the center, although capitalists refused to admit this fact and arrogantly claimed victory. The cost of the survival of capitalism before and during the Cold War was the creation of poverty-stricken societies, many of which had been colonies whose resources and cheap labor had served for decades or longer to stabilize the capitalist societies. Even today, the cheap labor of China, India and many others, the colonies that have gained independence from the West, serves as a stabilizer of capitalist economies of the West.

According to a study, in the year 2002, the Saudi Arabian government, including 250 Saudi families, had approximately $600 billion in the U.S. in the form of investments and cash; it is estimated that this wealth is approaching $1 trillion today. This wealth, which is generated by the revenues from the sale of petroleum, instead of being used for the development of Saudi Arabia or investment in neighboring Arab countries, has been invested in U.S. economy, helping the economic growth of the U.S. and creating jobs for U.S. citizens. Saudi Arabia is not the only wealthy society that contributes to the stability of the capitalist economy of the West, but most of the oil rich countries located in the Persian Golf and Arabian Sea. There are thousands of rich people around the world with no national interest that would prefer to keep their money in American, British and Swiss banks rather than reinvest in their own economies and create jobs for their people.

The pouring of foreign capital into Western societies that has helped the growth and stability of Western economies has also been responsible for minimizing the tension between the working class and the capitalists in Western societies, despite the widening gap of wealth among social classes. In return, this created a much bigger problem, which is a huge prosperity gap between the rich and poor nations, so wide that the tension is exhibiting itself in the form of terrorism today. This phenomenon is nothing short of an economic class struggle between prosperous and non-prosperous nations, which is taking place on a higher system level in the hierarchy of social system (the global society), analogous to socioeconomic class struggle among members of a society. Fighting terrorism without taking action to minimize the prosperity gap between the rich and poor nations will not root out this phenomenon. In contrary, it will create more resentment among the populations of poor societies toward the rich, that will help terrorist organizations to attract and recruit more young men and women who are willing to die for their cause.

There is no doubt that Marx's theory of history would have been exactly as he predicted it in a closed economic system. But when economic systems are open to one another and influence each other's evolutionary process on all subsystem levels, it is more difficult to predict the outcomes of their interactions. It is also difficult to predict how and when the historical processes will shift from one system level to another to achieve equalization. Globalization is the last stage of the growth of the social organism on earth. Its economy will become a closed economic system once again, with subsystems struggling for equality at their respective levels. This time, economic class struggle will take place at many different system levels much more complicated process than Marx envisioned, but the principle of the struggle will remain the same. (A quick reminder to those who believe that Marx's theory of history based on socioeconomic equality was unscientific—must remember that this theory is supported by the laws of nature and systems theory. Moreover, social evolution has not come to its end yet.)

The Cold War and its impact on the socioeconomic development of East and West: We who live in the United States, often hear from our leaders about the greatness of our political system, which is based on democratic principles and policies that have brought justice to our people and economic prosperity to our society. That is not quite true. When we review the history of U.S., or any other society that claims to have installed democratic principles in its governing philosophy without carnage, we learn that none of the democratic reforms in these societies was instituted through peaceful processes but rather through violence. In the U.S., for example, the human rights violations started with the genocide of the Native Americans, followed by the era of slavery, and the Civil War. Later in the nineteenth century, exploitation of workers led to the formation of labor unions. In the twentieth century, segregation and discrimination against blacks and other minorities led to the civil rights movement. It has cost a great deal of suffering and pain for the people of the U.S. to achieve the level of justice they have today.

Civil rights and labor movements in U.S., during the first half of the twentieth century, were not instigated and organized by the internal forces only, but influenced by the socialist ideology propagating from the East, after October Revolution in Russia. During this period, the socialist way of life appealed to many oppressed people living within the capitalist systems of the West, which were far from being democratic societies. Western societies, controlled by the wealthy, who were under internal and external pressures for democratization, had no alternative but to change or have a revolution on their hands, which would have resulted in confiscation of their wealth and nationalization of the means of production they owned. In reality, communism and the Cold War forced socioeconomic evolution of the capitalist societies of the West into a new direction and made them more democratic. Achieving such levels of democratization in capitalist societies, in the absence of communism, would have been through much more complicated processes, with greater sacrifices and it would have not been accomplished in that time frame. We can imagine that capitalists would have not softened their position on progressive forces within their societies as easily as they did during the Cold War. Such resistance on their behalf could have polarized their societies into two socioeconomic classes, resulting in communist revolutions in the end.

Thus, it is reasonable to believe that as soon as the first communist revolution had taken place in one of the industrialized societies of the West, it could have easily propagated to others and change the course of history completely.

However, decades after the first socialist revolution in the world (Russian Revolution 1917), most European societies have adopted a middle ground between communism and capitalism in conducting their social and economic affairs. The question is: can the West take all the credit of choosing its own political process to this stage of democratization without giving credit to those forces (socialist movements across the globe) who pushed them into this evolutionary path? Can we imagine what would have been the course of socioeconomic evolution and political process in the West without a communist Soviet Union exporting and sponsoring socialist movements throughout the world, and being strong enough to stand up against the West? In addition, if the socialist revolution in Russia had never taken place, would the Europe or the U.S. have been the first communist societies trying to export their revolution to the rest of the world?

The answers to these questions are not easy. Analyzing this issue of hypothetical history from the systems point of view shows that the inequality within a system produces stress among its members and elevates the system's internal energy, making it unstable. Natural laws, which apply to all systems (living and non-living) and their evolutionary processes, are beyond human control and are in command of the processes that take place within a system. These laws dictate that systems seek optimum stability in their evolutionary process. This is only possible when their internal state of energy is at a minimum level, which is possible only when their subsystems stop exchanging energy with each other, meaning that they hold an equal amount of internal energy. Therefore, when some of the politicians in the West claim that the West won the Cold War and defeated communism, they seem very naïve in their perception of historical processes.

In reality, what happened during the Cold War was that both camps softened their positions towards each other by actual changes that took place in their societies, after decades of conflict and interaction with each other (energy exchanges from the system's point of view), accompanied by the loss of millions of lives (dissipated energy). At the end, leaders of the two sides realized that they were much closer to an understanding than ever before, meaning that the level of tension had been reduced among them, by qualitative changes that had taken place in both systems. Moreover, the dangerous path of star wars and implementation of new weapon systems in the space had to be halted, because the inclusion of these weapon systems to the weapons arsenal, were starting to reduce the retaliatory response times for both sides to fractions of a minute. If irresponsible leaders had been allowed to continue along that dangerous path, the whole world would have been on the edge of a war, triggered by an accidental circumstance or miscalculation that would have wiped out our civilization with no advance warning. After both East and West realized the doomsday was waiting for them in that evolutionary process, they agreed to peaceful coexistence. They killed all the labels, such as capitalism and communism that had annoyed them for decades, replaced them with other labels such as market economy and economic justice, and signed a non-intervention treaty. But do such agreements stop the process of equalization at all subsystem levels in our social evolution? Do treaties change the intended goals of the global social organism, which still wants to achieve its lowest state of internally energy and optimum stability? Not really. The only thing that will change is that the global social organism will achieve its goals through different processes and at different times.

From the system's point of view, the global social organism has not yet reached its optimum stability. Energy exchanges among members of societies, and the societies themselves, independent of the labels we choose for their processes, are still in progress and unstoppable. In the human body, the brain controls all of the biological activities and treats all of the cells and organs equally and indiscriminately; otherwise, the body would have not functioned optimally. Members of the society must also be treated in the same way; otherwise, the society would not be healthy, optimally stable and operationally efficient. The process of socioeconomic justice will not only continue its progress within each society, but will also continue on a global scale, among societies as well.

To conclude this section, we can argue that the West did not really "win" the Cold War, as some western historians like to believe. In reality, the two sides compromised and terminated their hostility after numerous qualitative changes that had taken place within their societies. When we look at the types of governments that European societies had prior to the October revolution in Russia, and the nature of these governments at the termination of the Cold War, we see that most of these governments were either ran by socialist or social democrats. We cannot deny the impact that socialism has had on the socioeconomic evolution and the social consciousness on the global scale. This impact will last into the future and socialism will continue to play a central role in future socioeconomic developments.

Is communism dead or in hibernation? The main goal of ideologies such as socialism and communism, as well as labor unions and civil rights movements, has been to correct unjust socioeconomic relations between people and to eliminate the treatment of blacks and other minorities, as practiced by some governments. Human societies and the global social consciousness have undergone tremendous changes in their attitudes toward slavery and the establishment of a safety net for the working class (even within the capitalist systems) just in case a worker loses his job or suffered from a disability. A good example of this was the participation of U.S.A., once a practitioner of slavery, in the international campaign to end the apartheid regime of the South Africa, to eliminate forever the last stand of slavery in modern history. Thanks to all ideologies and political campaigns conducted for equality among humans, particularly during the last century.

From system's point of view, however, what matters at the conclusion of a political process is the outcome that would take the system one step closer to its optimum stability (by attaining equality among its subsystems), regardless of how it was achieved and under what political label. Labels such as *communism* strike fear and paranoia in the hearts and minds of capitalists, but labels such as *campaign for equality* do not. Why should the social organism concern itself with the labels, as long as both political processes provide the same outcome that it wishes to attain? Today, communism is in hibernation, and due to the collapse of the Soviet Union, which was the nurturer of this ideology from theoretical, ethical, and financial points of view, it is no longer supported. This has created a great deal of concern and disappointment within intellectual circles around the world as to why such regression in the historical process had to take place because it may undermine all the accomplishments and sacrifices that had been made over decades for the benefit of the working classes. The intellectual circles will eventually come out of their shock with an explanation for these developments and find a new thought process to continue their struggle for equality, as social organism desires. Today, capitalism may be under the illusion that it is in control of history and has buried the communism. Capitalism may have killed the label of the political process, but it did not kill the process itself. Capitalism did not kill communism, but merely forced it into hibernation. If those in control of history develop a compassion for humanity and the natural environment, they will keep this giant in hibernation forever. If they do not, they will be haunted by it once again. This giant may not come back under the same label or flag, but social organism does not care, as long as its intended goals are achieved through any substitute process. Let us not forget that it is not always the subsystems (human beings) that set the rules of social evolution for the system (social organism) itself, quite in contrary, the social organism is capable of manipulating its subsystems to achieve its intended goals.

The ideological void after the end of the Cold War: After the end of the Cold War, which resulted in the breakup of the Soviet Union and abandonment of the communist ideology, a great deal of disappointment and disillusionment was felt among intellectuals throughout the world. Alienated from their belief systems, these intellectuals were (and still are) looking for a substitute ideology that has a solid scientific foundation that promotes the notion of equality in the fabric of society. Such ideology can only be constructed by using the undisputed natural laws and their implications in the system's evolutionary process. Treating the social organism as a self-organizing system that is acquiescent to natural laws, we may apply these laws to its evolutionary process and predict its deterministic finality. A finality based on equality among its subsystems, each at its respective level, as we have extensively discussed throughout this book. Such an ideology supported by the laws of nature would naturally embrace humanitarianism and internationalism, as they have always been synonymous with equality. Bear in mind that establishing equality among subsystems is not the only objective of the social organism in its evolutionary process. This system also tries to establish a meaningful relationship with the environment that supports its structure. At the same time, that it strives to improve its operational efficiency and restructure itself organizationally to resemble the human body's structural organization.

Based on these notions, we may be able to predict some of the properties of the global social organism in the final stages of its evolutionary process. We will have a global community that is assimilated and homogenized culturally, economically, and racially. It will be a community in which people will enjoy the same standard of life, be treated equally, and participate equally in advancing human knowledge and technology. At the macro system level, this organism will be centrally controlled and regulated to achieve optimum operational efficiency. This organism will also establish a harmonious relationship with its environment and will monitor its own growth in order to avoid unnecessary abuse of its environment and endangerment to its own life.

These are only few properties of the social organism nearing its finality. We can concede that there is a wide range of processes, all involved in the realization of these properties that can be assisted by human involvement. Consequently, the most appropriate political ideology for progressive movements is an ideology that supports all of the properties of the social organism at its finality, as predicted by the laws of nature and evolutionary laws pertaining to the living organisms. For example, strengthening the bonds among nations through international agreements must be supported, since unification and harmonization on the international level can only be achieved through a single central control mechanism and a single set of laws. Energy-producing technologies and energy resources, whether they are gas, oil, or nuclear, must be globalized and shared by all nations; otherwise, they may become major obstacles to the integration process and pose a danger to our civilization. Appropriate use of energy-producing technologies in conjunction with a particular climate must be enforced to minimize environmental pollution and ecological damage. Science and technology must be shared among nations in the global community, as being a human heritage that has been handed from one nation to another over the course of our history. Eradication of hunger and disease and providing a secure environment for humans must become a priority because it will promote rational behavior both on human and societal levels. The social organism's evolutionary process is composed of numerous sub-processes that help the organism to achieve all of the properties associated with its final state. Guardians of the integration process must be watching for anti-integration processes that would damage or reverse earlier accomplishments. Anti-globalization and isolationism are ideologies that are doomed to fail in the integration process of history. They can only prevail in the disintegration process, in which there are not enough energy resources left on this planet to support the global structure, which is not the case at this time. In general, there is no better sequence of historical processes and stages, or preferred order of sub-processes; therefore, any combination in any sequence is acceptable, as long as the sequence is in line with historical evolution and leads the social organism to its predetermined finality. When a sub-process has been initiated within the historical process, it may or may not be completed before the historical process switches to other sub-processes. However, this does not mean that the evolving social organism will never come back to that sub-process to complete it at a later time. Similar to the unconcluded process of socialism that has been interrupted temporarily. Constructing a political ideology to guide us in taking an active role in the process of social evolution should be based on the realization of the properties associated with social organism's predetermined state of finality, which are enforced upon the social organism by the laws of nature and evolutionary laws of living systems.

Could the Cold War ever return? Most nations need a military force to defend their territory from aggression by other nations. Nowadays, most military forces are composed of highly sophisticated weapon systems and rely heavily on their effectiveness in the battlefield. But due to competition in weapons development, most advanced weapon systems lose their effectiveness within a few years or become obsolete. Most new developments come from the advanced nations that try to stay ahead of their rivals not only to protect themselves, but also to expand their domain of political and economic influence. This puts these societies in charge of the markets for the sale of their products and services in both commercial and military sectors. As new weapon systems are developed and proved effective, the stockpile of the outdated weapon systems must be replaced. But what do these countries do with their outdated weapons? Obviously, they try to sell them to other nations, as long as these weapons do not pose a danger to themselves if someday their buyers turn against them. As one would expect, creating an atmosphere of hostility in the regions where these buyers live and make them further insecure, will certainly help to boost the demand for these weapons. The funds generated by the sale of these weapons, will then be allocated to the development of a newer generation of weapon systems, and the cycle goes on and on. Since the security of every nation is, unfortunately, tied to its military force, it becomes crucial to keep this segment of the industry financially strong, so that research and development in this field continue. It is a well-known fact that the military-industrial complex thrives even more when world circumstances are a threat to peace, by getting larger number of military contracts from the government. If this sector of the industry is supported by the government, which is true in most societies, then budgets are not a worry and the manufacturers do not interfere with the policies of their state. However, when the weapons manufacturers are privately owned companies, then they have no choice but to engage in the political process by bribing government officials, conspiring with them against their citizens, and designing foreign policies to best serve their interests. As we know, the best environment for the survival of weapons manufacturers is a hostile and confrontational environment. This makes their involvement in the design of foreign policy a logical sense, as they create one enemy after another and confront them afterwards. In other words, weapons manufacturers become provocateurs of hostility and war.

A good example of this is the United States. During the Cold War, the threat of communism was a great justification for huge military budgets. After Cold War ended, U.S. lost its main excuse for justifying the allocation of huge sums of money for military projects. That is why the "axis of evil" was invented. Today, military-industrial complex representatives are either government officials or have close affiliations with the government. These officials are heavily involved in formulating the U.S. foreign policy by defining the role and relationship of the U.S. with other societies in the world. It seems that part of that grand strategy in the new century is to put the U.S. in charge of the world's affairs by building an unmatched military power. It is also part of the same plan that the U.S. should periodically demonstrate its power to its rivals in an actual battlefield by picking on one of these evils. First of all, this would allow these weapons to be tested in a battlefield before large orders are placed with these corporations, and second, it would leave no room for miscalculation of U.S. military power by its rivals. Clearly, the last thing the weapons manufacturers and government officials have in mind is the loss of tens of thousands of innocent lives in the conflicts they create, as long as the outcome of the process results in international subordination to U.S. policies, which paves the way for future economic gains for U.S. corporations throughout the world.

This behavior on the part of the U.S. is being watched with resentment by the rest of the world, and if it continues, it would result in formation of alliances against U.S. by almost every society that feels threatened by U.S. aggression, aimed not only at their economic interests but also at their cultural heritage. If resentment continues to grow, these alliances might expand to include the terrorist organizations that are currently operating independently. Unfortunately, U.S. policy planners who are influenced by war profiteers have developed a shortsighted view of world affairs. They think that they can fix any problem, militarily, as it arises. If the Cold War ever returns, it will be because of the policies of U.S. and its lack of respect for the rest of the world. It will be because other nations would refuse to abide by the rules of the U.S. and its denunciation of international laws. It will be because other nations refuse to take a shot of "American social fabric DNA" in their veins and transform themselves culturally and economically to please the U.S. Next time, U.S. will not find many allies by its side to fight the cold war that it creates. U.S. foreign policy planners must be aware that continuous engagement in war with other nations, in time, will erode U.S. power both economically and politically. This will provide an opportunity for second powers to rise to superpower position and push back the U.S. as a second power.

An argument regarding the efficiency of centralized and decentralized economic systems: Theoretically, when a system is optimally efficient at the highest level, this necessitates that the operations of all subsystems down to the lowest level in the hierarchy be optimized as well. However, when all subsystems are optimized at their respective levels, it does not necessitate that the system itself be at its optimum efficiency. We can clarify this argument by the following example. Let us assume that a system is composed of two individuals, each considered a subsystem. The task of one individual is to dig a hole in the ground as efficiently as possible, and the task of the other is to fill it up as quickly as he can. At the end of the day, both individuals have spent a great deal of energy digging and filling the hole. Each individual has accomplished a great deal, but the system encompassing both has accomplished nothing.

We have been taught that a decentralized economic system brings good things to consumers, such as new and innovative products at lower cost, plus better services, and over all, this economic philosophy is more efficient when it is compared to centrally controlled economies. However, what we are not told is that there is a huge cost associated with a decentralized economic system that is not visible at the first glance. Let us imagine a product that is manufactured by a multitude of companies, each competing for a larger market share by reducing the price of their products and at the same time, trying to provide a better product to their customers. A better product needs research and development, the cost of which gradually becomes overwhelming to some of the competing companies, as their profit margins start to shrink due to fierce price competition. Eventually, some of these companies will no longer be able to sustain the cost of research and development, and will be driven out of business by companies with greater financial strength. What we have lost here are huge investments of money and time. Skills acquired by the employees of these failing companies will most likely go to waste, and dismissed employees will soon begin a new round of job searching, relocation and acquiring new skills. As we know, this pattern is not limited to one industry alone, but the entire economy. At the end, those who survive this unhealthy competition and monopolize the markets will raise the prices of their products, giving consumers better products, but not necessarily cheaper ones.

The purpose of this example was to show that a decentralized economy can be inefficient on the macro level. In the next example, we will show the contradictory logic that the capitalist economy applies at two different system levels and yet claims that centrally controlled economies cannot be efficient. To understand this a little better, let us consider the operation of a corporation. Can we imagine what would be the outcome or the output of a corporation if the business were not centrally controlled and its employees were left on their own to plan independently and in disharmony? We can surely agree that a decentralized operation in a corporation would miserably fail. If this is the case, then why is it that in a capitalist economy, central control of the economy is regarded as dysfunctional, while the same notion has been rigorously researched and applied to the subsystem levels?

If an economic theory is valid, it should be valid for all system levels, including the economy at the macro level. Knowing that in a capitalist economy, subsystems are not in harmonious relationship and compete for survival by trying to destroy their competition (the so-called rule of the jungle), it is hard to provide a compelling argument on the theoretical basis that these economic systems are more efficient than systems optimized on the top. If so, then the big question in front of us is, why did centrally controlled economies adopted by communist states fall so far behind their capitalist rivals in terms of productivity and improvement of the standard of life for their people? Was it because their economy was mismanaged at the micro or subsystem level? Was it because the leaders of socialist societies were so deeply caught up in their ideological battle with the West and in exporting revolution that they did not see they were falling behind in the economic race? Was it because human nature in its current evolutionary stage is incompatible with communist way of life and Marxist-Leninist philosophy? Or was it perhaps because the ordinary people started seeing the corruption in the highest level of government officials, and this made them lose faith in their leaders and enthusiasm for their revolution?

The answers may be "all of the above." To show some of the poor ideological judgments made by the leaders of Soviet states, let us turn to further examples. When the computer was first invented in the West, Soviet leaders and Communist Party ideologues perceived it as a machine that was invented to replace workers. For this reason, they opposed it categorically. In a state-run economy, where new jobs could have easily been created for workers who lost their jobs to computers, rejecting computers was a very poor judgment on behalf of the party ideologues. Instead, they should have embraced the idea to improve their economic efficiency and its output without having a single individual out of the job. Western management techniques were also rejected because they were seen as exploitative, a taboo from an ideological point of view. In China, during the leadership of Mao Zedong, no farmer was allowed to have more that ten pigs or he would have been considered a capitalist. Highly educated individuals were sent to farms for many years so they would learn to empathize with the harsh work of manual labor before they could get back to their real professions. They could have been much more effective if allowed to use their education to help the state and the economy. These were just a few examples of ideological misconceptions of socialism by the leaders and ideologues at the time. On the political side, the Soviet Union spent part of its gross domestic product (GDP) to export and support revolutions throughout the world. It also supported the economies of countries that joined the socialist camp, the money that could have been used to further develop the economies of Soviet states. In addition, communist governments, particularly Russia, were forced into defensive positions by subversive activities the West sponsored and conducted inside these countries to destabilize their political and economic system. It took a great deal of energy for the socialist and communist states to defend themselves against these outside threats.

There were also positive aspects to these economies and many great achievements on the macro level that affected the lives of the people and the strength of these nations. For example, Russia was able to rise from the ashes of the World War II and become a superpower only within 30 years. Something that none of the European capitalist societies that claimed to have efficient economic systems were able to achieve, which demonstrates the operational efficiency of a centrally controlled economy. Free (government-sponsored) education in Russia produced a great many educated people who built Russian industry in every segment of the Russian economy. Allocations of funds to prioritize investment in basic industries, such as electric power generation, steel mills, mining and metallurgy, cement factories, housing and health care, and in many other fields, resulted in the creation of a virtually self-reliant economy that would have not been possible in the post-World War II without a centrally-controlled economy. However, at the end of the Cold War after decades of ideological and political war between East and West, the economies of West turned out to be more prosperous than those of the East. It could have been the other way around if the leaders of the state-run economies had not fallen into traps of ideological dogma, if they had adopted and embraced new management techniques and rewarded their hard working people and overachievers. Their economies could have been more efficient if they had demanded that their economic systems at the micro-level continually renew themselves to reach higher levels of efficiency and productivity while the government was applying the same concepts at the macro economic level. Marxist-Leninist doctrine did not succeed in bringing revolution to the industrial West, but it did cause significant socioeconomic reform that made Western societies to place a greater value on humanity, equality, and workers' rights, which produced positive results in strengthening their economies and left those who originated the idea in poorer economic standing. The communist leaders and their ideologues underestimated human nature and mankind's unyielding genetic memory formed by millions of years of evolutionary process. In China, they thought they could change man's instinctive behavior within a few generations through the Cultural Revolution. The glorification of work with no incentive promoted by the Cultural Revolution worked well for about fifty years, but has lost ground to human nature as Chinese people learned about capitalism. Citizens of communist states took the basic services that their governments provided to them for granted. They felt too secure, and in the absence of additional financial rewards for overachievers and outstanding performances, the work force became lazy, demoralized, and unproductive. Nevertheless, there is no doubt, that the Soviet economy was more efficient at the macro level when compared to the economies of Western societies at the same level.

When compared to the behavior of humans living thousands of years ago, the behavior of modern humans has not changed significantly. As we have argued earlier, due to shortages of life support systems throughout our evolutionary process, we have learned to save and accumulate for our future security. This fact is not only evident from our behavior as dictated by our genetic memory, but also by the adaptation of our bodies, which store excessive and unused energy in the form of fat in case food would not be available in the immediate future. Human survival today depends as much on natural environment as before. However, there is a new element added to his modern environment that comes from the economic system that he is part of.

The life support systems in the modern human environment that is connected with the economic system manifest themselves into one thing—money. With money, we can obtain shelter, food, medicine, a greater degree of freedom and every service imaginable for the support of life and security. In an economic system such as capitalism that is unpredictable and unreliable, humans may feel as insecure as they feel in their natural environment. This explains why, humans struggle to get rich and accumulate wealth in a capitalist economy. In general, no one desires an insecure environment, but because we have evolved in one, we are capable of adapting to it. Capitalist economy creates the insecure environment that we are familiar with but not necessarily like it. A human being surviving in such an environment will work harder and be more productive in order to take charge of his own security because no one else will do it for him. This is in contrast to the environment created by socialist economies, in which states provide unconditional security to the people and then expect them to work hard and be productive. As we have argued earlier, capitalism is not managed well at the top-level system, and as a result is chaotic and far from efficient due to adversarial and inharmonious relationships among its subsystems. On the subsystem level, however, namely in a corporation, the creation of harmony and teamwork is strongly encouraged and emphasized by the board of directors, which is the central control system of the corporation. We can reason from this fact that there is still an opportunity to make capitalism a more efficient and humane economic system by creating greater harmony and central planning at the top-level. In the human body, a few organs have duplicates, but they are not in competition with each other. They cooperate and work in harmony to enhance the operational efficiency of the body. The harmonious relationship between economic institutions on the subsystem level brings efficiency to the economy as a whole, and a prerequisite for that is to have a centrally planned economy. It seems that China may have found this magical blend of capitalism with communism in its new economic model, which has led to economic growth surpassing the growth of any economy in the West, for over two decades. This demonstrates that China's economic model is not only efficiency at microeconomic level but also at macroeconomic level. Capitalist economies, steered by deterministic forces of social evolution, will gradually gravitate toward central planning to satisfy the social organism's search for optimum operational efficiency, while keeping their subsystems motivated by financial rewards as the best compromise to deal with human nature for the time being.

Is the competitive behavior of social systems constructive or destructive?

Competitive behavior has been considered a healthy and acceptable behavior in most cultures and economic systems and a key to the success of both individuals and social system's economic advancement and growth. But what is the origin of competitive behavior? In their evolutionary process, human beings, like other animals, have learned to compete so they can control and protect the scarce resources of their territories upon which their survival depended. Modern human beings who are not so pressed to find the basics of their survival needs, continue to exhibit competitive behavior in every aspect of their lives. These behaviors are also exhibited in the higher-level social systems as human characteristics transcend to that system level. As a result, social systems and some of their subsystems, such as corporations, engage in competitive behavior to control their environment and its resources. To these corporations, markets are their environment and money its resource, so it is not surprising that competition and expansion to capture larger shares of markets has become the primary corporate goal and a source for their growth and expansion.

The *market economy*, which is the dominant economic theory of the current stage of social evolution was founded on the principle of capitalism and is extremely competitive at all of its subsystem levels. As discussed earlier, this economic system could be inefficient and chaotic at all macro economic levels, which includes the economies at the society and global levels. This can be observed clearly from the instability of stock markets, bankruptcies of corporations due to fierce price competition, and bankruptcies on a national level in third-world societies because of their inability to pay their debts to the World Bank and International Monetary Fund. In general, the market economy has created tremendous pain and chaos in the operation of the global social organism, especially for underdeveloped societies. However, one of the positive by-products of this economic system, which comes from the greed of multinational corporations and financial institutions, is that it acts as a catalyst to facilitate the integration of social organisms on a global scale. But would this economic system last when social organism grows on a global scale?

Economic theories evolve as quick as social systems advance in their evolutionary process, and we can be certain that when the entire world unites and forms a single global organism, out of necessity new economic philosophies will emerge, to bring harmony to the global economic system and to replace the unhealthy and destructive competitive behaviors of its subsystems. Harmony requires cooperation and collaboration—not competition—among the constituents of an organism, and this will be the theme of any new economic theory, when global social organism matures in its evolutionary process. Therefore, it is only logical to presume that in the long run, economic competition will subside and the few winners in the international arena will emerge to take responsibility for providing a single product or service worldwide. These economic institutions will be managed under tight regulations set by the international community to protect the rights of consumers and allow reasonable profits for these institutions. It is at this stage that a central control system will monitor all economic activities and invest in new ventures and enterprises in a controlled manner rather than through the old, chaotic process. The notion of central control of economic systems that was once adopted by socialist governments but did not produce the expected results will eventually prevail to bring about stability and efficiency to all subsystem and system levels. Its success this time around will be based on the implementation of new management techniques, the emergence of technologies that control and supervise economic activities at every system level, and take human nature and his genetic memories into consideration. After all, human nature cannot be changed by slogans over night, and the designers of a global economy must consider that fact as they create a dynamic and stable economic system. Creativity and hard work that are financially rewarded in a capitalist economy do not necessarily need a hostile environment to materialize. Similar results can be achieved by combining smaller financial rewards with greater recognition in a centrally controlled economy. The only things to watch for in a harmonized and centrally controlled economy, is to design a central control system that remains dynamic and aggressive in implementing new ventures and ideas and to prevent it from becoming stagnant.

The chaotic economic system we have today on the macro system level and the destructive power of competition (at least in some of its aspects) are transitional stages toward economic systems that are based on cooperation and the establishment of harmony and stability in the global economy. These transitions will start taking place gradually as global social organism starts maturing in its evolutionary process.

Underdeveloped countries and those responsible for them: Underdeveloped countries are countries whose economies are heavily dependent upon the support of advanced economies for materials, equipment, machinery, and all advanced technical services. These countries either have no resources of their own to attract imperial powers to colonize them (in which in this case they are left alone to live their tribal lives) or they (more usually) have one or two resources in abundance, which causes advanced nations to enter into fierce competition to control them. In underdeveloped countries, only a small percentage of the population benefits from a higher standard of life, while majority of people live in poverty and struggle every day to survive. The economies of these societies run into serious problems if advanced nations decide to interrupt their services or place the countries under international sanctions, which is the best way to keep them under control. The policy of control further extends into the life of an underdeveloped nation when an imperial power installs a puppet government or a dictator with a trained army to suppress any opposition or uprising on the part of the rest of the population, which may disagree with the policies of the puppet government—giving away their resources. The puppet government gives the imperial power ultimate authority and the final say-so in the affairs of the state, which protects the interests of the imperial power rather than the interests of the native population. The imperial power in control of the country's resources pays an incredibly low price for the raw materials simply because the colony lacks the know-how to extract and process the resources itself, nor does it have the authority to sell them in the international marketplace. The imperial power not only gains all the profit generated by the sale of the colony's resources, but also it gains the political upper hand in controlling other powers that may need the colony's resources.

However, this is not the end of the story of robbing the resources of people living in the colonies of imperial powers. Let us explore what happens to the funds generated by the sale of the raw material. The puppet government that enjoys a luxurious life protected by the imperial power has no alternative but to listen to every instruction coming from imperial power, or face the consequence of being removed from power by a *coup d'état*. One of these instructions is regarding, what the puppet government should do with the funds generated by the sale of the raw material. These funds usually end up being invested in the economy of the imperial power or deposited into its banks in accounts bearing the names of officials of the puppet government. The money is thus circulating in the economy of the imperial power and helping its economy to grow while the underdeveloped nation's economy remains in turmoil. Moreover, most of the people that the puppet government trains in higher levels of education end up fleeing their homes and going to the imperial country or other advanced nations, serving them rather than their own people, simply because they refuse to live in an environment of political suffocation created by their corrupt government and supported by the imperial power. This leaves the rest of the population of the colony angry and helpless because they know they have no control over their own destiny and the affairs of their society. The outcome of such repressive policies leaves behind a struggling economy in the underdeveloped nation while helping the economy of the imperial power to flourish.

During the Cold War, the economies of underdeveloped societies took another hit and eroded further when they fell victim to international politics and the ideological battles fought in their territories. Among these battles were internal power struggles between factions affiliated with various imperial powers, revolutions, and coup after coup, most of which were influenced and manipulated by superpowers.

Within the last few decades, when the socialist way of life impacted the social fabric of the capitalist societies around the world and gained more rights for the working classes in these societies, such as social security, unemployment benefits and health care. The cost of labor in these societies went up, which lowered the profit margins on manufactured goods and services. As a result, a new trend started to emerge in which the capitalists of the imperial powers started to look for cheaper labor elsewhere and began to invest in underdeveloped societies, which lacked labor laws, so that they could benefit from larger surplus values generated by native labor.

Today, cheap labor and new markets have become new sources for the generation of wealth for advanced nations and their multinational corporations. This trend may be positive for the economic development of the underdeveloped nations because corporations seem not to recognize borders and nationalities anymore. One thing they will never give up doing, however, is the policy of control in their territories. Natural resources, raw materials, and investments made by these corporations must be protected by all means possible. That is why today, in every corner of this world, the imperial powers have military bases with significant numbers of personnel and advanced military equipment, to allow them to strike anywhere within minutes or hours, if an undesirable political process threaten their investments or regions under their control.

For centuries, these policies of domination and control have been resented by the populations of underdeveloped nations, resulting in an unprecedented uprisings and resistance that is widely sympathized among the population of these nations, or at least within regions of similar cultures, and has created the new phenomenon of international terrorism. Underdeveloped nations are determined to free themselves from political captivity by any means possible, even if they have to resort to violence and terrorism. But why is it that imperial powers do not let go of these societies if they have to pay such a hefty price defending them? The answer is that the price for letting them go is even higher. Imperial economic systems, operating mainly on the basis of capitalism, have avoided instability at home by feeding themselves on the wealth pouring in from their colonies and offshore investments. If it were not for the influx of this wealth to the economies of the imperial powers, the ever-increasing gap between the rich and the poor would have driven these economies to instability, resulting in a class struggle that rich would have lost. This influx of wealth has been helping the rich get richer while keeping the working class from sliding into poverty, which has helped to maintain a stable economy.

But someone has paid for the economic stability of developed nations: the underdeveloped societies and their people. Repressive economic policies have led to the largest prosperity gap between advanced and underdeveloped nations in our history. Due to the increased level of tension between rich and poor nations, these systems need to exchange energy and equalize. This is done through international terrorism, which is a class struggle between underdeveloped (non-prosperous) and developed (prosperous) nations on a higher subsystem level in the hierarchy of social system, with global social system being at the top. The main purpose of this struggle is to equalize economic prosperity among nations, even though on the surface it may seem to be a religious or cultural clash between civilizations.

In earlier discussions, we argued that one of the reasons why Marx's prediction of the socioeconomic clash between classes did not happen in industrialized nations was due to the influx of wealth pouring into these societies, which means that the openness of these economies saved them from falling into chaos and socioeconomic transformation. Let us imagine, that for decades to come, the historical processes focus on equalization of prosperity levels among nations until this gap is closed and a global economy is ran on the basis of capitalism. In these circumstances, the global economy will become a closed system and a true environment in which to examine Marx's economic theory as it applies to socioeconomic classes. This time, capitalism will find no external system to exploit in order to stabilize itself and escape its destiny. At this stage of social evolution, the social organism will focus on equalization among socioeconomic classes on a global scale, thus paving the way to a true socialist way of life on our planet.

Let us now examine the behaviors of social organisms from the perspective of systems theory. Looking back at the history of the world, none of the classical empires—Roman, Egyptian, Turkish, Assyrian, or Persian—behaved any differently than the modern empires. Like the empires of recent history, they also dominated, enslaved, and exploited their surrounding nations. Ironically, today some of the ancient empires are underdeveloped nations struggling to free themselves from the political, cultural, and economic captivity imposed upon them by modern empires. Empires have risen and fallen throughout history, and it is only a matter of time before the modern empires fall as the old ones fell. Systems and living organisms, such as human beings and their societies, that have the lowest state of internal energy have always resisted the concept of equalization demanded by the top-level system, in this case the global social organism. These living organisms continue to seek an even lower state of internal energy by passing the high-energy states to the other systems. To achieve this, they continue to enslave, oppress, exploit, and pollute other systems. The lowest state of internal energy in living organisms is synonymous with prosperity, wealth, and control of the environment. Based on these arguments, it seems that we can justify the behavior of the rich against the poor and the powerful against the weak by simply proclaiming that their behavior is only natural and supported by the laws of nature. This may be true, but these same laws give supremacy to the top-level system in the hierarchy, the global social organism, which imposes equality among its subsystems through violent or nonviolent processes, whichever works, to minimize its own state of internal energy. Due to resistance to equalization at the subsystem level, the global social organism is left with no alternative but to impose violent processes upon its subsystems in order to achieve its goals. It seems that the designed-in selfishness of systems, which include human beings and their societies, has led us to all of the chaotic and violent evolutionary processes in our history and has been a good justification for everything that empires have done to their colonies and underdeveloped nations and what some people have done to other people.

Yes, we have fallen victim to the system design, but are we capable of changing it? Are we capable of moderating the violent processes that the global social organism is imposing them upon us and all other sub-organisms? Are we capable of responding to the demands of the global social organism and achieve a state of equality among ourselves through non-violent processes? Violent evolutionary processes for the integration of living organisms do not have to be the first choice for global social organism, if all humans and social organisms understand the finality of the process. As the evolution of the social organism and history as a science become better understood, this knowledge base will change the attitude and the consciousness of humans and social organisms, and make them more receptive to the idea of equality as an inevitable reality of historical process. At the same time, subsystems will become less resistant to the intended goal of social integration on a global scale and may even assist its process in that direction. Imagine the day when the advanced nations and empires, under the pressure of public opinion, acknowledge their contribution in the stagnation of economic development of underdeveloped nations, and to end their hostility, join forces and help to lift these nations out of their current socioeconomic situations one at a time.

Closing the gaps in economic prosperity and moving toward globalization:
Population growth in the nations of Asia and Africa is growing out of control. On one hand, the economic growth of the advanced nations that provides a

higher standard of life to their slow-growing or non-growing populations, and on the other, the stagnant or slow growing economies of the underdeveloped nations that cannot catch up with their population growth, continue to widen the prosperity gap among them. This trend will eventually put advanced and underdeveloped nations on a collision course that is unavoidable and in fact has already started. If a full-blown collision occurs, a great deal of energy will be dissipated in the form of collateral damage and loss of human life. To avoid such a calamity, the advanced nations must seek the cooperation of the leaders of the underdeveloped nations to close the widening prosperity gap before it is too late. This can be achieved if the advanced nations invest heavily in the economies of the underdeveloped nations, on basis of sincerity and not for the purposes of exploitation, while setting up plans to reverse their population growth through tough laws pertaining to family size.

Economic assistance, along with long-term population control policies, is the only way to close the prosperity gap between rich and poor nations and minimize the build-up of tension between them. If economic growth or prosperity is measured by indicators like the gross domestic product (GDP) or genuine progress indicator (GPI), then the ratio of this indicator over population (per capita) is probably a better indicator of the rate of progress towards prosperity. For example, a depressed economy that is accompanied by a growing population has a negative rate of progress toward prosperity when compared with a growing economy with population reduction, which has the fastest rate of progress toward prosperity. In another example, if two societies have the same GDP, the one with the smaller population is more prosperous. Evidently, the fastest way to close up the existing gap of prosperity between advanced and underdeveloped nations must include population control. An illustration of progress towards prosperity is shown in Figure 7-1.

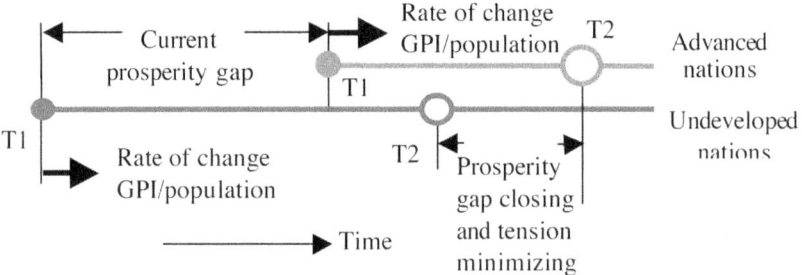

Figure 7-1 Closing of the prosperity gap.
(T1 and T2 are cross sections of time.)

It is important to emphasize that the build-up of tension between rich and poor is measured by their relative distance and not by their absolute position. For example, if we assume that the advanced and underdeveloped nations helping each other, were able to improve the prosperity level of the underdeveloped to the current prosperity level of the advanced nations in the next thirty years, which the advanced nations has doubled or tripled their own prosperity level in the same time period, the tension will continue to remain between the two blocs despite tremendous improvement in the lives of people living in the underdeveloped nations. Therefore, it is the closing of the prosperity gap that reduces the tension and minimizes the possibility of confrontation between these blocs, and not just an improvement in the prosperity level of the underdeveloped nations, yet leaving the gap still wide open.

In recent years, we have witnessed numerous terrorist activities that have taken place around the world against the interests of the advanced nations as an indication that the first phase of confrontation between the two blocs has already started. Unfortunately, the advanced nations have paid no attention to the widening prosperity gap between the two blocs and have made no attempt to correct it, in order to prevent such violent reactions between them. Now, the advanced nations have no choice but to resort to force in order to suppress this uprising and stop the violence. But can they really control it by force? The American government has been declaring victory over Al-Qaeda by claiming to have either captured or eliminated most of its leadership, believing that if the leadership is eliminated, the whole organization will fall apart. This assumption is probably inaccurate and it does not take a military genius to figure out that by now a whole new generation of leaders has probably been installed in the ranks of this organization. Let us look at another part of the Middle East to make our point. Israel has been eliminating the Palestinian leaders for almost four decades, but have they been able to stop the movement for the liberation of Palestine? Not really. Eliminating a layer of leadership by no means leads to its destruction and deters its members to fight for their survival. To win the war on terrorism with minimum casualties and collateral damages on both sides, the leaders of the advanced nations must rethink their approach in dealing with this phenomenon, and eliminate the root cause of this uprising.

The true solution to reducing the tension between the rich and poor nations and win the war on terrorism would be to start lifting these nations up economically. When poor nations start to prosper, their population growth will follow the pattern of advanced nations, and some sort of balance will emerge between their economic growth and population growth. At the same time, recruitment of young men and women to join terrorist organizations will fall because the root cause of resentment and hopelessness due to poverty has been eliminated. The policies of economic assistance and investment in the economies of underdeveloped nations will cost less for the advanced nations, than keeping these nations suppressed and from time to time, spend huge military expenditures to confront them as tension builds up. In addition, in each confrontation, tens or hundreds of thousands of lives are lost and the entire infrastructure of these societies are destroyed or damaged, putting them even further behind from catching up with the advanced nations. These brutal policies against underdeveloped nations, inflames the hatred of their populations for the advanced nations and adds to their determination to fight them to the end.

When hatred reaches its highest level, it closes all the doors to diplomacy and rational behavior. It is at this stage that military confrontation becomes unavoidable. One of the reasons why Israel is resented so much in the Middle East is not just because of religious differences between Jews and the Muslim world surrounding Israel. Among Muslim societies of the Middle East and Africa, Israel is perceived as an extension of the advanced and prosperous nations, in the form of an island within their territory, that exercises the same policies of aggression against their economic, cultural and territorial interests. If Israel had extended a helping hand to Palestinians during the past four decades and built schools and hospitals in Arab communities with a small part of the American aid dollars it was receiving every year instead of destroying them, by now Israel would have won the hearts and minds of the Palestinians and the whole Arab world. As a result, Israel would have been safer today than at any time since its establishment. In the later process, all of the radical and fanatical approaches toward the annihilation of Israel by some radical Muslim organizations would have been discredited, and over time, their organizations would have been dismantled due to lack of a theoretical and moral principle for their struggle. Let us not forget that radical and extreme measures always generate other extremes, regardless of who started the conflict. This applies also to Muslim organizations and some Middle Eastern governments that have not given up the idea of the destruction of Israel. No need to mention that behind all of these conflicts (apparently due to religious differences between Jews and Muslims) lies the powerful economic factor that unfortunately has been overlooked.

Isolationism vs. globalization: Isolationism in the political sense means that a nation closes its doors to any cultural, economical, and political exchange with other nations and sets itself to be self-supporting inside its own territorial boundaries. Before we go further, let us remind ourselves that a society is an organism, and any organism must exchange mass and energy with its environment in order to survive and grow. In the past, primitive societies with unsophisticated economies have survived in relative isolation from other societies because their needs were limited to food and shelter that were available within their territorial boundaries. Modern societies with sophisticated economies and advanced technology, however, can no longer survive in isolation from other societies. The diversity of their needs for materials, energy resources, technology, knowledge, and even food is so vast that they have no alternative but to seek them elsewhere by active engagement with other nations. As a result, the process of "openness out of necessity" that may have started merely for the purpose of survival has facilitated other exchanges among nations in the areas of culture, life style, sociopolitical and socioeconomic arenas, leading to a full-scale assimilation and merger of these societies in the long run.

It is the law of systems that when channels of communication open up between two or more systems, the final state of these systems will become a homogenous mixture or compound of these systems with a unity of physical characteristics and unified boundary conditions. In the case of social organisms, "homogenous" means speaking one language, assimilating cultures, forming common sociopolitical and socioeconomic views, and eliminating territorial boundaries and more. This deterministic process dominates social evolution on our planet by forcing societies to merge and form a global social organism with the characteristics of a single organism. Naturally, at this stage of our social evolution where the dominant course of history is integration process (which means that nature has not turned against us yet), isolationism as a political ideology will never prevail unless society is willing to regress economically and technologically. As we know, this is not a possibility. There is no need to mention that there are no systems in the entire universe that are isolated from their environment and other systems in an absolute way.

The hidden forces of equalization and homogenization in today's profit-driven capitalism: As the focus of corporations has shifted from internal markets to the world market, a new culture has emerged that is different from capitalism in its traditional sense. Traditional capitalism once had a tint of nationalism, but not anymore. It is still true, however, that almost every strategy or policy that has been adopted by any economic institution in the capitalist world, both in the past and present, has been to improve profitability of the institution. In the past, corporations earned their profits mainly from unfair purchase of raw materials from poorer nations and the surplus value that they generated from their employees on the mainland. Their products were then sold in limited markets, generally within the industrialized nations, because the poorer nations could not afford them. Later, price competition forced some corporations to use cheaper foreign labor to compete with their rivals, which was to build the product offshore and sell it in a restricted market within the industrialized nations. Today, they do not limit themselves to a restricted market or the nationality of their workforce because they want to capture the entire world market and its labor force. This aggressive force of capitalism may seem wicked on the surface, but it has also unintended positive consequences as it plays a major role in the historical process, particularly in the development of a homogenized global society and the transfer of technology to underdeveloped societies.

This is not to say that the globalization of the world economy on the basis of capitalism will succeed in establishing humane and just relational bonds among its subsystems at all levels and lead the social evolution to its finality. Certainly, this will not be the case, and the continued greed of the capitalism that can find no external resource to exploit (in a closed global economic system) will intensify the exploitation of labor that will ignite other historical sub-processes to abandon capitalist economic system for the last time. In the meantime, despite its shortcomings capitalism will help to integrate the world. Countries such as South Korea, Malaysia, Singapore and Taiwan were initially used by the industrial world for their cheap labor, but in the process, knowledge and technology were transferred into these societies to produce higher quality products. This process improved their educational systems and produced first class scientists and engineers who were able to compete with their peers in the industrialized nations to advance technology. The best indicator of advancement is to compare the number of patents granted to individuals in these societies in recent years, as compared with any time in their history. When the populations of these developing societies start to become better educated and demand a higher standard of living, wages rise and eventually catch up with those of advanced societies. At this stage, the profit margins that investors used to enjoy in these developing societies start falling short of their expectations and they start looking elsewhere in the world where they can find cheaper labor. Theoretically, this process can continue until every society in the world becomes part of the global economic system and has, more or less, reached an equal level of prosperity on the national level. However, this process will not correct the profound inequalities within socioeconomic classes (human level) on a global scale.

In this argument, we have shown how technology and life style can be transferred and how prosperity among nations can be equalized. In the following discussion, we will show how this process also assists the homogenization process of the populations throughout the world. As we stated earlier, today's capitalism lacks nationalism and thinks on a global scale. Corporations do not discriminate against nationalities and they hire the most talented and qualified individuals to run their management and engineering teams. This new attitude of capitalism and the globalization of markets will eventually cause large populations of people to move from one country to another, searching for jobs and opportunities. This movement will facilitate assimilation of cultures and consequently the homogenization process of the population on a global scale.

This is part of the historical evolution in integration process of history and is consistent with systems theory. However, with all of these comes the widening gap between socioeconomic classes on a global scale that could threaten the stability of the global economic system. Is it possible that powerful multinational corporations of the future develop compassion for humanity and the environment and adopt new attitudes in conducting their businesses and help to minimize inequality among socioeconomic classes, or they will become arrogant and blind by their powers, trying to further exploit the environment and the working class for greater profits? In the latter case, corporations would reawaken the hibernating giant of communism, to reorganize the labor against them, this time throughout the world and take over the critical and top-level means of production. In conclusion, capitalism and the market economy may help the global social organism to achieve some of its intended goals, but certainly not all. Later, the global social organism will initiate other complementary processes to minimize the huge inequalities that capitalism and market economy have created between socioeconomic classes.

The unregulated market economy and modern slavery: Today's market economy has enslaved large populations of adults and exploited children in labor market in numerous underdeveloped societies. The lack of laws and regulations to protect labor and children from exploitation in these societies has given enormous freedom to the corporations to treat the labor as they wish. The greed of capitalism has no limits when it comes to increasing the profit margins and surplus values that it makes off every worker, just to make their stockholders happy and earn companies' board of directors millions of compensation dollars. Child labor can be bought much cheaper than adult labor in these societies and employers see this as an opportunity to get rich faster. In most cases, the benefits these employees receive from their employers are none or minimal, compared to those that the same employers provide to their employees in their homeland.

In recent years, there have been alarming signs that even in industrialized nations labor benefits have been on the decline. The elimination of pension and retirement plans and reduction in medical benefits, longer working hours without pay, and the exclusion of yearly salary increases, despite having an inflationary economy, are all indications that employers are under tremendous pressure to survive fierce price competition from developing societies that have cheap labor and produce cheaper products. If this trend continues, employers will have no other choice but to take their design and production centers to developing nations or ask for even greater sacrifices from their employees for mutual survival. Some companies have already taken advantage of these circumstances to squeeze more out of their labor force and increase their profit margins, even though they lack good justification for being financially threatened by outside competition. All of this means that in advanced nations the benefits of working classes will gradually shrink, working hours will become progressively longer, and pay cuts will lower their standard of living to levels below what they used to be. This new economy will produce an overstressed generation of employees who will spend more than they earn to maintain the life style they once had. With their credit cards filled to their maximum limits, they will finally become slaves to the global economic machine. As this economic system evolves along its current path, it will produce its own antidote: the lack of any protection for the very subsystem (human beings), which its survival depends on.

The turnaround will take place when global economy on the basis of free markets fail disastrously worldwide, and result in chaos and social unrest erupting all over the world. The regenerated world economy with a new social order will then be filled with laws and regulations to protect every system and subsystem in its organization. In other words, the economy will become a centrally controlled economy, dictated by the forces of necessity. It is inconceivable that economic planners do not see this coming down the line and are disregarding the economic well-being of the very subsystems (human beings) that the economic machine is built upon.

One way or another, the global social organism and its economy will be centralized. It does not matter who will be in charge, corporations with a changed attitude or a socialist world government, as long as there is stability and security for every system and subsystem in the hierarchy of global social organism. From the perspective of the global social organism and its intended evolutionary goals, it is irrelevant which sub-processes are executed and completed first. Societies may integrate economically and socially first, and then establish fairness in their socioeconomic relations at all subsystem levels, or they may establish fairness in socioeconomic relations first and then integrate socially and economically.

Managing the process of history: Early in our history, wars were fought on a much smaller scale and the loss of lives was proportional to the scale of the conflict. But after the conflict was over, the warring societies started to integrate by forming larger societies with common objectives. Our history clearly demonstrates this historical trend and how smaller societies that fought with each other eventually came together and formed larger societies, and continued to integrate following every interaction with other societies. In recent times, societies have grown into such large entities that their conflicts produce much larger number of casualties and greater collateral damages than ever before. Take World War II, for example, in which multitude of nations on each side were engaged in a war that produced 55 million casualties and destroyed cities throughout the European continent, including Japan. If we count every life lost in every nation throughout the world, as a result of confrontation between capitalists and communists, the casualties of the Cold War (starting from 1919 to the fall of the Berlin Wall) may not be less than those lost in World War II. During the Cold War, there was not a single country on the planet that was not affected by the ideological rivalry of the two superpowers and the regional wars that they provoked. For example, the total casualties of Chinese revolution, and the wars fought on Korean peninsula, Vietnam and Afghanistan alone will mount to over 10 million casualties. During this period, the two systems (Soviets and the Western societies with Americans in the forefront) exchanged enough energy to reconcile and start their integration process.

Today, most of the former enemies from the Cold War era that belong to the Northern camp are either unified or in the process of consolidating their unification. Today, the world is on the brink of another conflict much greater than World War II, one that can potentially integrate the entire world and bring about a new world order and stability to the world community, after it is ended. This is the conflict between North and South. As a reminder, "North" refers to the advanced nations, many of which are north of the equator, and "South" to the poor and underdeveloped nations south of the equator. This may be the last stage of world conflict because it encompasses the entire world community that divides every human and every society and puts them in either one of the camps. If the Northern camp continues to prosper and leave the South behind, the prosperity gap will continue to grow, and so will the tension between them. This growing tension will inevitably thrust the two systems into a clash of an instantaneous and violent form, with massive energy exchange and destruction that will lead to catastrophe and maybe endanger human civilization and life on earth. This will bring us to the realization that before any reconciliation takes place between the North and South, there will be monumental human casualties on both sides, possibly more than the casualties of World War II and the Cold War put together. It is unfortunate that the reconciliation and integration of societies requires the price of human lives and the destruction of order.

Human life is part of the dissipation energy that is needed for this merger to take place. The only interference with the process that human beings and their societies, with all of their wisdom and creativity, can have is to manage the rate of energy exchange and spread it out over a longer period of time. This will avoid major destabilization on the global scale that may lead to chaos and unpredictable reactions and consequences. The current conflict between North and South will be fought as the Cold War was fought for many generations to come until, gradually, the two camps start to reconcile and establish a new world order on a global scale. This seems to be the extent of human involvement in their historical process, which is to avoid unnecessary historical turns and management of the rate of energy exchange in conflicts; obviously powerless to put an end to the destruction of lives and order.

Governments and their leaders in the global community: About 2,400 years ago, the Greek philosopher Plato wrote (in an undeniably true statement) that a philosopher has to be the king or the king must be a philosopher to properly rule. Up until the late twentieth century, the people of United States were still electing leaders based on their popularity and ideological narrow-mindedness concerning other races and nations, but not for their wisdom. The same was also true with Soviet Union's leaders succeeding one after another with one goal in mind: to defeat the West politically, economically, and militarily. This adversarial relationship between the two camps dragged us to the brink of nuclear disaster many times after the World War II. The leaders on both sides thought that they could change the finality of history by changing its course. In reality, no one is capable of changing the finality of social evolution as set by the laws of nature. We can only change the course of events that accelerate or decelerate the process leading to that finality. We are destined to have a global society. Processes are at work to get us there, provided we do not annihilate ourselves fighting over energy resources when or if our current resources start to run out and we are unprepared to replace them with other resources. To accelerate the process of social evolution toward its finality, the future leaders of all societies must be a mix of economists, ecologists, technocrats, scientists, social scientists, philosophers, and historians. Unlike those who form the U.S. government today, we do not need mainly lawyers. By nature or by training, lawyers are argumentative and uncompromising. These characteristics may become unhealthy factors when it comes to building constructive relationships among nations and peoples. Unbelievers can look at the domestic politics of the U.S. for the past 25 years, which largely consist of scandals, accusations, charges, and countercharges brought against each other by members of the political parties. Scientists, on the other hand, are driven by logic, the thirst for knowledge and facts that make them a better choice for leadership, and to construct fair and lasting relationships among nations and peoples on a global scale. Again, unbelievers can look at the cooperation between NASA, Russian space agencies, and other partners in the exploration of space. The leaders of the world must understand and accept the finality of social evolution as a stage that terminates the struggle of nation against nation and man against man, a finality that brings equality and justice to all nations and peoples and stability to the global social organism. This finality is by no means the end of our history, but a stage we need to put behind us to focus on our struggle with the environment. With the help of wiser leaders, we can get to the predetermined finality of our historical process faster and with fewer human casualties and destructive processes along the way. If we do not behave wisely, we are doomed to pay for it with our lives…yet at the end, we will find ourselves at the same destination that we tried so hard to avoid.

The ambition of the United States after the Cold War: The United States and the European Union both continue to be suspicious of the Russian democratization process. They continue to believe that Russia may bounce back at any time to an authoritarian system of government and become an obstacle to NATO's expansion of its domain of influence in the world. This is why the NATO alliance considers Russia to be the last barrier to overcome before it (NATO) takes control of the entire world and its historical evolution by expanding its principles and so-called 'democratic values'. Since Russian military might cannot be easily defeated, the NATO alliance has adopted other strategies to defeat the Russian federation, which is to destabilize it politically and economically and surrounding it militarily.

It all started from Eastern Europe after the end of the Cold War when NATO, and in the forefront, U.S., began to provoke and arm ethnic and religious secessionist groups across Federal Republic of Yugoslavia against the central socialist government for so-called 'liberation movements'. But the main purpose behind this policy was to divide the Eastern European alliances and break them into smaller societies, particularly within the Federal Republic of Yugoslavia, so that each individual nation would lack sufficient power to confront the NATO alliance. When humanitarian disasters took place because of ethnic clashes for independence, NATO justified its involvement with military action against the central socialist government, which was mainly composed of Serbs, and succeeded in dividing the country into pieces based on their ethnic majority. The heads of the socialist government and military were either assassinated or removed from power, blaming them for all the humanitarian disasters that took place in the region, although NATO leaders themselves were equally guilty for initiating these ethnic confrontations.

The defeat of the Federal Republic of Yugoslavia and its disintegration opened the gates to western borders of the Russian Federation. In the meantime, from the south and using the same tactics, Muslim separatists were armed and trained to conduct attacks on Russian soil for so-called 'independence' in Chechnya and other Muslim states in the southern parts of Russia, which resulted in two major wars in that region. Again, hoping that Russia will fall apart without a war. NATO's long-term plan was (and still is) to surround Russia militarily and try to destabilize it politically and economically. Interference in the Russian Federation's affairs by NATO and in particular by the U.S. and Britain, has not been limited to supporting Muslim insurgents and separatists but also financially supporting political candidates with greater leniency toward western values in every republic of Russian Federation, such as Armenia, Azerbaijan, Georgia, Chechnya, Ukraine and others. Following the declaration of the war on terrorism and using the pretext of fighting terrorism, the U.S. has been very aggressive in its foreign policy and in deploying military bases in Afghanistan, Iraq and other states along the southern border of Russia. Hoping that those bases will remain there for the foreseeable future and be used to destabilize Russia, if and only if, Russia moves away from the democratic process and adopts an authoritarian political system unapproved by the NATO alliance.

But there are also other reasons why the presence of these military bases are so important to U.S. and NATO alliance, and that is to secure the region's natural resources of oil and gas that are so badly needed by every NATO member. Before we speak further on this subject, we need to state that NATO members do not always agree on every policy and occasionally, when their individual security and interests are threatened, they compete with each other and form smaller alliances. Such divisions and differences of opinion regarding the conduct of world affairs have become very clear during the administration of George W. Bush, particularly when U.S. unilaterally invaded Iraq and removed Saddam Hussein from power, claiming that he was a threat to the world peace with his weapons of mass destruction (WMD).

On the surface, it seemed like a noble cause, since U.S. not only reduced the threat of terror in the world, but also freed Iraqis from the rule of a tyrant. But the untold story is different, which is why it has displeased most of the NATO members, including Russians, at the unilateralist policies of U.S.. After conquering Iraq, U.S. canceled all construction contracts European nations and Russia had held with the former Iraqi government and granted them to American corporations. After Cold War ended, U.S. government has come to believe that because it is the sole remaining superpower on earth, it is possible that it can emerge as the central control system of the global social organism, and has designed its aggressive foreign policy to achieve that status. But U.S. is not alone in this political adventurism, and we know that there are two political factions in U.S. that have tremendous influence in the design and execution of the nation's foreign policy, which may not be constructive in terms of the nation's own long-term interests. These two factions are the British and Israeli fifth columns in the U.S. government, which occasionally use the American military muscle to advance their own economic and political interests around the world that may be in conflict with the interest of other alliance members, namely the European nations. This is why, from time to time, European counterparts in NATO do not approve of U.S.'s foreign policies, for refusing to be a partner and an honest broker in handling global problems. Examples include the uncertain and unmoving peace process in the Middle East and the American refusal to participate in important international treaties, such as the ban on nuclear testing, the Kyoto Accords on global warming, and participation in international criminal court. For these reasons, Europeans have lost faith in the U.S. as a partner; considering it a superpower that plays by its own rules in the international arena rather than by the rules of the international community, designed to enhance security and stability around the world.

In reality, the plan to invade Iraq had been drawn up years prior to the September 11th of 2001 attack on American soil by terrorists. There were also plans to get rid of the Taliban government in Afghanistan, all for the following reasons: Israel wanted the Iraq war primarily to get rid of Saddam, a sworn enemy of Israel, in order to improve its own security. For Britain, the Iraq war was to safeguard Kuwait's oil resources from ambitions of Saddam, who claimed Kuwait as part of his country. Finally, the Iraq war intended to serve the long-term foreign policy of the U.S. and Britain, aimed to control all the energy resources in the Persian Gulf and, eventually, those not fully explored in the Caspian Sea Basin, which are located in the Northern Caucasus region of the Russian Federation. This region of the world contains so much oil and gas that we can think of it as the heart of global social organism that pumps the much-needed blood (oil) to all of its sub-organs (nations) that they need for their survival.

These things make it clear why the U.S. and Britain have been so heavily involved in the destabilization of the Russian Federation and have supported the Northern Caucasus nations in their independence movements because their oil exploration and distribution will fall into the hands of British and American oil companies. If this becomes a reality, Caspian Sea oil will be delivered through pipelines running across Afghanistan and Pakistan and distributed all over the world. When we consider the economic growth of China and India, we will realize what a unique position and lucrative business will it be for any company that distributes these energy resources. With China and India emerging as superpowers, U.S. has begun to consider policies to deal with them if they start to challenge U.S. authority and its vital interests around the world. Therefore, it is reasonable to think that the long-term U.S. policy in dealing with China and India is to control their energy needs, in order to have an upper hand controlling their aggression and subdue their rivalry.

Obviously, the Russians were well aware of the activities of the Americans and British in their Northern Caucasus region. They had no choice but to act quickly to reestablish their dominance over the region after Vladimir Putin was elected president of Russia. For both political and economic reasons, Russia will try by all means in its disposal to keep the British and the Americans out of this region. Russia needs the cash generated by these energy resources for its own economic development, and it would supply them directly to the end users, which are mostly Europeans and the Chinese. At the same time, EU members may be encouraged to invest in the Russian economy to solidify their partnership, which would create an economic, political, and military power-house that would extend from the Atlantic, across Europe and Russia, and all the way across China to the Pacific, *forming Eurasian alliance.* This new alliance might weaken NATO, and that is why the U.S. and Britain are so nervous regarding these developments. In fact, part of the problem of EU members versus the U.S. and Britain arises from their basic differences in approaching world problems. Europeans have come to a better understanding of global affairs and take more rational approaches to solve them through international bodies such as the United Nations, whereas the U.S. and its close partner, Britain, continue to resort to early 20th century imperialistic policies that are outdated and will not serve them well in the long run. The unilateral policies of the U.S. and Britain aimed at controlling the world without the consent of other members of the international community would lead to divisions in NATO and will push the EU into the arms of the Russians and the Chinese as more reliable global partners. Economic cooperation among these nations will produce a political, economic, and military force that is strong enough to contain the aggressive policies of the U.S. and its closest ally, Britain.

Given these facts regarding high-level strategic planning by the U.S. and Britain, we can come to this conclusion that the invasion and occupation of Iraq were not so much about removing a dangerous dictator from power, nor liberating the Iraqi people—who did not have "freedom" by Western standards—as they were for the reasons stated above. The U.S. and Britain continue to brag about their human face and how they liberated Iraqis from a dangerous dictator who was killing his own people, but when 800,000 people in Rwanda were slaughtered in tribal clashes, where was that human face? None of the superpowers interfered or sent their troops to stop that genocide, probably because Rwandans are black or maybe they did not have oil and their country was of no strategic importance.

In conclusion, the US-British partnership in conducting self-serving global policies that are not internationally approved could polarize the world once again and trigger a new round of arms race between the superpowers. This race has already started with EU members thinking of having a strong European military with the latest technology, and Russians accelerating their research and development in designing new weapons systems. These new economic partners may even collaborate in developing new weapons systems to put themselves in a better position to contest and contain the aggressive policies of the U.S. and its close partners that are perceived as threats to world peace and security. To avert this dangerous process and avoid falling into political isolation from the rest of the world, the United States and its closest allies must set aside their ambitions to control the global social organism and join the rest of the world community in finding solutions to energy crises and other global issues through the UN. The United Nations is the only legitimate body that can emerge as the controlling organ of global social organism and its affairs, and not any other power.

World peace and global disarmament: Today's nonproliferation policies in regard to WMDs are unrealistic and based on a double standard. For decades, the U.S., Britain, France, Russia and China have been using these weapons as a force of deterrence and to impose their foreign policy agenda and political will around the world. Now these nations are terrified by the fact that the knowledge of building these weapons and the systems to deliver them is spreading around the world so rapidly, and nations who have been terrorized by these weapons and lost control over their own political life are willing to pay any price to acquire them in order to take back their own political life. Some of the nations who have succeeded in developing or acquiring these weapons in recent years that has concerned the oldest members of the nuclear club are India, Pakistan, Israel and North Korea, and it is possible that more nations may join this club in the years to come. To the oldest members of the club, it is terrifying and inconceivable to allow the nuclear technology to spread among socioeconomically depressed societies, particularly those of the Islamic faith, because most terrorist organizations operate from within these societies. The main fear that is legitimate is the fact that terrorist organizations may get their hands on these weapons and use them irresponsibly to kill the civilians and destroy military targets, and inflict as much damage as they could to the infrastructure of the advanced societies. As a result, the oldest members of the nuclear club have started a campaign of intimidation by resorting to force or imposing economic sanctions, against every nation that has a nuclear program and rewarding those who volunteer to end them. These policies may succeed in stopping some governments from pursuing these weapons, but it will not stop terrorist organizations from acquiring them. Terrorist organizations believe the destructive power of these weapons, if used against the advanced nations, will lead to prompt policy review and a change of attitude toward the suppressed nations they represent. Resorting to force and intimidation may work when dealing with a government, but it will not work with terrorist organizations. This fact dictates that, since these economically suppressed nations are the breeding grounds for terrorist organizations, a policy review in this regard is overdue. Preemptive and containment policies may not work one hundred percent either, as the terrorist organizations get smarter in evading them to carry out their missions, as they finally did in toppling the World Trade Center after many attempts.

The leaders of the terrorist organizations, at least those we have seen in recent years, are well-educated and politically motivated. Members of the organizations are likewise motivated to the point where they are willing to die for the cause they believe in, which makes them the most dangerous type of terrorists. The fact that they are willing to die for what they believe in requires an enormous build-up of anger and frustration with oppressive internal forces linked to external forces that have taken control over their political life for many years. This is an alarming sign that requires an immediate policy review and reconciliation if we are to start reversing this deadly confrontational process that may lead to massive casualties if it comes to the use of WMDs by one or both sides. When the superpowers unilaterally decide who can and who cannot have WMDs, they are sending a message loud and clear to the rest of the world: *We want to remain in control and dictate your faith.* This policy of double standards, combined with political and economical suppression of other nations, would not stop nations or terrorist organizations from seeking these weapons.

A true peace and disarmament policy can start when the superpowers allow other nations to control their own political and socioeconomic lives and participate in good faith with other nations in an international effort to eradicate all WMDs, regardless of who has them, and give international teams of investigators unrestricted access to every desired site in any nation.

This seems to be the only winning policy that will lead to world peace and disarmament. But the concern is that the policy makers in the U.S. and other powers may not come to this conclusion soon enough to avoid major disasters. If policy reviews do not come in time, it is only logical to conclude that, based on the number of the nations involved in this new confrontation between North and South, human casualties and the destruction of order, may exceed those of the World War II and the Cold War combined, before a new balance emerges on the planet.

Individual freedom: For centuries, the subject of freedom has been a topic of discussion among philosophers. There is as much agreement as there is disagreement regarding what constitutes individual freedom and liberty when an individual is part of a larger organization (the society he or she lives in). A basic and essential part of individual freedom starts with economic freedom, which is the ability of an individual to live with dignity as a member of a society. As we know, the most basic survival needs of a human being are food and shelter. In the modern society we live in, food cannot be gathered or hunted and shelter cannot be built anywhere one wishes, as every single square foot of habitable land on earth is taken, either by someone or an organization. This means that basic, primeval survival is impossible, and the only way one can acquire the essentials of life is through employment with an economic institution that requires skills. To obtain skills, one needs to be trained and spend many years in school. Attending schools and colleges in a capitalist society needs money, and as we know, most of us are not born with a wallet full of money. In societies where economic justice is lagging, children who are born to poor families have little chance to lift themselves up from their parents' economic class, regardless of how bright they may be and they continue to remain in a lower socioeconomic class, struggling to survive. As a result, the degree of individual freedom that people may enjoy living in these societies will become a function of their socioeconomic class.

The other part of individual freedom is freedom of religion, speech and expression and participation in election of the government officials, etc. etc. This is the luxury part of individual freedom that comes after economic freedom is achieved. How many homeless and hungry individuals, for example, would pick freedom of speech and religion over a warm meal on their table? In fact, the luxury part of individual freedom to those lacking economic freedom means absolutely nothing because they cannot enjoy it in the first place. Interestingly, all of those who are constantly worried about freedom of speech and choice, and get involved in intricate discussions about this concept, already enjoy their economic freedom and know nothing about being poor and economically suppressed. This is not to downplay the importance of the luxury part of the freedom, as it could be a powerful instrument in setting new directions for the evolution of social organism, by redefining the relational bonds among peoples and societies through new and fresh ideas. But a man who is hungry has other concerns before he starts thinking about how he can make this world a better place for everyone else. For example, freedom of speech may be used to teach people to understand why economic freedom should take precedence over other individual freedoms so that citizens of a society are provided with the basic rights for survival, which are education, health care, and employment. When a society provides economic freedom to its citizens, it is then that its operational efficiency and stability reaches optimum level. Moreover, it is in this environment that luxury part of the individual freedom works best because everyone can participate in free speech and the exchange of ideas.

Collective freedom versus individual freedom: Theoretically, an individual who lives in the wilderness, having no relational bonds with other humans, has a greater degree of freedom than a person who lives in a community. As soon as communities are formed, so are relational bonds among individuals, which restrict their freedom for the sake of others' freedoms and the community itself. In fact, as soon as a community or a social organism comes to life as a living system, it takes charge of its own course of evolution, and in order to survive with a maximum degree of freedom, it restricts the freedoms of its own subsystems (humans), because without such restrictions the social organism would cease to exist. In other words, for the social organism to have a meaningful existence, it needs the relational bonds among its constituents, but for constituents having these relational bonds translate to the loss of their freedom. The degree, to which a subsystem loses its freedom to the system itself, is a function of both its position in the hierarchy of the system and the complexity of the system at that evolutionary stage. For example, the lower the position of a subsystem in the hierarchy of a system, the greater the loss of its freedom, as all of the higher-level systems would impose their own conditions upon that subsystem. To make this clearer, let us look at our own lives. How many of us feel that our lives are no longer in our control, with the ties that we have with our employer, commitments toward our family and other members of our society. How do we feel about the laws and regulations that keep us in order and take away our freedoms in every way for the betterment of our society? Restrictions such as not being able to park our cars wherever we want, or turn our music louder because our neighbors may be bothered by it, and for hundreds of other reasons why we cannot do this or that. In today's society, people are imprisoned in small cells that connect their homes to their jobs, as they spend most of their time living and working in those cells, similar to the cells in our body. The loss of freedom at the subsystem level equates to gaining harmony, functionality, efficiency, and finally a greater degree of freedom and security for the social organism, but not for its subsystems. As the social organism becomes more complex, so do the laws, regulations, and restrictions it imposes on its subsystems. One thing that makes perfect sense with the ever-growing complexity of the social organism is the awarding of economic freedom to every subsystem and individual within the social organism at its maturity. Analogous to a socialist way of life because the social organism's own health, functionality, and stability would be highly dependent on the health of every functioning organ within its organization, similar to human body. However, as far as who and how many of its constituents would be involved in making high level decisions on its future evolutionary processes, it would be limited to a handful of subsystems and individuals. What this means is that the majority of the individuals may be cut off from making decisions on the complex affairs of the social organism, because social organism would not risk letting these affairs be decided by the simplistic individuals who make up the majority and their vote may be easily manipulated. There is no need to mention that in the very complex social organism, everyone would be highly restricted in his individual freedom for the sake of the social organism's security and collective freedom.

The decline of human freedom with the maturation of the social organism: For more than a century, politicians have exploited the notion of freedom in order to sell their political system around the world. But freedom means different things to different people, depending on their socioeconomic status. The communist version of freedom emphasized on the economic freedom that has an immediate connection with survival of human beings in their society; which covers healthcare, free education, guaranteed employment, affordable housing and retirement with dignity. From the viewpoint of communism, no human being can ever be socially free until he is economically free. However, for political reasons during the Cold War, there was no freedom of expression or speech granted to citizens of Soviet Union if it meant to criticize the government and the establishment. Communist governments also outlawed practicing all religious and ideological beliefs other than Marxism-Leninism. During this period, the West launched a propaganda war against communist governments, criticizing them for denying their citizens the rights to freely practice their religion and engage in free political debates, while kept quite regarding their own serious human rights issues. In much of Europe and the U.S., a significant portion of the population was segregated by color and socioeconomic status, and those who demanded basic human rights for this segment of the population were often accused of being communists and were harshly punished. In fact, a hungry, discriminated-against, and undignified human being would care less about freedom of expression, which he is unable to enjoy after all. For this human being, stepping out of his economic misery is gaining freedom, and he would accept the communist version of freedom with open arms at any time. Obviously, in both camps, there was only a fraction of the population that was content with what their political system was able to offer them in connection with their perceived notions of freedom.

Now let us take a look at the latter generation of the Russian population ruled by communism, who had already been lifted from the economic suffering and poverty that feudalism and Tsar's ruling imposed upon them prior to their revolution. This generation of Russians was well-educated and no longer poor and without jobs, and was receiving other benefits that were not easy to come by in Western societies, but they lacked freedom of expression. Often, their most honest expressions and participation in improving Russia's political system were considered treasonous by the authorities followed by some sort of punishment. Part of the hysteria on the part of Russia's communist government was understandable, which was the result of several decades of subversive activities conducted by the West within Russian territories with the aim of overthrowing their revolution. Later on, when younger generations of leaders came to power, they felt the need for change and greater openness, similar to those practiced in the West, because this generation of Russians as well as people throughout the Soviet bloc were waiting for this change that had not come in the earlier stages of their revolution.

Naturally, every human being desires both economic freedom and freedom of expression, but freedom of expression is meaningless without economic freedom. Human beings need to survive in a transformed environment that is no longer a wilderness. In earlier days, necessary survival skills pertaining to the life in wilderness were taught by parents, and after coaching them for a while they were let go to survive on their own. But survival skills within today's complicated societies cannot be taught by parents alone, but rather through educational institutions that must be made available to every member of the society so that they can develop their full potential. In return, it is expected that those who were helped to acquire necessary skills assume responsible roles in their society. This mutual responsibility of society toward its members and members toward their society (for mutual survival) echoes the relationship that exists between human body and its cells. There is no doubt that one day, when social evolution starts to approach its finality, a similar relationship will develop between the social organism and its members and the economic freedom of every individual will be observed and guaranteed by the society. However, at the finality of social evolution the faith of the luxury part of human freedom, which comprises of freedom of expression, choice and movement, etc. etc. may be in serious conflict with the freedom of the social organism itself because the social organism will be in a commanding position over its constituents. Measures to enhance the harmony both within the social organism and with its environment will result in the loss of freedom for human beings and other subsystems of social organism. Any measure to improve the security and operational efficiency of the social organism will further deprive individuals of their freedoms. For example, overpopulation and congestion will bring more laws and regulations aimed at establishing order and harmony in the society, which will further erode human freedom. Laws to protect the environment and the security of our societies will have the same effect. As we know, the human body is constantly under attack by viruses and bacteria that enter its system. In addition to fighting these invaders, the human body continuously protects itself against internal enemies, such as malfunctioning cells that need to be contained or eliminated. Can we imagine our survival in a hostile environment without an effective immune system to protect us from viruses, bacteria and cancerous cells that grow within our own bodies?

Society is continually evolving and building defensive and offensive mechanisms to protect itself against internal and external enemies. It is developing methods to attack and surgically remove its enemies. Today, surveillance equipment and listening devices are being rapidly deployed to every corner of our environment; these are society's detection and defensive mechanisms. Our communications are being randomly checked and overheard to protect the system from those who intend to harm it. In this process, we are losing our freedom of privacy without even knowing to what extent. For greater efficiency, a society needs greater harmony, whether at the national or a global level. Greater harmony translates into greater uniformity, which comes with the disappearance of diversity of philosophical and religious beliefs, cultures, and languages among the members of a society. Greater operational efficiency in the level of society, which comes naturally in its evolutionary process, may lead into smaller operating cells, causing restrictions on mobility, consumption, and conservation on the human level. With the diminishing of natural resources and overpopulation, these restrictions can only become more severe. None of these paint a pretty picture for the luxury part of human freedom in a highly organized and advanced society where human freedom has been compromised to a large degree to enhance the freedom and security of the society. It seems that gaining operational efficiency and a state of security for the social organism means a loss of freedom for the sub-organisms, including individual human beings. The question is, is there a middle ground between the social organism's security matters and its operational efficiency and the freedom of human beings? Or will human beings eventually turn into functioning cells within the complex organization of the social organism?

Technological advancements and their interference with human freedom:
In the field of science and engineering, every discovery or development can be used for constructive or destructive purposes. For example, nuclear energy has been used to generate electricity but also to build nuclear weapons with enor-

mous destructive power. Radio frequencies can be used to promote or disturb communication and to destroy electrical and electronic circuits. Radio frequencies can also be used to tinker with the human mind, as well as control human behavior. Knowing that the mass media have already been used to control the social consciousness and influence the behavior of the masses, what would happen when the human subconscious mind comes under attack by radio frequencies with subliminal messages propagating from the sky over the cities and nations? With all the surveillance equipment and listening devices around us and with mass media and radio frequencies controlling our minds and conforming the social consciousness, what will happen to human freedom if these discoveries and the means of their delivery are in the hands of few? Will the majority of humans one day become nothing more than functioning cells within the social organism that do not think for themselves and only a group of elite individuals conduct and control their behavior and the affairs of the social organism? Would the majority of humans lose their freedom without even realizing it? We cannot and should not stop research activities in the fields of science because we need the knowledge we gain to use it for constructive purposes, but what we cannot afford to lose is control over who would own and take charge of these scientific breakthroughs.

Globalization of knowledge and technology: Knowledge and technology are not the creation of a single nation alone. Throughout history, knowledge has been handed down from one nation to the next. The Assyrians, Persians, Egyptians, Greeks, Indians and Chinese are among few civilizations that have laid out the foundations of science and technology for the rest of the world to enjoy. Today, however, some of these societies are no longer at the forefront of science and technology and are, in fact, ranked amongst the poorest and most underdeveloped nations. Looking at the population of scientists and engineers in the Western Europe and particularly the United States, we will find that a large number of their scientists and engineers are not native to these nations and have come from abroad to participate in the grand human endeavor of advancing knowledge. These societies have become magnets that attract the most brilliant scientists and students from all over the world, including those from underdeveloped nations. Consequently, western societies have been growing stronger, both economically and technologically, leaving the rest of the world behind. This trend is not a healthy trend because it is creating a much greater prosperity gap between advanced and underdeveloped nation that has elevated the level of tension among them. The future of the world community as a stable and peaceful society would largely depend on the creation of equally prosperous nation members. This stipulates that advanced nations must start sharing their knowledge and technology with others so that they have a chance to prosper as well. It is simply unjust that certain nations monopolize and control the knowledge that is really an international property as everyone has contributed to its evolution from time to time. It is obvious, however, why the advanced nations are not willing to share their technological expertise with others. Nations with strong economic and military powers, which are manifestations of the strong knowledge base in these societies, have always used their power to impose their will upon others in order to facilitate their own survival. Even though this behavior is supported by the natural laws on the sub-organism (national) level, it is challenged and rejected at the organism (international) level by the same laws. As we cannot allow the scarce energy resources on our planet to be manipulated by a few, we should also forbid the monopolization of technology and knowledge by few others. Those who can appreciate the purpose behind the socioeconomic struggle at the human level can also appreciate similar processes at the societal level, which is between nations that possess the means and resources to achieve prosperity and nations that lack them to achieve the same. Clearly, without sharing our knowledge, technology and resources a stable global community can never be built.

Overpopulation and its consequences: One of the technological advances that have contributed to our overpopulated world in recent history is the field of medicine, which has saved or prolonged our lives, perhaps against the intentions of nature. Many of us would not be alive today if it were not for life-saving drugs (such as antibiotics), or the skills of a surgeon who operated on us and saved our lives. Overpopulation will get worse as we go along because the average life expectancy in advanced societies continues to rise due to improvements in health care technologies and discoveries of new drugs.

But when we compare reproductive rates, the highest rate of population growth does not come from advanced nations but from third-world societies. Higher rates of population growth in these societies are directly related to the primitiveness of their economic systems, the average level of education and the influences of cultural and religious beliefs in regard to contraception. Traditionally, in societies with primitive economies, which are the majority of world societies, women bear many children in order to assist them with the farm's intensive labor required for survival. Since the populations of underdeveloped nations still live primarily on farms and in villages and small cities, the population growth rate for those segments of society continues to surpass those segments of the population living in the larger cities. Therefore, it becomes crucial for the governments of those societies to establish sound economic development to accommodate their population growth year after year. But this is usually not the case and the populations of those societies continue to live below poverty levels by any international standard. It has been shown in both laboratory experiments and the real world that when living space for animals becomes too tight, or food and other life support systems fall short, violence erupts among them. Human beings are no exception to this rule. The trend in population growth in third-world countries is alarming, not only to those societies that put them on the brink of economic and political instability, but also to their region and to the rest of the world.

In a world where globalization and economic integration have become inevitable processes, population growth can no longer be considered a national problem but rather a global problem. When we become globally connected, overpopulation will eventually affect the life of everyone on the planet, regardless of where that person lives. To keep the global social organism stable and its growth healthy, socioeconomic planning on a global scale must be carefully crafted based on the population growth, otherwise it will eventually erupt into chaos. But a better plan is to stop the growth of population and improve the standard of life for people as global economy grows. In this approach, the chances of conflicts and wars occurring among peoples and their societies will be reduced drastically, putting the global social organism in a much better standing in terms of its stability, while creating a new balance with its environment, as well as giving other species space in order to survive in that environment. Moreover, environmental pollution is also directly related to the size of our population. If we allow the global social organism to grow out of control, beyond the ability of our environment and our economy to support its needs, it is possible that for a short time, the process of history switches from integration to disintegration process until balance is regained. In this process, wars and civil unrest will destroy large parts of the global population and its infrastructure in order to achieve this new balance. Moreover, our environment will not sit back and watch quietly, and in order to have a chance to replenish itself it may eliminate a large number of us. We may face epidemics of deadly diseases caused by mutated microbes and viruses that have evolved in the environment that we polluted ourselves. Technological advances, as some of us believe, will not be able to catch up with an ever-growing earth population, to house and feed every person on earth in the limited space and with the limited resources of our planet, and at the same time, maintain the delicate natural balances among all species living on the planet. Therefore, population control by whatever means is an absolute necessity for the political and economic stability of the world community and is essential for ecological balance.

Pollution and its consequences: There are at least two reasons why we pollute our environment. One is associated with technology and its unwanted by-products, and the other relates to the size of the population on earth. Technological by-products, such as carbon dioxide (produced by burning coal, oil, and gas), sulfuric gas (produced by burning fossil fuels), and radioactive waste material (the leftovers of fuel from nuclear power plants), are unwanted by-products that are polluting our environment. In earlier discussions of the second law of thermodynamics, we stated that both the formation of ordered systems and the cost of maintaining that order produce disorder in the environment surrounding systems (in the form of pollution), which is totally unavoidable. We also argued that as ordered systems evolve into larger structures and organisms, such as a global social organism with its huge economy and connectivity, the energy requirements to maintain their structure and their operation would increase tremendously, leaving a much greater impact on the environment in the form of pollution, again unavoidable. Therefore, the question of fighting pollution is not to eliminate it because scientifically it is impossible to do so, but rather to minimize and contain it.

In the future, as more nations join the ranks of economically developed societies and produce more ordered structures in the form of goods and products and build their own advanced infrastructure, they will further pollute our environment. Ethically, it would be wrong to stop the economic development in these nations and deny them the opportunity to improve their standard of life in order to control pollution. It would be also risky to leave large prosperity gaps between nations because global social organism will become an unstable system, ready to erupt into crisis at any time. So, what choices are we left with to minimize the level of pollution, yet allow economic development to proceed on a global scale? One is to expand the use of clean energy resources readily supplied by the nature, such as solar and wind power. This can be done by creating a worldwide energy policy through the United Nations to encourage (or even enforce) the use of certain types of energy resources that are more suitable for certain geographical locations. For example, territories located on the equator should be encouraged to use the solar energy as their main source of energy, and if they lack the technological expertise to implement it, this expertise should be provided to them by nations who possess it.

The other producer of pollution is the human population. Population growth is followed by greater demand for manufactured goods and products, such as construction materials, cars, and electronics, which in turn, produce more pollution in the environment. It is obvious that the world population cannot grow forever and needs to be controlled. The earth's resources are limited and they can support an ordered structure of only a certain size and scale. Planet earth can only replenish itself at a certain rate to allow life to sustain itself in the current form. If we grow unwisely, exploit our resources at a rate exceeding the rate of their replenishment, and do serious damage to our environment, sooner or later the planet will force us to scale down our overgrown structure. This may happen through warfare conducted to control the remaining resources, or dying from epidemic diseases that we created ourselves by abusing our own living environment. In polluting our environment beyond repair, we will also eliminate thousands of species and life forms on our planet that our lives are so dependent on. Therefore, careful analysis is essential in all aspects of an overgrown structure (the global community and its economy) as it interacts with the environment and other living beings that share this planet with us. Only when we create this delicate balance will we be able to have a sustainable global social organism and avoid bursts of disintegration in its evolutionary process.

Global energy policies: As we proposed earlier, integrated systems composed of multitudes of subsystems at different levels require much more energy to maintain their ordered structures than the combined energy that their subsystems need individually. The difference is consumed by the infrastructures to establish relational bonds and connectivity between subsystems in every level. It also seems that the natural tendency of living systems is to combine and integrate when there is an abundance of energy resources in their environment and disintegrate when energy is deficient. This deterministic process of integration and disintegration of living systems in relation to the availability of energy resources seems to be unchangeable and applicable to all subsystem levels of a living organism. When energy resources are abundant and able to support the integration of smaller organisms to form larger living organisms, we humans, as subsystems of that organism, adopt policies to support that process and obstruct it when energy resources fall short. Seemingly, disintegration and integration processes have no boundaries in any direction, from disintegration to the complete annihilation of humans and all ordered structures, to integration on a planetary scale if one day we encounter civilizations that are willing to live with us in peace. Knowing all of these and understanding the dependency of the social organisms on the energy resources of their environment, we must be extremely careful not to let these organisms starve for their energy needs because they will react instinctively to the situation they face.

Before we advocate the idea of globalization of energy resources and their technologies, let us discuss some undesirable circumstances that would elevate the tension among nations and create the risk of military confrontation. To clarify this point, we can ask ourselves what we would do if we were hungry and desperate. Obviously, many of us would start thinking about breaking the law and stealing food from those who have more than they need. It is just this unfair distribution of food or wealth in a society that foments civil unrest and revolution in that society. The same is true with the societies that make up the global social organism but in a higher system level. As human beings need food to survive, so do the social organisms (societies). But there are only a handful of societies in the world who possess an abundance of energy resources that everyone else needs. Can we imagine what would happen if these resources are denied from those who need them? The answer is that they will be taken by force and by breaking the international laws.

Hopefully, this analogy will convince us that the behavior of societies as living organisms do not differ significantly from human behavior when it comes to their survival. Consequently, if we believe that the equal distribution of wealth among members of a society will bring about more stability to that society, then it should be true for the societies that if their energy needs are secured, they, too, may live in peace and harmony. Obviously, this suggests that a comprehensive energy policy on international level is needed if we are to avoid the catastrophic consequences of competition to control energy resources that may endanger our civilization and change the course of our social evolution. International agreements may include: (1) Globalization of all discovered and undiscovered energy resources around the world. (2) Globalization of all technologies related to the generation of power. This would include not only the current technologies, but also those of the future. All future research and development activities on new energy resources and technologies must be budgeted and conducted internationally for the benefit of all peoples and societies. (3) To avoid monopolies, the transportation and distribution of the energy resources around the world must be monitored by international community. (4) Other policies would include enforcement of the use of specific types of energy resources suitable for particular environments to minimize pollution. For example, communities near the equator must be encouraged to use solar energy as their main source of energy, even if they own natural gas, petroleum or fossil fuels. Regions not near the equator, would use energy sources other than solar, such as nuclear or gas. Since most of the world's natural energy resources are in underdeveloped territories, in return for the participation of these nations in this global endeavor for peace and stability, advanced nations must help to build the infrastructure of these societies and provide them with the technology base to elevate their standard of life to equal that of the advanced nations.

Based on these policies and mutual commitments, no nation or territory will be denied its energy needs, which is the exercise of socialism among societies within the global social organism. These policies may seem to be idealistic and non-pragmatic solutions to the global energy crisis, but if the energy resources and technological know-how are available for the further integration of social organisms, we may witness the emergence of such policies or proposals in the future, to avoid conflicts that may engulf the entire world.

Global economic growth and pollution in connection with social organism's stability: Because the environment is the life-support system on our planet, any imbalance created in the earth's ecosystem by human activities would trigger a round of chain reactions that might lead to catastrophic consequences for some life forms, which might then propagate to others on whom they depend on. For example, the emission of greenhouse gases by industries in industrialized societies not only makes the air unhealthy to breathe but also creates a planet-wide rise in temperature, or global warming. Rising temperatures will melt polar ice, leading to the rise of ocean levels around the world that would drown some of our major cities, which occupy seacoasts. But these perils do not seem to worry our politicians. In a market economy where economic institutions operate in a competitive environment, businesses do not concern themselves with the environmental issues because building and using appropriate technology to avoid damages to the environment would add to the cost of their products and make them less competitive in the world market against those without this cost burden. This lack of sensitivity is pervasive in governments that generally represent business interests and manifests itself in the policies that these governments adopt in regard to environmental issues. As of today, from the fear of economic and political consequences, the U.S. government has refused to cooperate with the rest of the world in the reduction of greenhouse gas emissions in the atmosphere, knowing fully well that U.S. industry is the main contributor to air pollution. This lack of vision and sensibility regarding environmental issues can lead to other forms of instabilities in the life of humans and the social organisms when damage is done, which will have their own economic and political consequences, enormously larger than those that the government tries to avoid today by not participating in this international endeavor.

To some extent, it is understandable that when a system is relatively stable, it refuses to undergo changes, particularly when changes are radical and vigorous. A vigorous change throws the system off-course and into chaos for some time, until new relational bonds start to evolve between its subsystems and the system becomes stable again. This explains why U.S. government refuses to participate in this international effort, which is a short-term solution to keep the U.S. economy competitive and stable. U.S. government seems to be comforted by the idea that environmental pollution is not an imminent danger to humans and their societies yet and it can wait. But it lacks the vision and logic that long-term abuse of the environment would threaten the life of every species on earth and it would take a much greater toll on the economies of the world to cope with its consequences when damage is done, not to mention that it may take decades or a century to reverse these problems. Therefore, it is critical for governments to have a plan of action to deal with environmental issues while they are not totally out of control. Such plan of action can only be drawn and enforced on an international scale and must impose political consequences on governments that disregard it. One concept that can be extremely helpful in fighting the emission of greenhouse gases is the notion of globalization of energy resources of the world and policies related to their usage with respect to different climates and environments. Only through such international cooperation, human beings and their societies can become environmentally friendly while growing and prospering economically.

World peace and the necessity of globalization of life support systems and energy resources: Over the course of their evolution, human beings and animals have learned to be territorial to protect the limited energy resources available to them and to defend their resources vehemently against the incursions of others. This territorial characteristic of humans has manifested itself in the characteristic of society as well. Like human beings, societies also live within territories that are separated from each other by imaginary lines called borders. In the past, these borders were subject to change, from time to time, when one empire defeated the other and conquered its territory and resources. However, after the devastation of European societies as well as all others who were involved in World War II, most nations in the world agreed to respect each other's borders and sovereignty in order to create greater stability and peace in the world. In today's world, international agreements prohibit conquering other territories by means of military. However, installing of friendly government in another nation through political processes continues to be a general practice by the major powers, to assure the flow of goods and resources between these nations and enhance their vulnerability against other competing societies that have an eye on their resources. Obviously, these attitudes lead to the design of foreign policies that are self-protective only, which creates tension among societies. To change these attitudes and policies, societies and humans must feel that they will never be left without energy resources that they need, which requires global cooperation to secure and distribute these resources to every society in need. Such global cooperation that secures the survival of every society and human being in the world will result in major foreign policy changes, and will lead to the development of harmonious relationships among humans and their societies and paves the way for their full integration into the global society.

If we intend to build a global social organism that is stable and its constituents live in harmony and peace with each other, then we need to focus on several activities that are managed by the union of nations. First, we must take action to control population growth, particularly in third-world societies. Those who believe that technology can continue to support the needs of an ever-increasing population are only dreaming. Therefore, it is crucial to maintain a balance between population and resources to avoid conflict between societies and instability in international community. If the balance between world population and its resources is not maintained, international agreements and laws will not prevent societies and humans from doing what they need to do in order to secure themselves. Second, developed nations must start investing heavily in the third-world countries to help them prosper and reduce the existing tension that has resulted from the prosperity gap. The war on terrorism can never be won until the standard of life of people living in third-world societies are improved. Third, we must continue our research and development in technological areas to replenish our resources and improve the life support systems of the entire world population. Then we will witness the emergence of rational thinking in all ranks of subsystems within the global community that will start coming together for a peaceful coexistence and full integration, rather than engaging in competition to manipulate the resources. Rational behavior can only be expected when security and survival of societies and humans are not threatened.

Democracy in practice: As we know, Western societies are very proud of their democratic principles, which allow all members of the society to participate—at least in theory—in electing their governments, which could vary ideologically from far right to far left. However, the validity of this process depends on how well-informed the citizens of a society are, in order to elect a government that they think is more appropriate for the circumstances of their time. In today's world, where mass media and information flow to the public are controlled by special interest groups and the government that represents them, ordinary citizens can be easily deceived by falsified information. Naturally, when one receives inaccurate information, he/she will form inaccurate judgments that would lead to inappropriate decisions or behavior. The desire to control the affairs of the state by special interest groups for personal gains is in conflict with the democratic values of Western societies and their constitutions that protect individual freedoms. However, there is nothing in these constitutions that says governments cannot lie to people, mislead them by feeding them falsified information, or manipulate their minds in order to produce favorable opinions toward predetermined policies. The big question concerning our opinions of critical issues of our time is whether these opinions are formed out of truthful knowledge, or they have been planted into our minds by the mass media under the control of special interest groups. If the latter is the case, then democratic process has failed. Polling plays a major role in informing the government or special interest groups of the direction that public opinion sways, and allows them to strategize for the next round of information to adjust and tilt public opinion in a direction that gratifies them without public even knowing it. Human brain is capable of accurate judgment between right and wrong if it is provided with correct and comprehensive information, but it cannot form an accurate opinion if the truth is concealed from it. That is how the governments and special interest groups get what they want; by controlling the sources of information.

In recent times, governments have learned that their citizens have become increasingly suspicious of being fed with falsified information, and as a result, they do not stop at giving their citizens inaccurate information alone. They go a step further to fabricate realities that correlate with their lies to make those lies more credible. These governments have no problem with planning an attack on their own soil and against their own people and blaming it on someone else in order to gain the affirmation of their public for their follow-up conduct against the so-called perpetrators. If a powerful country or alliance plans to attack another country to seize control of their valuable resources or for mere geopolitical advances, it can set the stage for the realities of their choosing to emerge, so that their responses to the new realities look like humanitarian intervention in the eyes of their public. The attacks on Yugoslavia and Iraq in recent years are two examples of this kind of public manipulation.

The mind control games in the so-called democratic societies of today, will soon go beyond providing misinformation and fabricating realities and will reach a new level that, if implemented, will turn every human being into an android. Researchers are working on technologies to tap into people's unconscious minds through audio/visual signals that carry subliminal messages that will reprogram their minds or give them instructions to act upon. Researchers are also involved in designing mind control weapons for future confrontations. These are psycho-energetic weapons that will use powerful electromagnetic or acoustic waves to either kill or turn the whole population of a society into zombies. Who can predict what will be the fate of democracy, despite all of its shortcomings today, if these technologies are perfected and fallen into the wrong hands? With today's technology, which can fabricate the visual images to seem real, who can believe what he sees or hears anymore? All we can say is that when a mind is tinkered with, the principle of democracy has been violated, and the societies that act in this manner are not any better than authoritarian governments that force their policies upon their citizens by means of terror. It is unfortunate to see that the novel concept of human freedom has been weakening and transforming into an illusionary freedom. In summary, a democracy without well-informed citizens that receive truthful and accurate information from their government in order to form independent opinions and freely participate in political process is only a deceiving concept.

Restriction of human involvement in the affairs of an advanced social organism: In reference to our earlier arguments, we know that a system and its subsystems have conflicts of interest when it comes to their desired goals and intensions based on the laws of nature and systems. For example, the greater degree of freedom for the system equates to lesser degree of freedom for its subsystems. The lowest state of internal energy for a system prohibits the same for its subsystems and forces them into a state of equality. In our discussion of freedom, we also noted that if a subsystem's degree of freedom were greater, it would result is chaos, disharmony and instability in the operation of the system itself. If we agree with these notions, then it becomes clearer that the further a social organism progresses toward its finality (which accompanies greater stability), the more it will restrict the freedom of its subsystems. What this means is that what is good for a system may not necessarily be good for its subsystems, and vice versa.

Since we like to use analogies, we can use the human body once more to further consolidate our theory in this regard. Human body organs have a very limited degree of freedom. They do not choose from time to time what organ will control the operation of the body as a whole. They have no freedom to relocate from one part of the body to another, and neither they have the ability to change the nature of their functionality if they are tired or bored with what they do. If human body allows this to happen, we can imagine what would happen to the operation of the body as a whole. Human brain is in control of every process in the body and cannot be replaced by any other organ. Similarly, a sophisticated social organism in its advanced stages of evolutionary process may turn every one of its subsystems (human beings for example) into a functional element of its systemic operation, giving them little or no chance to participate in conducting its operation, unless they are qualified and assigned to do so.

Does this mean that democratic principles that we have created are only transitional concepts that will fade away as social organism advances in its evolutionary process? Again, it depends on what we mean by "freedom." If we mean the basic freedom, then that freedom will be inherent in the structure of the advanced society and no one will have to be worried about his basic survival needs. If freedom means the participation of every single human being in setting up a new course of evolutionary process for his or her society, then that would be an optimistic view. This part of the democratic principle will not be part of the characteristic of an advanced and mature social organism. One of the failures of the democratic process in our time is that the vote of a highly-educated individual that understands the world around him can be easily wiped out by someone who can hardly read and write, simply because the two votes are equally weighted. We can imagine the outcome of an election and its consequences if the second group overwhelms the first. Even though it is important for every member of a society to participate in the political process, but the judgment of the majority does not always equate to greater legitimacy and accuracy.

Let us clarify this with the following example. Suppose a patient seeks treatment for his illness and decides to take the advice of three of his closest friends, only one of whom is a trained physician. He gets one diagnosis and course of treatment from the doctor and two similar courses of treatment from other two friends different from the course proposed by the doctor. What should the patient do? Follow the course of action proposed by the majority (his two friends) or take the advice of the doctor? This is where democracy fails, when the voters are either misinformed mobs or they do not have sufficient knowledge about what they are voting for. But why have we created democratic processes in the first place? Because we knew that individuals or governments could become corrupt and insensitive to people's needs, and we had to create a process to replace them if necessary, despite creating interruptions and temporary chaos in the operation of the social organism during the election season and the reorganization of the government after the election. We thought it would be better to endure these interruptions than to allow a corrupt government to rule for an indefinite period of time.

But what if we had a government that was sensitive to the needs of people and systems of all levels? Do we need to replace such a government? Do we mind at all that such a government rules our society indefinitely? Referring to our analogy example, we know that the human body has evolved in such a way that every single organ and sub-organ in its organization receives its basic needs so that it can function and support the rest of the organs and the body as a whole. Human brain is the central control system that organizes all of the activities within the human body and its function does not change for the entire life of the body. Human body has evolved with a democratic principle inherent in its design and we do not hesitate for a minute that our brain would discriminate against some of our organs in favor of the others, unless it is necessary and a crucial measure for our survival. Would the social organism at its advanced stages of evolution become so democratic in its core that we need not to worry about electing a new government from time to time? Would this government be able to manage and provide the basic survival needs to all of its constituents? It probably would, and in the course of the evolution of the social organism, the organism would limit the interference of its constituents in crucial issues of its operation, with the exception of constituents that are qualified to interfere. Government officials in this social organism will not be elected by the people, but rather replaced from within the government as needed, by highly intelligent and knowledgeable individuals who have been carefully hand-picked from their childhood to serve in these positions and raised with the highest degree of ethical standards. An advanced social organism that approaches the complexity of the structural organization of the human body needs continuity, harmony, stability and operational efficiency. This social organism would not allow everyone to interfere in its evolutionary process and derail it from achieving its intended goals. Can we imagine the level of chaos that would erupt if we try to elect a new world government and ask the entire population of the world to go to the voting booths and cast their votes? Moreover, what would be the level of disorder while world government is being reorganized after every election? Following the arguments we have presented here and in previous discussions, it seems unlikely that individual human beings will be able to retain all of their freedoms (particularly those not directly related to their survival and security), as society moves forward to more advanced stages in its evolutionary process.

Does history repeat itself? We use the phrase "history repeats itself" to point to repeated historical events such as wars that are caused by humans' poor judgment. For some of us, history is merely a random process with no directionality. That is not quite true. History is the story of the social organism's evolutionary process, in which its growth or diminution is set by the support systems present in its environment, among them, energy resources. In the growth process, the organism continues to grow by integrating with other sub-organisms and forming a multi-level living organism that plans its own evolutionary process toward a predetermined destination that is set by the laws of nature and systems. Social organism and its sub-organisms (societies and human beings), like other systems, engage in energy exchange with each other and behave violently in order to keep the state of their internal energy at a minimum level, which is achievable by controlling as much energy resources or life support systems as possible. As a result, violence becomes part of the historical process irrespective of its main evolutionary trend, whether it is integration or disintegration process. Violence results in destruction of order and loss of life, which can be considered dissipation of energy, a requirement set by natural laws that lead to equilibrium, stability and equality within a system. In integration process of history, every time a channel of communication opens up between two social organisms, a new process is initiated to integrate the two systems, which is likely to be violent if prosperity levels in these social organisms are not equal. Merger and integration of social organisms will continue with the opening of new channels of communication between social organisms to include the entire world community. The historical process that makes global integration possible contains historical sub-processes and events that are violent and seem to be repeating from time to time. Naturally, when we observe this succession of events, all accompanied by violence, we may presume that history repeats itself. While it could very well be that the eruption of violence in the life of the social organism may be part of the next level of integration of social organisms, all designed to establish equality between subsystems of the social organism as it grows. The big question is, can we avoid the losses and casualties associated with violence, yet achieve the stability and harmony (a byproduct of equality) that the greater organism ultimately seeks? In other words, can we replace the violence and war inherent to the evolutionary process of the living organisms and systems with peaceful processes to allow social organism to attain its intended goals? Finally, can we learn from our historical process and not repeat the violent processes associated with the growth and integration of our societies? If we understand the process of social evolution and believe in inevitability of its finality, and if we are not naïve enough to think that we can challenge the laws of nature that support that finality, it is likely that we can. With a new consciousness, we may become wise enough to regulate our historical process and avoid repeated bursts of violence and destruction in our social evolution.

Can human consciousness assist in shortening the process of social evolution? Social evolution began with the formation of small groups and has grown to become a global community. Throughout this lengthy process of integration, human relations have been continually modified with every transition to a new stage of historical process and it is expected to do so until social evolution reaches its finality. Some of the most important elements that could influence these relations in the future historical developments are human knowledge, technology and the collective consciousness of humans, the so-called 'social consciousness.' A historical process could be a straight line connecting the starting and ending points of the process or any other course, as shown in Fig. 7-2 A through Fig. 7-2 C. Clearly, the historical process A (shown by the straight line), requires less time and dissipation of energy to reach its destination than processes B and C; destination being a utopian stable global society that has attained equality and harmony in all subsystem levels. As we know, dissipation of energy equates to human casualties and destructive processes that are the least in the historical process A, and the most in the historical process C.

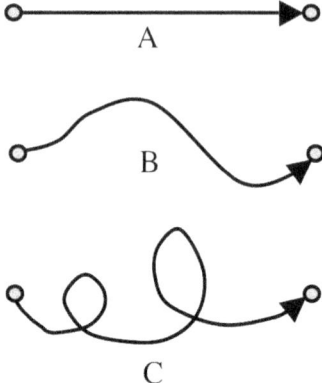

Figure 7-2 Alternative Paths of the Historical Process

To clarify this, let us assume that we are leaving our house and driving to a destination that we have never been to. The best way to execute this plan is to acquire a map, locate both the origination and destination points, and then find the shortest path to get there. An alternative approach would be to sit in the car and drive in the general direction of the destination, but in the process, encounter one-way and dead-end streets and roadblocks before we reach our destination.

The first approach in our example is analogous to historical process A, the second to historical processes B or C. It is clear that while process A consumes less energy and takes less time to reach the desired destination, there is still a minimum amount of energy that has to be spent in order to reach that destination, no matter how well this journey is planned. The question is, can the collective consciousness of humans assist them in picking a historical process, such as process A, that leads their social evolution to its finality in the shortest period of time and with a minimum number of casualties and destructive processes?

Most of us who believe that humans are capable of being rational creatures rather than behaving instinctively all the time would say *yes* to this question. Then what seems to be the problem? Part of the problem is related to human insecurity, which is a consequence of his evolutionary process and the other pertains to the most desired state of internal energy intended by any system. But the most important reason of all is that most humans are unaware that their historical process has indeed a deterministic finality, with well-defined characteristics at that state. Naturally, when the state of finality is unknown, designing a historical process that would lead them to that state becomes impossible, much less to design a direct path toward that finality. If we humans are convinced that our social evolution is leading us to one and only one finality in the integration process of history, regardless how we conduct its process, this might change our consciousness in such a way that it would affect our relational bonds at all sub-subsystem levels. Believing in the finality of social evolution will enhance the possibility that peaceful resolutions of our differences may become more dominant processes in our social evolution than confrontational ones. Since equality in the state of internal energy of all subsystems, each in their respective level, is a deterministic goal of social evolution at its finality, it makes no difference for the system itself how it is being achieved, through violence or through peaceful processes of choice. As a result, some of us may accept the notion of equality as an inescapable reality of social evolution and act upon it to make it a reality as soon as possible. Whatever the case, the ultimate factor influencing the process of history lies within human consciousness, and it is through this consciousness that we may find the shortest historical path to accelerate our journey to the finality of our social evolution. Let us use a historical example that created an enormous problem for the whole world. During the Cold War, both West and East used indoctrination techniques to promote hatred in their populations toward the opposing system and harmonize them against the enemy. Neither side knew that one day, still to come, their societies will merge into the global society when it reaches its finality. Similar mind-control techniques were used with the full support of Western alliance in the Middle East in the late seventies and early eighties by the radical Muslim communities to produce a whole new generation of radical Islamists to fight against the atheist Soviet army occupying Afghanistan. Today, that same Islamist faction has turned against the West that helped to create them a quarter of a century ago. After the elimination of active extremists, Middle Eastern nations and Western societies still have to deal with a huge population of extremist sympathizers brought up under Islamic fundamentalism, which will take many generations to moderate their views and change their attitudes toward the West. This process will not be easy and without casualties on both sides. But one day, still to come, these societies will merge and integrate into the unitary global society and become one.

These complex historical processes, which resemble B and C in Figure 7-2, run in circles and create enormous casualties and destructive processes with every turn. Those who are responsible for these unwanted historical turns are policy makers who serve the special interest groups and think they can change the course of history forever. Of course, in their minds, changing the course of history accompanies with a finality of their choosing. Yes, policy makers can change the course of history temporarily, but they can only dream about changing its finality. Politicians and people can change and derail the course of history, but they cannot keep it off track forever. Social evolution in integration process of history will correct its course one way or the other through historical necessities and with the support of social consciousness. In summary, if the course of history can be manipulated for the worse, it can also be manipulated for the better, by accelerating   its process toward its destination to prevent unnecessary casualties and destructive processes.

The roles of people and activists in driving the social evolution: The evolution of the social organism, as we said earlier, is a goal-seeking process. To achieve its goal, it needs to complete many sub-processes (each connected with a particular characteristic of the social organism), either in sequence or in parallel. However, there seem to be no preference in what sequence these sub-processes have to be completed. Sub-processes may even be left to be completed later, after other sub-processes are taken care of. We may ask, "what are these sub-processes that will take the social organism to its finality?" To create a list of these sub-processes, all we have to do is to remind ourselves of some of the laws of physics and thermodynamics that apply to systems and influence their behavior. Based on these laws, we know that all systems, including the social organism, are in search of the lowest state of internal energy, which is the most stable condition for the system in a given environment. Other sub-processes may be influenced by evolutionary laws pertaining to living systems like the social organism that tries to resemble the structural organization of the human body. In doing so, we can generate a list of items to help the social organism achieve its intended goals and characteristics and shortcut our historical evolution.

The first on the list is socioeconomic equality among humans and equality in prosperity among nations that meets the requirement of the law of the lowest state of internal energy for the top-level system (the global organism), which leads to the optimum stability and lowest stress level among its constituents in all levels. Attaining this state requires global cooperation in population control to create a balance between population and resources and the eradication of disease and hunger. Next on the list are:

- Globalization of energy resources and their usage policies in connection with environmental issues.

- Centralization of financial planning and economic development on a global scale.

- Global defense against space threats.

- Globalization of health care and education for every human being on earth.

- Strengthening international laws and the United Nations role in the world.

- Supporting research and development in technologies that would assist realization of the above mentioned goals.

- Cooperation in the preservation and protection of the environment not only for human beings but all other species.

Global social organism in its evolutionary process needs to complete all of the above-mentioned sub-processes and more to reach its maturity and finality. In order to achieve these goals without our guidance, it needs to find its way toward its finality through trial-and-error process, and continually challenge its own subsystems with which it presents a conflict of interest. The other process that would assist the global social organism to achieve its intended goals more rapidly is the active involvement of humans in each one of the sub-processes mentioned above, which is meant to reduce the conflict of interest between system and its subsystems and allow a smoother transition of global social evolution toward its finality.

During the era of the Cold War, a single process that got the attention of most activists was socioeconomic equality among peoples and liberation of countries oppressed by imperialist powers. Although progress was made in educating and empowering the working class and the poor, as well as helping oppressed nations to wake up and take charge of their political life, the process was not complete when the Cold War ended. This alienated most of the activists in believing that what they valued as a compelling historical viewpoint may have been wrong all along, otherwise, why would history take such a wrong turn. As we know, temporary setbacks are natural in the historical processes. They are caused by many factors, including conflicts of interest between the social organism and its sub-organisms. It is also possible that the social organism may shift its attention to different goals from time to time and adopt new sub-processes to achieve them, depending on the urgency of these goals and leave the partially accomplished goals with less priority to be fully accomplished in later time.

Today, we see the tension between North and South, which is mainly caused by the difference in the prosperity levels of the two blocs, one of which consists of generally rich and prosperous nations, the other of generally poor nations.

Doesn't this remind us of class struggle, but on a higher system level? Doesn't this tell us that inequality on the national level needs the urgent attention of the global social organism, more so than the residual inequalities left uncorrected on the human level in advanced societies? Regardless of what name we give to this new conflict, the fact is that it is between prosperous and non-prosperous nations and therefore, it is an economic war. This new struggle, labeled *international terrorism* by the North and *liberation* by the South, may continue for decades before a state of economic equality starts to emerge between these blocs. The only way out of this cycle of violence will be when the North acknowledges that the root cause of this struggle is the prosperity gap between these blocs of nations and starts taking steps to close it. It seems that social evolution is still on a correct path toward its intended goals, and all we have to do is to support it in its new course to achieve its objective, which is closing the prosperity gap among nations.

After the fall of communism, many intellectuals and activists who saw communism as the backbone of every progressive social movement became alienated from it, though they remain socially active; some got absorbed into other political organizations such as anti-globalization and anarchists who have very little theoretical backbone to support their ideologies. These activists must become aware that social evolution may not remain on the same course forever and as it shifts gear from one sub-process to another, the activists may also have to adapt. In its evolutionary process, social organism needs to achieve many goals before it reaches its maturity, establish harmony and equality at every subsystem level and becomes operationally efficient. Both ordinary people and activists should pick any goal from various goals that social organism pursues and work to make it happen because every step toward the finality of social evolution is an important step. Again, these goals do not have to be met in any certain order. They could be achieved in parallel or in series, through continuous or discrete processes. Activists, who think globalization should be abandoned because it is unfair to underdeveloped nations, should instead focus their activities on accelerating it, while at the same time pushing for the establishment of labor laws in underdeveloped societies that are at least comparable to laws currently in place in advanced nations. Whether we participate or not in bringing quicker justice to the underdeveloped nations, to their work force, and to their economic prosperity, in time, the economic forces will, but it will take a longer time.

In brief, the global organism has enough intelligence to achieve what it plans to achieve with or without our assistance. What activists can do is to identify the goals and sub-processes that are critical in creating a stable, just, and prosperous global community that is in harmony with itself and with its environment. The next step would be to get involved and influence the prosecution of every sub-process to facilitate the transition of global social evolution to its final state.

Ideology for the era of globalization: Throughout history, political ideologies have served human society and the social consciousness as a guide for building a better world, better at least in the minds of those who devise those ideologies. In some cases, these ideologies were progressive and meant to help the masses of people, whereas others (non-progressive) meant to serve a select few only. But how we can differentiate between a progressive and a non-progressive ideology? In general, progressive ideologies fall in line with the laws of nature and systems that drive the social evolution. This is why these ideologies have been more successful in finding acceptance among majority of people. It is expected, however, that as long as social evolution has not reached its destination, these ideologies continue to emerge and guide our social evolution. But the day that social evolution on a global scale reached its destination will be the day that ideology as a political thought process that led social evolution to its finality will perish all together and leave behind only an operational guideline for the affairs of the global social organism.

In the meantime, however, our quest to construct a scientific theory that explains our social evolution and our socioeconomic relations will keep scientists in all disciplines busy. If one day such a general theory were constructed, then it would become a new political ideology to alter the social consciousness and drive the remaining part of our social evolution. The progressive ideology for the twenty-first century should consist of everything that we have proposed so far to achieve the finality of human society on earth as an integrated and stable global community. The implementation of policies leading to that state rests solely on the shoulders of the advanced societies rather than underdeveloped nations for clear reasons. The underdeveloped nations are in no position to enforce their will upon the advanced nations, nor, in general, is their social consciousness as progressive as it is in the advanced nations, with exception of a small elite minority among them. In advanced nations, where most members of the society survive easily and enjoy a sense of security, social consciousness and social behavior have a much better chance of being influenced by rational thinking than by emotions and instincts. To give rational thinking a chance to succeed in making this world a better place for everyone and assist the social evolution attaining its goals, most activities must be focused on improving the security and survival of all members of global community. This requires economic development across the world, particularly in underdeveloped nations. When survival and security issues for both humans and their societies are resolved, social consciousness on the global scale will transform to assist the integration process of the societies in an accelerated manner.

Who is ultimately in control of history? We humans have always thought that we were in control of history and social evolution. We have never thought of society as a living organism that plans its own evolutionary process and takes us along on its journey. We may be able to clarify this by resorting to two examples. In the first example, which is more realistic than the second, we are trying to provide an analogy between social organism and human body, that may clarify our position on the authority of the social organism over its constituents and subsystems, in directing their activities. Let us assume that a human walks few steps and moves from point A to point B. At point B, someone asks all the cells of the body, assuming that they can talk, who was responsible for the transportation of the entire body to that point. Obviously, the cells in the legs would claim responsibility for the transportation process, as they were all involved and truly deserve all the credit. But did the leg cells really act independently? We know that this is not the case, and if the brain had not instructed the legs to move, they would have not moved. Is it fair to say that the cells in the leg, as well as all other cells in human body, are instruments of brain that its function is to coordinate and oversee the entire operation of the human body for the benefit of all of its constituents? Obviously, the cells do not know that brain manipulates their activities, as probably they are unaware of the complexity of the structure of which they are part; a structure complicated enough that is capable of planning its own evolutionary process and define all the relational bonds among its sub-organisms. Is it possible that the social organism plays the same game with us?

In the second example, which is an imaginary one, we intend to show how powerless human beings might be to prevent the social organism from reaching its finality. Suppose the social organism is sitting in the back seat of a car and a human driver is at the wheel. This human driver is extremely stubborn, thinks he is in charge. He refuses to listen to the guidance the social organism is offering him and does not follow directions. When the car arrives at the first intersection, the social organism points out the most direct route to their destination, but the driver refuses to listen and takes a different road and he does this at every intersection. After a long drive, the road finally ends and the driver has no choice but to stop. The social organism says, "Thank you. This is my destination and I will get out here." The human driver is now totally confused and thinks, "How did social organism manage to get to its destination in spite all of my efforts to prevent it." Then he realizes that all different routes, long and short, were leading him to the same destination and he just made his life more difficult by not listening.

In this hypothetical example, we intended to show that the forces involved in conducting the evolution of social organism are far more superior and powerful than those of its constituents. At the end, and as long as the environment supports the integration process of history, these forces will dominate not only the actions but also the relational bonds among the sub-organisms of the social organism. But how can the social organism achieve its evolutionary goals on its own and without the help of its constituent humans? That is a legitimate question, and the answer is that not every human being behaves like the driver in our second example. The social organism can inspire people to assist it in its evolutionary process. These people become the instruments of the social organism and the forces that support and drive social evolution to its destination. Some people who develop a better understanding of the process of social evolution and its evolutionary goals, may propose progressive political ideologies that may become major forces in reshaping the social consciousness and ultimately facilitating the transition of social organism to new evolutionary stages by reconstructing all of the relational bonds at every subsystem level. The term "progressive" applies to political ideologies that conform to the laws of nature that guide the social organism to its finality. What we are trying to say here is that, in reality, the social organism is in control of its own destiny and is assisted by its supporting environment and the laws of nature that guide it through its turbulent evolutionary process. In the process, the social organism uses individual human beings as its instruments to meet its evolutionary objectives through violent processes, if humans choose not to cooperate with its grand plan.